Teaching Reading in Small Groups

Differentiated Instruction for Building Strategic, Independent Readers

Jennifer Serravallo

Foreword by Lucy Calkins

HEINEMANN
Portsmouth, NH

Heinemann
361 Hanover Street
Portsmouth, NH 03801–3912
www.heinemann.com

Offices and agents throughout the world

Library of Congress Cataloging-in-Publication Data
Serravallo, Jennifer.
    Teaching reading in small groups : differentiated instruction for building strategic,
independent readers / Jennifer Serravallo.
        p.   cm.
    Includes bibliographical references and index.
    ISBN-13: 978-0-325-02680-0
    ISBN-10: 0-325-02680-7
    1. Reading (Elementary).   2. Group reading.   3. Small groups.   I. Title.
    LB1573.S454   2010
    372.41'62—dc22   2009039520

Editor: Wendy Murray
Production editor: Sonja S. Chapman
Cover and interior design: Lisa A. Fowler
Typesetter: Cape Cod Compositors, Inc.
Manufacturing: Valerie Cooper

Printed in the United States of America on acid-free paper
18   17   16   15   VP   8   9   10

Contents

Recommendations for Reading and Returning to This Book	
If You Identify with the Following Statements . . .	**You Might Find Help In . . .**
• I need help uncovering what kids are doing when reading . . . it just seems too invisible. • I need help figuring out how to group kids. • I need help putting some assessment measures in place for independent reading.	Chapter 2
• I've done everything I can think of to try to get my students reading. There are some who still just sit there during reading workshop. • My students do what I tell them in minilessons, but I don't think they really care that much for reading. • My students are fake reading and I don't know what to do about it. • My students need to figure out what they need instead of me just telling them all the time. • Some of my students feel like they aren't good at reading. I want to build their confidence. • Some of my students read below grade level, and none of the books in my classroom library appeals to them. Yet, they need to practice with these books if they ever expect to improve.	Chapter 3
• My students seem to understand what I'm teaching them in a minilesson, but I don't see the transfer of that knowledge to their own books. • Some of my students struggle and could use alternate strategies for the same goals. • Some of my students need more help from me before they can practice a strategy independently. • I don't understand what makes a demonstration effective. • I don't have a strong understanding of how the prompts I use when coaching help to release scaffolding.	Chapter 4

Recommendations for Reading and Returning to This Book	
If You Identify with the Following Statements . . .	**You Might Find Help In . . .**
• It feels like my students get together in partnerships and clubs and just share ideas. How can I get my students to talk in ways that push their thinking? • My students just aren't ready to function independently in book clubs. What's an intermediate step? • How can I use the natural groupings during clubs to teach reading skills and strategies? • Sometimes students in my book club pick a book to read that they need more help with. What can I do to help them with a new genre or provide background knowledge? • I feel like all of the partnerships in my K–2 classroom are going through the same moves and routines. Is there a way I could differentiate better?	Chapter 5
• Shared reading isn't right for all of my students, but I think that some could benefit from a small-group structure. • Some of my students have been stuck in a level for a while, and their fluency is holding them back. • I know the research about the value of rereading, but I can't get my students to do it.	Chapter 6
• When I look at my class assessment data, it seems like there are some students who are moving along at a regular pace and others who have been reading at the same level for a long time. • I find that most or all of my teaching is based on my unit of study. I'm not paying much attention to reading levels. • Some of my students read far below grade level and I want to help them to move through levels a little more quickly.	Chapter 7
• I don't have a vision for how this is all going to work. What are the rest of my students doing? • How do I keep track of what I've taught and stay organized? • How can I balance what I'm already doing (like guided reading and conferences with individuals) with the new ideas in this book?	Chapter 8

Foreword

*H*ere's what you need to know about this book. It is a book about all the new buzz words: differentiated instruction, data-based teaching, accountability, formative assessments, comprehension, fluency, small-group work . . . it's all here. Yet the really extraordinary thing about this book is that Jennifer Serravallo is able to harness the current pressures, and to use this momentum to help all of us teach reading with that magic combination of rigor and intimacy. Imagine reading instruction that depends on the voices of kids, their passions and foibles, hopes, and heartaches, and that depends on the face-to-face interactions between teachers and students around a book. Imagine reading instruction for which these moments of flickering amusement or amazed understanding are not happy offshoots but are at the root of how teachers teach reading.

This book will serve as a handbook to help you use a whole array of formative assessment tools to assess readers and lead small-group instruction within reading environments in which kids read tons and tons of self-selected books at levels they can handle. Your assessment tools will help you think about learning progressions as you support children towards their next moves as readers. The book will help you fashion small groups that are as rich and varied as your children and your purposes. Rather than advocating for one and only one form of small-group work—guided reading— Jen provides you with a repertoire of ways to lead small groups, and with suggestions for how to teach each well.

The book is a stand out for all sorts of reasons.

First, although it is a book about small-group work, it is written by a teacher-educator who is passionately committed to one-to-one conferring. I've always thought that educators' views on small-group instruction differ above all based on whether people see small-group instruction as a variation of whole-class instruction, only delivered to a smaller group, or as one-to-one instruction, done with several individuals at a time. Jen's approach falls squarely in the latter camp. Coauthor of the popular book, *Conferring with Readers*, Jen never waivers from her image of teaching as an intimate interchange that begins with a child, engaged in reading for her own purposes, and a teacher, leaning in to listen, to understand, and to extend what that child can do.

Jen's commitment to a responsive and personal sort of teaching is reflected not only in her content but also in her writing style. The book brims with kids—you hear their quirky, uneven language, you learn about the stuff that fills their pockets, you see them sitting, arms linked, two on a chair. The book brims with teachers, too, like those who aspire to keep Perfect Records and end up with records that might not be showy but can be used on the run, in real classrooms. But what shines through most of all is the sense of connectedness between kids and teachers. The instruction is imbued with connectedness. You'll see this connectedness as you watch teachers working within small groups while meanwhile, they keep their eyes on individuals and on data about kids. And you will feel the connectedness as you come to know the author, Jennifer Serravallo, and to sense that she hasn't tried to write a book, to make a monument, so much as she has tried to connect with you, a colleague.

The book is a stand out also because Jen shows that a teacher who is deeply committed to teaching reading workshops can not only deal with but embrace the contemporary pressures. For teachers who sometimes feel as if data-based instruction, differentiated groupings, and formative assessments somehow involve going over to The Dark Side, this book is a powerful antidote. It will help you know that in today's climate, you can hold tight to your deepest beliefs about children and literature, classroom communities, and good teaching.

Finally, the book is a stand out because Jen, as a part of the Teachers College Reading and Writing Project, has had the privilege of working with some of the most dedicated and brilliant teachers, superintendents, principals, coaches, graduate students, and teacher-educators that the world has ever known. This book shows the way in which this collective community gathers clusters of kids together, and listens, and loves, and learns.

—Lucy Calkins

Acknowledgments

*W*e are each a product of the groups to which we belong. I would like to thank *my* groups, and the individuals within those groups, for their support.

Thanks first to my professional group, the Teachers College Reading and Writing Project (TCRWP), and its founding director, Lucy Calkins. She is a generous leader who gives of her knowledge, her spirit, and her mentorship widely. Thanks to her for reading versions of this manuscript and giving encouragement and advice all along the way.

It is through the team of staff developers Lucy has worked to assemble, and the weekly Thursday think tanks she leads, that I have developed into the educator I am today. These think tanks help me constantly question my practice and force me to grow. Kathleen Tolan, Deputy Director of the TCRWP, has influenced so much of my thinking about the teaching of reading and small-group instruction and about staff development. She is a model teacher to children and adults. Amanda Hartman, leader of Primary Reading, was my first staff developer about eight years ago and, through her modeling, helped transform my classroom. She is the teacher who first helped it to "click" for me and she continues to make new things click regularly. Thanks also to Mary Ehrenworth and Laurie Pessah, two other influential, inspirational leaders of our work.

Every member of the TCRWP, past and present, has influenced me in immeasurable ways, and their footprints are all over this book. Specifically, I want to thank Carl Anderson, Mary Chiarella, Colleen Cruz, Brooke Geller, Cory Gillette, Ami Mehta, Elizabeth Moore, Alison Porcelli, Donna Santman, Emily Smith, and Joe Yukish. Thanks for keeping me thinking.

Thanks to the groups of educators at all of my schools across the country, but in particular the teachers at PSs 63, 158, and 277 in New York City. Thank you, Darlene Despeignes, Darryl Alhadeff, and Cheryl Tyler, the leaders of these amazing schools, for providing such an inspirational model of leadership and for hiring me to work with your school for so many days each year. Thanks to all of the teachers at these schools for allowing your classrooms to be lab sites and for talking back during meetings. You are all critical friends. Special thanks to Laurie Faber, Samantha Diamond, Rosie Maurantonio, Tara Goldsmith, Lisa Uhr, and Brooke Baron, who shared their children's work and their own conference notes for this book. Thank you to the principal, staff, and students of PS 63 for the beautiful images that fill the pages of this book, especially Darlene Despeignes, Brooke Baron, Jodi Friedman, Heather Madigan, and Amanda Ortiz.

Thank you to the group of people who read versions of this manuscript. Judy Wallis was a tremendous help from the beginning. She was always available and responded with urgency. You helped me get unstuck many times. Thanks also to Colleen Cruz, Kara Gustavson, Lucy Calkins, and Samantha Diamond for offering feedback along the way.

Thank you to the team of people at Heinemann who have helped to make this book possible. Thanks to Kate Montgomery for encouraging the initial proposal and for finding me a wonderful editor, Wendy Murray. Wendy is so much more than an editor. She has been a sounding board, a challenger, an advocate, a mentor writer, and a giver of much help and time. Thanks also to all of the people in the design, production, and marketing departments—Sonja Chapman, Lisa Fowler, Eric Chalek, and many others I have not yet met—for lending your creativity, time, and dedication to this book.

Last but not least, I'd like to thank a most important group: my family. Thanks to my dad and mom for reading to me so much as a child and being such great teachers in so many ways—reading and beyond. Thank you to Jen for being so understanding when this book took over evenings and weekends that belonged to you. Finally, thank you, little Lola, for not arriving until the manuscript was turned in, and for napping so that I could finish this book. I love you all!

Beyond Reading Groups, Beyond Guided Reading

Herbie Jones was an Apple. That was the name of the lowest reading group in Miss Pinkham's third grade class. Herbie hated the name. Margie Sherman suggested it the first week of school. Unfortunately, there were three girls and two boys in the Apples. The girls voted for Apples and the boys, Herbie and his best friend, Raymond, voted for Cobras. Miss Pinkham was pleased the Apples won.

Now it was March, and Herbie's group was still reading the red book (the one with the suitcase on the cover). His teacher said the stories were about people going places. Herbie didn't think his group was going anywhere.

—Herbie Jones (Kline 1986, 7)

*M*y elementary reading experience was similar to Miss Pinkham's class. We were grouped according to reading ability and we read out of a textbook. Once you were in a group, you stayed there for the year. Our class' Apples couldn't read many of the words on their own, so in order to stand a chance at the comprehension questions at the end of the book, someone had to read the stories to them. Those students in my group, the "middle" group, could read the story and probably got most of the questions correct. This basal reader was most appropriate for us in terms of readability, but we had no choice in what we wanted to read, and many of the stories held little if any relevance.

It soon became clear that our sole purpose in the group was to read the story and answer the questions. But this assigning and assessing in place of reading instruction was not beneficial. As Durkin (1981) points out, we were tested, not taught. We were also largely bored. We finished our assigned reading in short order and at times didn't even read the passage as we learned that we could just look at the questions first, skim the story, and get the correct answer. So many of the questions were literal and required little if any thought.

When I was a student teacher, I worked with a wonderful fifth-grade teacher who taught an evolved version of those groups. Instead of basal readers, the students in her class read real trade books. She grouped students according to reading ability but also by interest, and children spent their meeting times reading, discussing, posing questions, and sometimes even acting out their favorite parts.

These groups were far better than my own experience learning to read. The groups offered ways for the children to respond to literature authentically, different books were assigned for different groups based on what students were able to read, and students read many more pages across the week than I ever did in my basal reader. As Richard Allington said, sheer volume of reading helps kids get better at reading (2000) so this element of this model benefited these kids. The problem with these groups, though, is that the instruction was about the book itself. It was devoid of explicit teaching about how to transfer what students had learned to other books or other situations. In other words, the students in the groups weren't learning much about being a reader—they were learning mostly about a book.

In the first years in my own classroom in New York City, I relied heavily on guided reading groups. I scoured Irene Fountas and Gay Su Pinnell's many books and led groups by providing supportive book introductions, coaching students while they read, and leading a brief discussion afterward. I balanced these guided reading groups with one-on-one conferences and book groups, as I'd done in my student teaching experience. These two structures constituted all of my individualized reading instruction.

At some point in my third year, I stepped back to ask myself this question: Is what I'm doing a benefit to the student, to myself (teacher), or to us both? I had always thought of myself as a purposeful teacher, but a close look at my small-group reading instruction made me take pause. When I thought critically about what I was doing, I found that I was *checking up* on their comprehension more than *teaching* comprehension (Durkin 1981). I did more teaching of the *book* than teaching the *reader*. I spent more of my teaching time in what Johnston (2004) calls "telling mode" than responding to what they needed as individual readers.

I wanted to get better at differentiated reading instruction. I knew that to do this I needed to group children more flexibly and purposefully and to develop a repertoire of ways to meet their needs. I needed to find structures and methods that got at the heart of engaged, independent reading.

The small-group methods described in this book were developed, refined, and tweaked with the aim of supporting children as readers and thinkers and discussers of books. In contrast to the kind of instruction Herbie and the Apples group received, the small-group methods and structures I choose help children feel like they're going somewhere—specifically, small groups that will help children to:

- ❏ read with engagement and enthusiasm
- ❏ read strategically
- ❏ engage in meaningful, invigorating conversations about books
- ❏ read fluently and with expression
- ❏ read increasingly more challenging texts

QUESTIONS TO ASK YOURSELF AND TO EXPLORE WITH YOUR COLLEAGUES

- ✔ What were your own school experiences with reading groups?
- ✔ What are the small-group structures you rely on most in your classroom to teach reading?
- ✔ What are your fundamental beliefs about teaching in general, and the teaching of reading specifically?

All of the small-group work in this book comes from my personal experiences. Much of this work is informed by the work at the Teachers College Reading and Writing Project (TCRWP), by my work in schools where I serve as a literacy consultant, or from my own classroom teaching experiences. Much of the work has its roots in researchers and theorists from Pearson to Vygotsky to Marie Clay.

The schools, teachers, and children most frequently mentioned in this book are in New York City where I spend the majority of my time: PS 63 in the Lower East Side, a tiny school with large numbers of English language learners and receivers of free and reduced lunch; PS 158, which serves a largely middle- and upper-middle-class neighborhood of the Upper East Side; and PS 277 in one of the poorest congressional districts in the country, the South Bronx.

Although they have such diverse student makeups, these schools have a number of important things in common. First, they are strong communities of practice where teachers work, plan, and think together; constantly try to outgrow their best ideas; rely on research; and respond to children. The leaders and teachers of these schools believe strongly in professional development.

Second, they each have exemplary reading and writing workshops, conduct daily read-alouds, and use an assessment-based developmental word study program for phonics, spelling, and vocabulary. In concert, these balanced literacy structures support one another and create a well-rounded approach to literacy instruction.

Third, and perhaps most relevant to this book, is that all three schools are committed to small-group instruction, and these small groups have had powerful effects on their readers. At PS 277, the teachers had to order scores of new books for their classroom libraries because children were reading at higher levels than they ever had before. This year, their state English Language Arts exams results showed a 25 percent increase in one year for children performing at or above grade level. PS 63 also celebrated large gains. At PS 158, this year, they saw 98 percent of their students performing at or above grade-level standards on the same exam.

Small-Group Instruction and The Five Reading Tenets

In my first book, *Conferring with Readers: Supporting Each Student's Growth and Independence* (2007), Gravity Goldberg and I described our beliefs about what reading instruction should look like and what it should accomplish. We distilled our beliefs to five tenets. We believe reading instruction should:

- ❏ match the individual reader
- ❏ teach toward independence
- ❏ teach strategies explicitly so that readers become proficient and skilled
- ❏ value time spent, volume, and variety of reading
- ❏ follow predictable structures and routines

We wrote that in a reader's workshop classroom, we are reading mentors, and conferences are an opportunity for us to model the kinds of reading habits and skills we use to support student readers to do the same in their own reading.

Small-group conferences accomplish, and complement, these same goals. Although the one-on-one conference is an important weekly meeting between a teacher and a student, we can supplement an individual conference with small-group conferences to work more efficiently. This efficiency is especially important in today's classrooms with higher benchmarks, larger class sizes, and increasing demands placed on students and teachers. Working in groups helps children because teachers can see more children in the same time it takes to do one individual conference.

One-on-one conferences address individual student needs and foster the close relationship between teacher and student. Group conferences have the added benefits of helping children build reading relationships with each other, as well as helping teachers work more efficiently.

When children are part of a group with a common goal, it makes it more likely that they will reach out to peers when they encounter difficulty. Small groups give children the chance to hear other students' thinking about their reading process and responses to texts. Children's voices can serve as a counterpoint to the teacher's language about comprehension. This kind of culture also contributes to a student's motivation and engagement when learning new skills and strategies. Knowing that as readers they have tools to use to accomplish their goals helps students develop what Johnston calls *agency* (2004).

> ▶ **Some Benefits of Small-Group Instruction**
>
> A small-group conference
>
> - addresses instructional goals by matching student need with a purpose and method
> - creates efficiency: more children can be seen more frequently for intervention or enrichment
> - allows students to feel like part of team as they work on the same goal with other students
> - builds in peer support as students mentor one another toward their goals

Small-Group Instruction Should Match Individual Readers

What I learned from Lucy Calkins (2000), Kathy Collins, Kathleen Tolan, and others at the Reading and Writing Project about strategy lessons (Collins 2004) "clicked." It made perfect sense that sometimes we should pull a group of students together not because they were reading the same book or were reading at the same level, but instead because they would benefit from the same strategy (Duke and Pearson 2002). In these groups, students receive instruction in a strategy that is transferable to other books and contexts, not only instruction that would help them in the current book. Once I began using strategy lessons they became a foundational part of my reading workshop.

I find that teachers sometimes confuse *strategy lessons* with *guided reading*. Or, more commonly, some teachers call all kinds of small-group work "guided reading." Strategy lessons differ from guided reading in a number of important ways: what children are reading, how the group is structured, what the group is learning, and how the teacher responds to students. For example, strategy lessons work with students on their own independent level, in self-chosen books. In guided reading, the teacher chooses books at the students' instructional level and the students typically have little choice (see Figure 1.1 for more examples). More on strategy lessons can be found in Chapter 4.

Guided Reading	Both	Strategy Lessons
• Students practice in instructional-level texts. • Students practice in text chosen by teacher. • Structure often includes book introduction, reading with coaching, and teaching point(s) or discussion.	• Small group of students works with the teacher. • Combination of explicit and supported instruction used. • Teachers coach. • Students respond.	• Students practice in independent-level texts. • Students practice in self-selected or teacher-assigned texts. • Structure includes connection, explicit teaching, active engagement, and a link to students' reading.

Figure 1.1 Comparing Strategy Lessons and Guided Reading

Across the next years in my own classroom, and with teachers with whom I work in my current role as staff developer, I discovered that the strategy lesson is just one of many structures possible for small-group instruction that achieve the same essential goal of providing instruction that matches individual readers. Depending on the purpose, small groups might resemble another balanced literacy component like shared reading, or they might look more like a coaching conference that you would typically do one-on-one with readers. I ask myself, What am I helping the reader to learn about reading? and How much support does the student need from me to accomplish the task? My answers guide my decisions about structures and methods (Pearson and Gallagher 1983; Vygotsky 1978).

SMALL-GROUP INSTRUCTION IN READING IS REALLY CONFERRING To me, a well-run small group in reading seems more like a conference than anything else. I think of a conference as a structure that offers opportunities to meet with a student or students to support them as they work to acquire new learning and to support them as they transition to their own independent practice.

Even though children are grouped, I still need to see the students as individuals and differentiate my responses in the course of the small-group work to meet their needs. As Tomlinson (2001) teaches us, differentiation means that I need to understand how children take in information, make sense of ideas, and express their learning. Differentiated instruction, she writes, needs to be student-centered, rooted in assessment, and dynamic—we need to constantly make adjustments to match learner to learning. This differentiation is something that happens naturally in a well-run individual conference, and is the hallmark of a good group conference as well.

Because I put so much emphasis on differentiation and the quality of conversation that I strive to maintain in small groups, all of the small-group work structures and methods I describe in this book can really be thought of as *group conferences.*

Small-Group Instruction Should Teach Toward Independence

When I work with children during small-group instruction, I keep in mind what it will take to support each individual reader toward independent success with a strategy. I consider what I know about balanced literacy to ensure a suitable balance between teacher support and student independent practice. I also make sure I choose strategies to teach that are within the learner's zone of proximal development, and release scaffolding at an appropriate pace.

UNDERSTANDING HOW BALANCED LITERACY TEACHES TOWARD

INDEPENDENCE   The term *balanced literacy* appears throughout the literature in a number of different ways (Cunningham and Allington 1994; Cunningham and Hall 1998; Fitzgerald 1999; Dickinson and Neuman 2001; Pearson et al. 2007). Some use the term to refer to the *balance* in the children's literature chosen or the skills being taught; to others, *balance* is about instructional methods; to others, it is about taking a philosophical stance. Many would agree that the term *balanced literacy* originated during the whole language versus phonics debate. The term denounces the extremism on either side and instead offers a solution: a little of both (Pearson et al. 2007). Balance.

In this book, I use the term *balanced literacy* to describe methods and structures of teaching, and, more precisely, the amount of teacher support versus student independence expected in each method and structure of teaching. This view of balanced literacy captures reading's true complexity (Pearson et al. 2007).

In my concept of a balanced literacy classroom, there are opportunities for students to watch the teacher demonstrate, opportunities for the student to practice with teacher support, and opportunities to practice independently, offering a bridge to independence. This bridge is known as the *to*, *with*, and *by* of balanced literacy. That is, there are times when the teacher provides a model *to* the students, times when the teacher works *with* the students, and times when students work *by* themselves. I find the graphic in Figure 1.2 helpful in visualizing this, which I adapted from Pearson and Gallagher (1983).

It is important to be aware of where each component of a reading workshop fits into this bridge to ensure an equal balance across a week of planning, which will ensure an appropriate bridge to independence. For a review of terms relating to reading workshop, see Chapter 8.

Read-alouds and minilessons are examples of times when I offer heavy support, in the *to* category. During read-alouds, I read out loud to the students, offering glimpses into my thought process through think-alouds. I may also provide prompts to encourage discussion. Minilessons are also in the *to* category, as during most of the lesson, I model, explain, and demonstrate. During the independent reading portion of

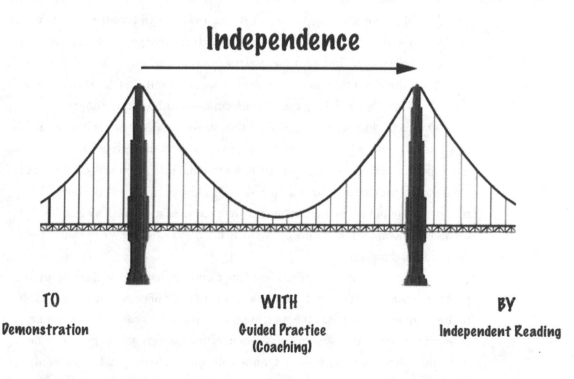

Figure 1.2 Bridge to Independence

the workshop, children work *by* themselves. They are expected to continue reading in their own spots, independently and for a sustained period of time, working to apply strategies they've learned.

In this book, I focus on the *with* part of this bridge—in particular, how I support students as they read, always moving students closer to independence. The theoretical underpinnings of this are discussed in the next section.

A LEARNER'S ZONE OF PROXIMAL DEVELOPMENT AND RELEASING SCAFFOLDING

During conferences—individual or group—I attempt to assess what the individual student currently understands and then I decide on a teaching point that is a slight stretch beyond what the student can already do independently. This teaching decision is made to support the student working within his zone of proximal development (Vygotsky 1978). Vygotsky called this "the distance between finding the actual developmental level as determined by independent problem solving and the level of potential development as determined through problem solving under adult guidance or in collaboration with capable peers" (86). Instead of assessing to find what the student can't do, and then teaching to a deficit, I find what the student is already able to do and I teach to move the student, always linking the new information with what is known.

> *. . . then I decide on a teaching point that is a slight stretch beyond what the student can already do independently.*

Once a teaching decision is made, I then provide support to the student in this new learning. After all, if the student is able to do it independently already, then there is no point in teaching it! Vygotsky (1978) asserts that new learning occurs when the child accepts the challenge to take on new competencies, not repeat old ones. The supports that I put in place are commonly referred to as *scaffolding*, a metaphor first used in developmental literature by Wood, Bruner, and Ross (1976) and later applied to educational contexts.

Just like the scaffolding around buildings under construction, there needs to be a plan for how to take it down. I used to make the mistake of providing excessive scaffolding—more support than the student needs—and held it constant rather than gradually removing it. I wouldn't see when my students were able to practice independently what I had taught them. I mistakenly referred to the children as "needy" and just kept putting more supports in place.

In fact, what I was missing was the gradual release of responsibility, or the slow takedown of the scaffolding, when planning for and executing conferences (Pearson and Gallagher 1983). I needed to teach toward the development of "inner control," so the child no longer needs external support from me and can function independently with the new learning (Clay 1991).

The idea of scaffolding can be applied when looking at the balanced literacy model presented in the previous section. *To* and *with* are scaffolds to get to the *by*. On a more microlevel, though, it's also important to study how we interact with students while engaged in a conference. Examining how we respond to student approximations, the amount of support we give through modeling and coaching, and the amount of time we spend supporting the student before she is expected to practice alone are all important aspects of scaffolded instruction. Balance, then, is not simply about the diverse structures we use, but the methods of teaching within each structure, the amount of support we give, and how we release that support, always in constant consideration of what readers need most.

Small-Group Instruction Should Teach Strategies Explicitly

When I first learned to draw figures in my high school art class, I had some trouble. My drawings usually ended up looking out of proportion. One day, the teacher taught me that in order to better proportion the people I was attempting to draw, I could sketch a series of ovals: one for the head, one for the neck, one for the body, three for each arm. Essentially, every segment of a person became an oval. He showed how after doing this, I could go back to these light ovals and draw the body's outline: the shapes of elbows and hands and clothing. When I used this strategy, I was able to create life-like drawings of figures that were in proportion.

I practiced this technique for months, always starting out with the ovals and then tracing over, until one day I tried to draw a figure freehand. As it turns out, all of those months of drawing ovals had helped me internalize the proportions, and I was able to draw a figure that didn't look distorted. The strategy—drawing ovals—became unnecessary. I was now *skilled* at drawing a human figure in proportion—without the scaffold of drawing the ovals.

In my community at the TCRWP, we believe that readers also need deliberate strategies to develop skilled performance. We believe that strategies are deliberate, effortful, intentional, and purposeful actions a reader takes to accomplish a specific task or skill in reading. As readers grow more and more proficient, the consciousness with which they do these actions fades as the skilled performance becomes automatic. *The strategy gives way to a skill.* However, when a reader encounters a problem, that strategic set of actions resurfaces in his consciousness to problem solve. Strategies, then, are the step-by-step how-tos for internalizing skills such as determining importance, questioning, inferring, monitoring for meaning, activating prior knowledge, visualizing, and retelling/synthesizing.

For example, instead of telling a reader that he needs to envision as he reads, we might instead tell him to think about how the character might be feeling and think about how that feeling would look on his face and body in order to help the student better picture the character. Eventually, the reader won't need to so deliberately form a mental picture of the character, but for now the intentional use of that strategy will help, just as drawing ovals helped me.

QUESTIONS TO ASK YOURSELF AND TO EXPLORE WITH YOUR COLLEAGUES

✔ How balanced is your literacy instruction? Is there a way to bring more balance to ensure a bridge to independence?

✔ When in your life have strategies helped you to acquire new learning?

Small-Group Instruction Should Value Time Spent, Volume, and Variety of Reading

Each of the small-group structures described in this book allow for quick practice with the strategy being taught. This allows children to spend more time reading, and to use less time listening to a teacher talk about reading.

Because I meet with students whose books are self-chosen, I am likely to need to support volume of reading. According to research, when students are allowed to choose their own reading materials, they tend to read more. Instead of assigning books as guided reading or reading groups do, most small-group conferences work with children's self-selected reading material (Allington 2000).

Small-Group Instruction Should Follow Predictable Structures and Routines

Although each chapter outlines small-group instruction options that are unique, all have a common structure. These predictable structures allow children to come to know what to expect. They are clear on their role within the group, as well as the teacher's role. The structure of these groups is firmly rooted in balanced literacy philosophies where there is an "I do it" part of the lesson and a "you do it" part of the lesson—a "to" and a "by" (Pearson and Gallagher 1983).

The groups begin with the teacher stating a purpose for the group and reinforcing a strength. In subsequent chapters, I refer to this part of the lesson as "connect and compliment." The teacher orients the children to why they've been gathered for the small group, and sets the agenda by stating the strategy. In this part of the lesson, the teacher also gives a compliment. This helps to foster a sense of agency: that the children *can* learn what is being presented because they already have strengths that preclude them to learning it (Johnston 2004).

The next part of each lesson is the "teach." In this portion of the lesson, the teacher quickly demonstrates, gives an example or explanation, acts as a proficient partner, or acts as a ghost partner. The teacher sets the children up to begin their practice, keeping in mind the amount of support, or scaffold, that the students need.

The most important part of the lesson is when the children practice. The students in the group are actively involved in trying the strategy that the teacher just set them up to try. I refer to this part as the "engage" section of the conference. The engage part of the small-group instruction described in this book is what makes small groups more similar to conferences than minilessons as each child is responded to as an individual. The teacher gives one-on-one attention and tailors the focus of the lesson to the individual's needs. The teacher also differentiates by changing *how* he interacts with each child and the type of output expected (Tomlinson 2001). For example, the teacher might vary his responses to student attempts at the strategy based on learning-style preferences. Verbal/linguistically oriented children might practice out loud, whereas kinesthetically oriented children might act out a part of their book when practicing the strategy, and spatial/visually oriented children might sketch.

The final part of each group conference is the "link." This part links the work that students do in small groups to the work that they do at their independent work spots. The teacher reiterates what was taught and encourages the children to practice independently. This is an important, though quick, part of the conference because it is essential that children transfer what they've done in the ten-minute small group to their independent reading. It is through repeated practice in multiple contexts that children solidify new learning.

Although the structures remain the same, there is nuance in what happens in each type of small group. As you read each chapter, use the predictable common structures to focus your reading, and look to see how the differences support the goals of the group.

The Last Word

There is nothing better than one-on-one conferring with readers. The impact these conversations have on our young readers is long lasting: the undivided attention we give our students and their reading benefits them personally and academically. Of course, in a class of thirty or more children, you can't rely solely on one-on-one instruction to meet the diverse needs of the class. The next best thing is to get our small-group instruction as close to the motivational bonding that one-on-one instruction offers.

Differentiated reading instruction is best attained through flexible, purposeful groupings and with attention to the repertoire of ways to meet students' needs. By holding firm to the five reading tenets of good reading instruction, I can ensure that I match individual readers' needs; I teach toward independence; I teach strategies explicitly; I value time, volume, and variety of reading; and I follow predictable structures and routines. These tenets will be revisited at the close of Chapters 3–7 to reiterate how the specific methods and structures from the chapters align.

Forming Groups: Making the Invisible Visible Through Assessment

Several years ago, I taught a third grader with a magic hobby. He sometimes came in from recess or from home having read about a new card trick or how to make three segments of rope magically become one again. With his magic hat and the wave of a wand, he often baffled me.

"Pick a card, any card," he said one afternoon. He fanned out a whole deck in front of me. I chose my card and held it close to my chest. He made the cards return to a nice neat stack with a tap on each side.

"Put your card back in this deck," he said, splitting the deck in two, "and I'll tell you what card you pulled." I did as told. He flipped every card over, one by one, until he got to my queen of hearts. "That's it! That was your card. The queen of hearts."

My first impression was, Wow! He did it again. Tricked me. But today I was determined. It was only a trick. There was a way he did it. I just had to figure it out.

"Do it again," I said. As he did, I started asking questions in my head. Was he marking the card with ink on his finger? Did he bend the corner? Did he leave the card sticking out a bit so that he'd know which was which? I watched closely, scrutinizing every tiny movement.

And then I caught it. "Aha!" I said, and a look of worry spread across his face. "When you split the deck in half and had me place mine in the middle, you peeked at the card right on top. That way, when you went to flip them over, you'd know which card that would come right *after* that one." Then, as soon as I'd said it, I felt terrible for ruining his trick.

As teachers of reading, it often seems that what happens inside a student's head when he reads is like the card trick my student performed. What we see on the surface is one thing—arriving at the right card or arriving at the word or thought while reading. But what lies beneath is really what we're after.

To be a good teacher of reading, we need to know the student's tricks and what makes her tick. We need to better understand everything from the student's book choices to how she plows through each page. We need to get underneath how she does what she does so that we can help her to engage with texts and think with more sophistication as she reads. We need to be able to assess well, and make teaching decisions based on those assessments.

The goal of this chapter is to offer advice on how to make the magic behind reading a little more visible. Accurately assessing and gaining insights about individual students allows me to group them according to their strengths and needs.

So in a book about groups, *this is a chapter about how to see children as individuals.*

The insights I glean from my assessments can literally help me differentiate instruction the very next moment, or in a small-group setting later that day, or in the days to come. These groupings tend to be flexible as my constant assessment using the measures described in this chapter allows me to move students in and out of groups as appropriate.

I begin by reviewing some principles of assessment. I then discuss ways to assess students'

- ❏ engagement with reading
- ❏ fluency and intonation
- ❏ print work strategies
- ❏ comprehension
- ❏ conversational skills

In examining these five aspects of reading, I get a more complete picture and am able to make goals for students that move them ever closer to engaged, proficient reading. The subsequent chapters in this book offer structures and methods for supporting children in developing increasing proficiency each of these five aspects. In each section ahead in this chapter, I explain the dimension, then lead through a structure that I find helpful for assessing the dimension. I use specific examples of children with whom I work so you can have practice making sense of the information gathered from the assessment measure.

What's Ahead

- • a review of principles of assessment
- • assessing *engagement* through engagement inventories, book logs, and reading interest inventories
- • assessing *fluency* through shared reading, running records, individual conferences, and partnerships/clubs
- • assessing *print work strategies* through running records and individual conferences
- • assessing *comprehension* through reading portfolios, writing about reading, conversations about books, minilesson active involvements, and individual conferences
- • assessing *conversation* through whole-class conversations, partnerships, and clubs

Some Principles of Assessment

Ongoing assessment is a critical part of teaching reading. As teachers in a reading workshop, we constantly and consistently assess readers to match them to just-right texts; to craft whole-class, small-group, and individual teaching opportunities based on readers' needs and strengths; and to understand what effects the instruction has had on the learner. Although you are likely familiar with much of this vocabulary, I review it here so that we can begin with a common language. This language allows you to categorize the types and purposes for assessment for yourself, your students, your parents, and your administrators. Reading assessments can be categorized as diagnostic, formative, or summative; informal or formal; quantitative or qualitative.

Diagnostic assessments help us gain a baseline understanding of a reader. Diagnostic assessments may be used to determine a reading level, to determine a reader's strengths and needs, to understand what a reader already knows and can apply, or to figure out a reader's attitudes toward reading. In a reading workshop, this type of assessment often helps us determine unit of study goals or may provide initial information affecting how to form groups.

Formative assessments are on-the-go assessments that give us information about what readers do when they are in the process of learning. Often, these types of assessment are frequent and provide ongoing and continuous feedback about work in progress. Formative assessments allow us to revise, alter, and tailor instruction to meet the learner's needs.

Summative assessments are end-of-learning assessments. After a unit of study or a set period of time, a student will have the opportunity to demonstrate the new learning. Summative assessments offer an opportunity for both the student and teacher to celebrate the accomplishments from the time being assessed. In small-group instruction, these types of assessment can be used after students have worked in a group on a goal over time and are ready to show their new understandings. For example, I worked with a group of third graders who spent several days working on describing what they pictured as they read. On Thursday of that week it was clear when I coached them that they were close to cementing their understanding. So to confirm that each child had gotten it, and that this would be our final time together with this skill, I asked them to describe on a large sticky note what they pictured, which then stayed in their reading portfolio.

Any of these three types of assessment—diagnostic, formative, or summative—can be formal or informal, although it is most common for formative assessments to be informal.

Formal assessments are typically those that are standardized. Standardized assessments have been tested on students and report the data as statistics, percentiles, or stanines. Examples of formal assessments are the Directed Reading Assessment (DRA), state standardized tests, or IQ tests.

Informal assessments are not data driven, but instead are content and perform-ance driven. Examples of informal assessment are checklists, rubrics, and listening to a conversation about books to determine comprehension skills being used. Most of the small groups I form are based on informal assessments, but this is mostly because by the time I receive results from most formal assessments, the data are old. That is, what a child was able to do in January when the state English Language Arts test was given is likely very different from her skill level in May when I receive the results. If you work in a district where formal assessment data are turned around quickly, this will not be such a conflict for you.

Assessments can also be categorized as quantitative or qualitative. Quantitative measures yield numbers. Quantitative data in reading can refer to a reading level, a percentage of accuracy on a running record, or a test score. Qualitative measures, on the other hand, attempt to offer descriptions for what is going on. These measures may include descriptions of the kinds of books a child likes to read or may analyze the reading skills a child uses when talking about a book in a book club.

It is important to have a repertoire of ways to assess reading. Standardized tests are not enough. A running record is not enough. A questionnaire about reading inter-ests is not enough. It is through multiple assessment measures—formal and informal; quantitative and qualitative; diagnostic, formative, and summative—that we can begin to understand the complexity of a reader's process and offer appropriate instruction to meet the reader's needs.

Assessing Engagement

Like any activity, reading is something that one gets better at with practice. It is not surprising, then, that for children to become better readers, they must read for long stretches of time, with just-right material, joyfully engaged in their reading (Allington 2000; Calkins 2000; Serravallo and Goldberg 2007). Without engagement during reading, this "time spent reading" doesn't count. As responsible reading teachers, it is important to be vigilant when it comes to our students' engagement and to offer them strategies and techniques to help them stay motivated and engaged while reading (Guthrie and Wigfield 1997).

Assessing for engagement can be both qualitative and quantitative. Certain behaviors are observable when it comes to determining whether a child is engaged or not: giggling at the funny part, keeping eyes on the book, turning pages at an acceptable pace. There are also measures, though, that help quantify how fully a child is engaged. We can look at the number of pages students read per reading workshop period and the number of books they read across the course of a week. Engagement inventories, book logs, and reading interest inventories provide both quantitative and qualitative data to help us plan for individuals and small groups (see Figure 2.1).

The Engagement Inventory

My staff developer, Mary Chiarella, woke me up one day out of a dream world. I had worked hard to create all of the conditions for a productive reading workshop for my thirty-two third graders and was quite proud of the silence. I felt strong at conferring with individuals and groups, and had children tucked away here and there across the classroom in their own self-chosen spots. Sounds nice, right? I was in denial, I guess, until Mary came into my classroom and said, "Half of your kids aren't reading. This is an emergency." My cheeks flushed as I looked around the room and realized she was right. Kids were quiet, sure, but they weren't reading. They were looking around the classroom or looking at me or looking out the window. They weren't looking at their books.

Something needed to be done. So, like any good daughter of an analytical chemist, I decided to observe closely and collect data. I expected and hoped to see that students were engaged in their reading work, that they were either engrossed in a

Assessing and Measuring Reading Engagement: What Information Can We Get from Engagement Inventories, Book Logs, and Reading Interest Inventories?	
Qualitative	**Quantitative**
Engagement inventory • Are the child's eyes on print? • Is the child giggling at the funny parts? • Is the child turning pages at an acceptable pace? • What types of things distract a child from reading? *Book log* • What types of books (genres, authors, levels) does the child tend to choose? *Reading inventory* • What are a child's attitudes toward reading? • Whom does a child like to share his reading with? • What types of books (genres, authors) does the child report liking and disliking?	*Engagement inventory* • How many minutes can a child stay engaged with a book? *Book log* • How many pages is the child reading per minute? • How many books does the child read per week? • How much time is spent reading at home versus reading at school?

Figure 2.1 Assessing Engagement Through Qualitative and Quantitative Measures

book—brow furrowed in concentration, or laughing at funny parts—or they were writing about their reading on sticky notes or in their notebooks.

I developed a checklist with my students' names along the left-hand column and time intervals along the top. My plan was to record exactly what I observed during each of the five-minute increments that I watched. I developed a quick coding system for myself so that I wouldn't spend a lot of time looking down at my clipboard, but would instead keep sweeping my eyes across and around the classroom. I decided to write a checkmark if students seemed engaged, a *W* if they were looking out the window, a *T* if they were looking at me, and *NB* if they were jotting about their reading in their notebook or on a sticky note. I also looked for signs of engagement, so I included

R for reacting to the text or *S* for smiling. After a day of watching closely, I analyzed my data. It spoke for itself, and was not very promising (see Figure 2.2).

From looking at the table, you can clearly see that many of my students were looking at me or out the window every single time I looked at them during the independent reading block. Some children lost steam after about fifteen minutes (Mark, Erin, Maria, Charlie, Elizabeth). Others sustained their attention the entire time (Mehak, Ramon, Desiree, Michael, David, Pete, Kenny, and Margaret). Clearly targeting the length of time that a student can stay engaged in reading helps develop a plan for how to help the child. One important piece of data, then, is to determine the stamina that a child has for reading. This stamina can be measured by how long a child reads before losing focus. I also am interested in looking at what the distracters seem to be, as that will also help me to identify an intervention plan. Students doing anything

Engagement Inventory

	10:05 (10 min)	10:15 (20 min)	10:25 (30 min)	10:35 (40 min)	10:40 (45 min)		
Mehak			R				
Melissa		NB			T		
Jenny				T			
Jose		looks tired	T		T		
Ramon							
Mark	T	T	T	T (look down)	T		
Desiree							
Luke			NB				
Selma		T			T		
Michael				Switched book	S		
Erin	W			T	T		
Maria	T		T		T		
Verona			NB	NB			
Rebecca							
Charlie	T	T		T	W		
David			R				
Pete		Switched book			R		
Kenny							
Elizabeth	T			T			
Margaret	S		S				

✓ = engaged
W = window
T = looking @ me, teacher

NB = writing (nt1k or post-it)
R = reacting to text
S = smiling

Figure 2.2 Completed Engagement Inventory

but reading every time I looked over (Mark, Charlie) are readers that I suspected had problems with choosing books that will interest them and problems refocusing themselves if they get distracted.

Book Logs

Book logs are invaluable tools for identifying many things about a reader. From a well-kept book log, you can learn about a student's reading tastes, habits, and stamina. We've long known the importance of book choice in reading. As far back at the 1960s, Daniel Fader's book *Hooked on Books* discussed how to get even the most reluctant students to read by helping them choose the right books. The book logs that the Teachers College Reading and Writing Project (TCRWP) recommends for upper elementary readers are logs that contain the date, title and author, start and stop time, and pages read.

I look for a number of different indicators of engagement in a child's book log. I look to see the types of books a child chooses, the length of time she is reading in home and in school each day, and her page per minute rate. Often, I can state what I notice but I also have some questions spring up from the information on a log. This information informs conversations I'll soon have during conferences.

Book Logs: What to Look For

- types of books a child chooses—is there a good variety or is it time to broaden the child's reading tastes?
- time spent reading at home
- time spent reading at school
- page per minute rate

Looking at the March book log of Samantha from Miss Rosie's second-grade class (Figure 2.3), I can glean some information about the kind of reader Samantha is, and I can formulate some questions I have about her. I notice that she reads several different kinds of series books, and when she finds a series she likes, she will seek out another within that series. She seems to like the Zack Files by Dan Greenburg, I can deduce, because she has chosen more than one. I also notice that she tends to read for

Name: Samantha

Miss Rosie's Class' Reading Log

Date	School or Home (S or H)	Title	Amount of Time	Pages Read (p. # - p. #)
2/24/09	h	hang aleft at Venus zack files	20 min.	p.1-p. 17
2/25/8	S	hang a left at venus	22 min.	P.17-P.41
2/25/09	h	hang a left at venus	20 min.	P.41-P.56
2/26/09	S	Hefi Jones 2#	20 Min	p.1-p.45
2/25/0	h	Herbie Jones 2#	20 Min	P.45-P.75
3/2/09	h	Hehbie Jones2#	20 Min.	P.75-P.91
3/4/09	S	Hehbie Jones 2#	#min.	P.91-P.94
3/4/09	S	Zack files	15 Min.	P.1-P.10
3/4/09	h	Zack files	20 Min	P.10-P.54
3/5/09	S	zack Files	20 min	P.54-P.58
3/5/09	x S	Judy mudy the docter is in!	20 min.	P.1-P.17
3/5/09	h	Judy mudy	30 Min.	P.17-P.31
3/9/09	S	Judy mudy	18 Min.	P.31-P.46
3/9/09	h	Judy mudy	20 min.	P.46-P.71
3/10/09	S	Judy mudy	20 min.	P.71-P.97
3/10/09	h	Judy mudy	20 m'.	P.97-P.135

Figure 2.3 Second Grader Samantha's One-Week Filled-In Book Log

about twenty minutes at a time whether in home or at school. Her reading rate at school (two pages per minute) seems to be faster than at home (less than one page per minute), which might mean that she is not really reading for twenty minutes at home, or that she has some things that distract her at home. All of the books on her log are pretty funny, so I think that she might also gravitate toward books with a good sense of humor.

This year, I worked with some colleagues at schools in New York City to create a book log appropriate for younger children. Of course, when children read books below level J/K, it is too much for them to record all of that information because it takes away from their time spent reading. However, they could easily use a tally system to record the number of times they've gotten through an entire book. In this example, a reader tallies under either the "home" or "school" column each time he reads a book. This reading might be a reread of a familiar book or a first read of a new book. In either case, he simply tallies once after reading. This system for logging could also be handled by putting a sticky note on the back cover of each book and having the student mark a tally on that sticky note. In this way, I can see how many times the child has read each book and how many books were read across the week.

In Isaiah's book log (Figure 2.4), it is apparent that he was inconsistent with how much (and probably how long) he read at home each night, whereas in school he was much more consistent. Also, he seemed to read less at home than at school. You can note from his teacher Ms. Lewis' comments that she gave that feedback to him and to the parent signing his log each night.

When looking at book logs with an eye toward engagement, it is helpful to think about the expectations for reading rate based on the level that the student reads. Harris and Sipay's (1990) research offers guidelines for reading rate based on grade level and reading level (Figure 2.5).

Name: *Isaiah*	Level: *E*	Monday's date: *11/3*
Monday (in school) IIII I	**Monday (at home)** III	**Parent initials:** *JBL*
Tuesday (in school) *no school – election day*	**Tuesday (at home)** IIII III	**Parent initials:** *JBL*
Wednesday (in school) IIII II	**Wednesday (at home)** IIII I	**Parent initials:** *JBL*
Thursday (in school) IIII I	**Thursday (at home)** IIII	**Parent initials:** *JBL*
Friday (in school) IIII III	**Friday (at home)** III	**Parent initials:** *JBL*

Teacher comments: *Isaiah – try to read as much at home every night as you do in school. Just like Wednesday. Good job also on Tuesday when we had no school.*
Love, Ms. Lewis

Figure 2.4 Isaiah's Tally Book Log

Grade Level	Reading Levels	Reading Rate (words per minute)
1	C–I	60–90
2	J–L	85–120
3	L–O	115–140
4	P–R	140–170
5	S–U	170–195
6	T–V	195–220
7	V–W	215–245
8	W–Z	235–270
9	Z	250–270

Figure 2.5 Reading Rate According to Reading Level (Harris and Sipay 1990)

With reading rate in mind, it is then helpful to think about how long it should take a child to finish a book, and, therefore, how many books a child should read in a period of time. We can compare these expectations against the child's book log to see if the child was engaged during reading in school and at home. For example, a level L text like *Horrible Harry in Room 2B* by Suzy Kline (1998) has about 4500 words in the entire text. If this is a beginning third-grade reading level, the child should be able to read it at about 115 words per minute. This means it should take that child about forty minutes to read the whole book. That's about one day's worth of reading. If the book log shows that it took the child even two days to read this book, that means that either the child is reading at half the speed that is expected for that level or the child was not engaged during reading. Further inquiry would be needed, but book logs are an important first signal to an issue with engagement.

Of course, all of these measures are only important if we also know about how a child understands a text. The information gleaned from book logs allows us to have conversations with students during conferences, or to use other assessment measures to understand not only how much time a child spends reading and how many pages are read, but what's happing during that time and in those pages. No one measure will give a full picture of what a reader is doing. The information gleaned here will also need to be understood in the context of how a student comprehends a text, whether the student has any difficulties with print work, and how fluently the child reads, in particular. These other dimensions of a reader are mentioned in subsequent sections.

Reading Interest Inventories

Reading interest inventories are questionnaires. In my classroom, I always began the school year with reading inventories, and repeated them a few times across the year. With these inventories, I hoped to get a sense of a student's attitudes toward reading, to learn who they considered themselves to be as a reader, and to find out about their book tastes and reading habits. In upper elementary and middle school classrooms, interest inventories can be completed by most students in writing. For younger children, or for children who aren't likely to accurately represent themselves in writing, these same questions can be asked during a conference.

My first attempts at reading inventories were modeled after published examples that suggested I ask questions like "What is your favorite series?" and "Where do you like to read?" Inherent in those questions, though, is the presumption that children actually enjoy reading. If my goal was to really crack open my students' attitudes about books, it was important that I didn't set them up to lie to me. Hopefully, many of my students did in fact love to read and couldn't wait to get their hands on the classroom library I had so carefully assembled for them. For some children, though, it was likely that reading time was met with an internal groan, a sinking stomach, and a clock-watching unique to that time of day. From the beginning of the school year, and all across the year, I was less interested in my students telling me what they thought I wanted to hear, and more interested with them being honest. With help from Donna Santman, a staff developer and author of a book on inference and interpretation called *Shades of Meaning* (2005), I developed a questionnaire with a slightly different tone. Questions included:

- ❏ When you hear it's time for reading, what do you think?
- ❏ Do you read outside of school? Explain why.
- ❏ Can you recall a positive experience with reading? Tell me about it.
- ❏ Do you have any negative experiences with reading? Tell me about them.
- ❏ If you could request anything to be part of the classroom library, what would it be?
- ❏ I'm planning on units of study this year in character, nonfiction, fantasy, historical fiction, poetry, and reading between the lines. Do any of those interest you? Which ones? Do you dread any of them? Which ones?

❏   How do you feel about having a partner who reads the same books you read, or a club to talk to about your reading?

❏   What do you like to do when you finish a book?

Nanako, a fifth grader in Lisa Uhr's class, completed an end-of-year interest inventory (Figure 2.6) that said a lot about who she was as a reader. I think because of what she said about her cousin, she understood that "lost-in-a-book" feeling. I love how she said she felt "adventurous" when she heard it was time for reading, and she liked Harry Potter books because they "dig you into another world." She understood that reading can take you places. She said she dreaded nonfiction and historical fiction because they were real things—but as a teacher, maybe I can teach her about how to get lost in those story worlds as well. She was very independent and I'm not sure that she was using her partnerships or book clubs to really push her thinking; she thought it was only "fine" to have a partner, and she thought that the purpose was mostly to agree or disagree. Maybe strengthening her work with peers would help her engagement in genres other than fantasy.

When I gave this questionnaire to students, I told them that I really and truly wanted them to answer honestly and completely. The results I got told me a lot about how to begin forming groups, how to modify my unit plans for the year, and how to reorganize my classroom library. I repeated these inventories at the end of the year as a way to help children make plans and goals for themselves as readers, and to send on to next year's teachers.

> **Ways to Assess for Engagement**
>
> •   Take an "assessment inventory" to see how long individual students can sustain reading.
>
> •   Look at book logs for evidence of engagement and stamina.
>
> •   Take a reading interest inventory, encouraging honesty.

The Take-Away: Implications for Grouping

Being able to form a small group based on needing work in engagement does not end with identifying a group of children who seem disengaged. Instead, it is important to ask why each student is not engaged, and then put them in a group

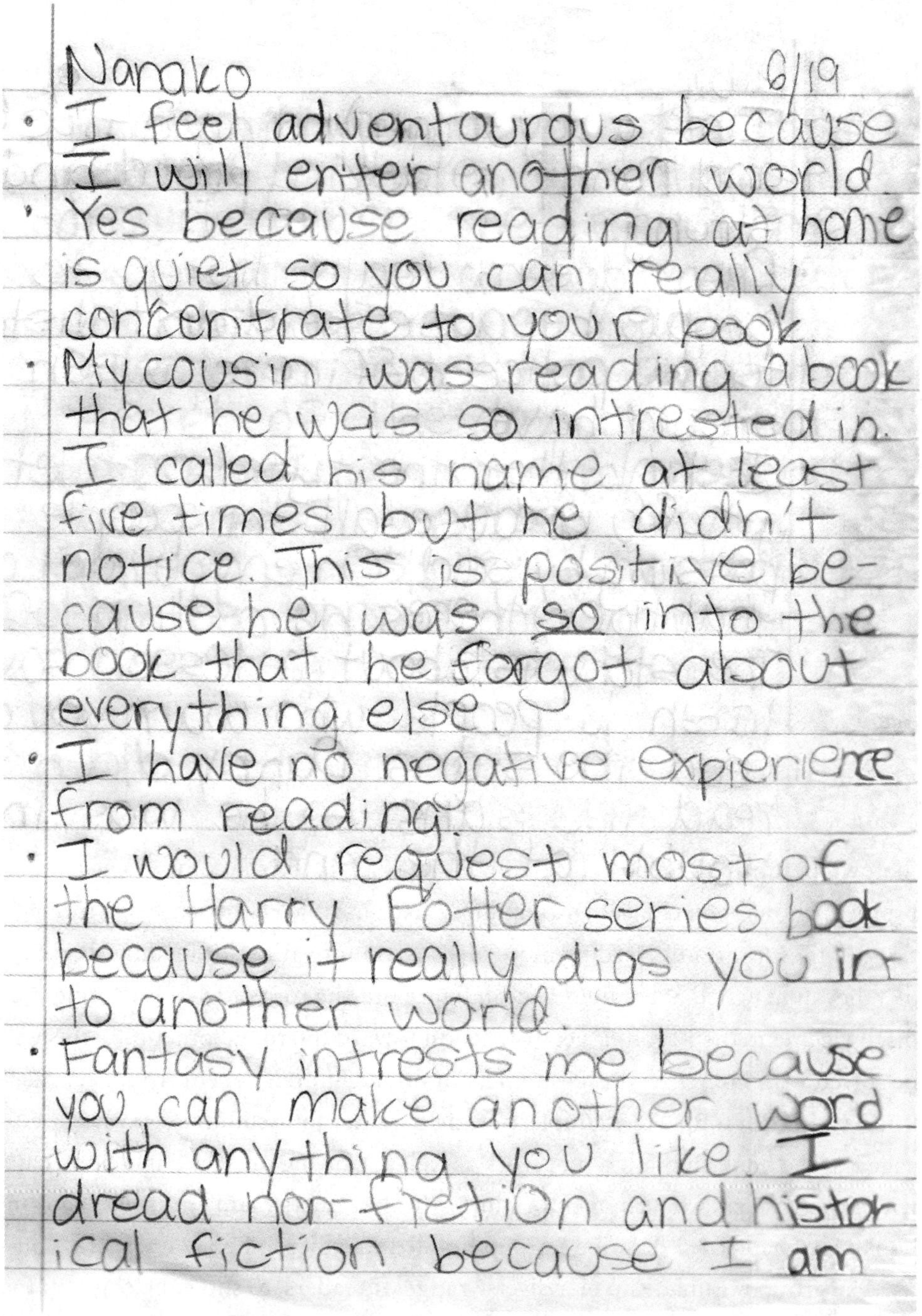

Nanako   6/19
- I feel adventourous because
  I will enter another world.
- Yes because reading at home
  is quiet so you can really
  concentrate to your book.
- My cousin was reading a book
  that he was so intrested in.
  I called his name at least
  five times but he didn't
  notice. This is positive because he was so into the
  book that he forgot about
  everything else.
- I have no negative expierience
  from reading.
- I would request most of
  the Harry Potter series book
  because it really digs you in
  to another world.
- Fantasy intrests me because
  you can make another word
  with anything you like. I
  dread non-fiction and histor
  ical fiction because I am

Figure 2.6 Nanako's End-of-Year Reading Interest Inventory

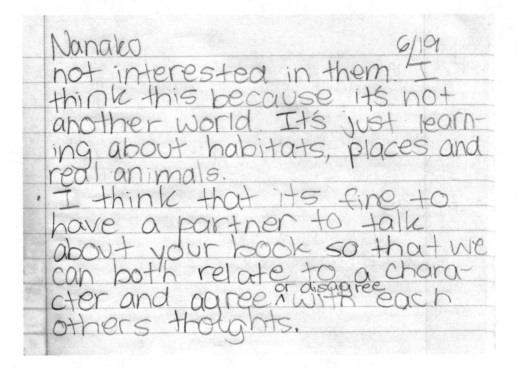

Nanako   6/19
not interested in them. I
think this because it's not
another world. It's just learning about habitats, places and
real animals.
• I think that it's fine to
have a partner to talk
about your book so that we
can both relate to a character and agree ^or disagree with each
others thoughts.

Figure 2.6 *(Continued)*

that will best help them past this bump in the road. Is the root of the engagement problem about book choice? Distractibility? Not having a clear sense of expectations in the classroom? Needing more of a social motivation for reading? Feeling like they aren't good at reading? If I can figure out the root of what is causing the disengagement, then I can target instruction toward the root. Sometimes, this will be solved with homogeneous grouping, but often children benefit from peer mentors within the group. For example, putting together four children who are disengaged into a book club might not work as well as putting one child in a book club with other readers who can mentor him with some energy and enthusiasm around books. In Chapter 3, I describe a group I pulled together to help with distractibility. The group was made up of a diverse range of readers, to show the children that all readers get distracted from time to time and benefit from strategies to help them to stay focused.

Assessing Fluency

Fluency and intonation are important signals as to the extent to which a reader makes sense of the text as he reads. Fluency tells us about comprehension. Through reading smoothly and expressively, a reader also communicates that meaning to a listener. Fluency affects comprehension, comprehension affects fluency (Kuhn 2008; Rasinski 2003). As with any of the other four dimensions mentioned in this chapter—comprehension, engagement, print work strategies, and conversation skills—it is not enough to look at fluency in isolation. Fluency tells us about how well a child comprehends, how automatic the child's word recognition is, the ability of a child to use print work strategies when encountering new words, and the ability to stay engaged in a book. This section looks at fluency, but any information gathered from the suggested assessment measures must be looked at alongside the other measures as well.

In analyzing a child's reading with an eye toward fluency, it is essential to go beyond just the speed with which a child can read and look at the qualities and dimensions within her fluent reading. In particular, I consider accuracy, automaticity, expression, prosody, and parsing and take note of each aspect. See Figure 2.7 for a partial glossary of terms explaining dimensions of fluent reading.

Accuracy: The ability of a reader to identify words in text correctly or with precision.

Automaticity: The recognition of words in text instantaneously without the use of strategy or other conscious effort.

Expression: See *prosody*.

Fluent reading: Reading that incorporates automatic as well as accurate word recognition along with the use of appropriate phrasing and expression.

Prosody: The aspects of reading such as stress, emphasis, and appropriate phrasing that, when taken together, create an expressive rendering of a text.

Parsing: Maintaining appropriate syntax when reading; breaking a sentence into appropriate phrase units. Correct parsing aids comprehension.

Phrasing: See *parsing*.

Figure 2.7 Fluency: A Partial Glossary of Terms. Adapted from Kuhn (2008).

It is important, then, to assess a student's oral reading of a text. Depending on the child's independent reading level, a different level of fluency is expected. Rasinski (2003) adapted a National Assessment of Educational Progress fluency scale (Figure 2.8) to aid in understanding how fluency develops. By using this scale, I can first determine the stage of fluency that the reader is in, and can then read the descriptor of the next level to see what types of behaviors to teach to support the child's move to the next stage.

Level 1: Fountas and Pinnell levels A, B, C (correlates to DRA levels 1 and 2)
- Reads primarily in a word-by-word fashion.
- Occasional two-word and three-word phrases may occur, but these are infrequent. Author's meaningful syntax is generally not preserved.
- Passage is read without expression or intonation.
- Reading seems labored and difficult.

Level 2: Fountas and Pinnell levels D–E (correlates to DRA levels 3–6)
- Reads primarily in two-word phrases with occasional three- or four-word phrases.
- Some word-by-word reading may be present.
- Word groupings may be awkward and unrelated to the larger context of the sentence or passage.
- Passage is read with little or inappropriate expression or intonation.

Level 3: Fountas and Pinnell levels F–I (correlates to DRA levels 7–17)
- Reads primarily in three- or four-word phrases.
- Some smaller phrases may be present. Most of the phrasing is appropriate and preserves the author's syntax.
- Some of the text is read with appropriate expression and intonation.

Level 4: Fountas and Pinnell levels J–Z (correlates to DRA levels 18 and up)
- Reads primarily in longer, meaningful phrases.
- Although some regressions, repetitions, and deviations from the text may be present, these do not appear to detract from the overall structure or meaning of the passage.
- The reading preserves the author's syntax.
- Most of the text is read with appropriate expression and intonation.
- A sense of ease is present in the reader's oral presentation.

Figure 2.8 Fluency Scale. Adapted from *The Fluent Reader* (Rasinksi 2003).

Shared Reading

When most of the children in my class were reading levels J and below, I had a daily whole-class shared reading time when everyone read from the same text (either a big book, a chart, or an overhead projection). During this time, I found it hard to listen to children as individuals. To remedy this, I had portions of the class read together, and I listened carefully to them as individuals. For example, I divided the carpet into four squares and each section took turns reading pages.

It was important during this shared reading for me to listen for different aspects of fluency, and to take notes on the children as individuals. For example, I had a check-list with children's names along the left-hand side and the fluency descriptors along the top (reads in two- or three-word phrases, attends to ending punctuation, phrases preserve the author's syntax). During the shared reading lesson, or after the lesson was over, I quickly checked off what I heard from each of the students (see Figure 2.9).

Running Records

Another important opportunity to assess fluency is during running records. When administering running records, I created a space on my form to record how many words the child read before pausing, whether the child paid attention to punctuation, and how the child's voice sounded during dialogue or during narration. When I collected these data on running records, I could go back and sort children based on where they fell along the fluency scale.

	Two-Word Phrases	Three-Word Phrases	Attends to Ending Punctuation	Phrases Preserve Author's Syntax
Isabella				
Marcus				
Emma				
Louis				

Figure 2.9 Sample Checklist Used During a Small-Group Shared Reading Lesson, Assessing Fluency

From Grace Lee's running record (Figure 2.10), I noticed that she read at a fluency level 4, as was appropriate for this level L text, *Meet the Molesons* by Burny Bos (1995). She preserved the author's syntax as she read, and often stopped to create meaningful phrases when she paused within a sentence ("One morning"/ "Dusty and I"/ "were getting ready for school"). Most often, though, she paused only at the end of sentences. She attended to punctuation, noticing exclamation points and question marks and making her voice match the marks she saw on the page. She was also very accurate and automatic with her word recognition, miscuing only twice, which helped her fluency.

One-on-One Conferences

When conferring with children reading below level I, I often ask the child to read aloud to me as part of the research of the conference. With children above this level, I research by asking the child to read aloud only when I know from past assessments that fluency or print work strategies may be an area of concern. During this time, I listen for the child's print work strategies as well as how fluently and expressive his reading sounds. Even if I decide in the one-on-one conference not to teach something relating to fluency, I make a note as to what I heard during that reading.

In the excerpt of the transcript below, notice how I began the conference with the goal of talking about the student's comprehension, but soon got the hunch that he was not really that engaged with the book. I wondered if he read it expressively in his head, and whether he really understood what was going on. I then decided to assess his fluency by having him read aloud. The slashes in the student's part of the transcript are to help you hear what I heard during the conference, and in brackets I give commentary on how he read the lines of the text.

Me: Hi, Jonah. How are you liking *Henry and Mudge Under the Yellow Moon*?

Jonah: It's OK. I like Halloween.

Me: Oh, it takes place at Halloween. Is it spooky?

Jonah: I don't know.

Me: Why don't you read a little bit to me?

Jonah: OK. [*Reads in a monotone*] Henry / loved Halloween. He loved / to make / jack-o-lanterns. He / loved / to make / paper bats. / And most of all / he loved to dress / up. But there was one thing / about Halloween / Henry did not like: / ghost stories.

Grace Lee   November 16

Meet the Molesons, by Burny Bos

One morning/Dusty and I/were getting

ready for school/ I found Mother's red

lipstick/ in the bathroom./

I opened it up/ I made/red dots on my

face/I put/some more on/ Great! / *(on)* ← good expression

Dusty noticed/ "You look like you have

chicken pox."/

"Ooooh," I said/ "I don't feel well/ I think   *changed voice to sound like character*

I have to stay home from school."/

"Give me that!"/Dusty took the lipstick. ←

Soon we both had "chicken pox."/

We went back to bed/

"Time for school!"/ Father called/

"Oooh!"/ we moaned/   *(Mo-ned)*   ✓?

Father ran in/ "What's wrong?"/he cried./   *didn't read in "weak" voice.*

"We are sick,"/ I said in a weak voice. ←

Figure 2.10 Grace Lee's Running Record Listening for Fluency. Slashes Indicate Pauses.

At this point in the conference, I decided to teach Jonah that he could think about and match his expression to how the character was feeling. When Henry was excited about Halloween, Jonah's voice should sound excited. When Henry was scared, Jonah's voice should sound nervous and afraid. I coached Jonah to try this on a few pages, and wrote notes to myself to follow up with him in another small-group conference soon with other students who could benefit from practicing this strategy.

Partnerships or Clubs

When children are grouped with and spend time reading out loud with same-ability partners or clubs, I can assess fluency. In primary grades, children have these partnership opportunities daily. In upper elementary school, children might meet with partners or clubs two or three times per week. During this time, I make my way around the classroom, assessing fluency and comprehension.

Often, during partnerships or book clubs, children read aloud parts of their text. They may read aloud to share a favorite part with their peers, to reenact a scene, or to prove a point they are making about an idea they had when reading. I can listen in, seeing if the way they read matches the emotion of the character on the page, if it matches the dialogue tag telling the reader how to read the dialogue, and if it is appropriately fluent for the level, according to the fluency scale. I teach in the moment, responding to what I see, and make notes for follow-up in subsequent small-group conferences.

Following is an excerpt from a transcript from two fourth-grade children who read *Junebug* by Alice Mead (1995) in a reading partnership. They discussed ideas they had about the characters; the students read excerpts aloud to prove their thinking. As I listened to them talk, I was interested to see if the children chose appropriate parts in the text to support their thinking, and if they were able to read those parts with intonation that supported their thinking. I saw with these two boys a nice intersection between evidence of their comprehension and evidence of strong fluency and intonation skills.

Jonas: Well, one thing I'm thinking about Junebug is that he acts one way around his friends, but, like, really feels different.

Malik: What do you mean?

Jonas: Right here, where he's talking about how he's nervous about his tenth birth-day cuz he's worried the kids are going to ask him to run errands. But I don't think he really means runs errands, he means do bad stuff like maybe steal. He says . . . I mean, he doesn't say it, but he's the narrator so he kind of says it. He says, "I don't want to think about that." And "Maybe he did. Maybe he didn't. I don't know" [*reads this part in a very dismissive tone as if the character were speaking, brushing off his own comments*].

Malik: So you think even though he says he doesn't care, he really does?

Jonas: Yeah. What were you thinking about?

Malik: I was thinking about the sister character.

Jonas: What are you thinking about her?

Malik: Well, it's weird how she doesn't talk. It says here, "She starts off up the stairs. She doesn't say a word. She can talk. She just doesn't" [*reads this part slowly, pausing dramatically at each period*]. This makes me think it's going to be a big problem later on in the book. It's the last thing he says in this chapter.

Jonas: That's a good prediction.

▶ **Opportunities to Assess Fluency**

- in the midst of whole-class or small-group shared reading
- while administering running records
- during conferences
- when children read aloud during partnerships or clubs

The Take-Away: Implications for Grouping

Just as with grouping for engagement, it's important that the children in a group on fluency have a common need, not simply that they all read choppily. It is more helpful to listen carefully to how many words they are able to put together at a time, and work to move them toward more meaningful phrases or more words read at a time. Perhaps I'll group children because although they read smoothly, their intonation could use some work. The common need of the group could also be that they read through ending punctuation. The more precise I am with why I pull them together, the more productive my group will be. In Chapters 4 and 6, I give concrete advice for a variety of structures to support readers in developing their fluent, expressive reading. Keep in mind, though, that group makeups constantly shift. A group may start out having four members for the first and second meetings, and then go down to two, then add a third for the fourth meeting. These groups are flexible and ever-changing, requiring constant formative assessment.

Assessing Print Work Strategies

Readers use print work strategies to "attend to the visual information in print" and to utilize phonological, semantic, and syntactic information for "word-level problem solving" (Clay 2001, 145, 126). For the youngest readers to be successful, they must be able to make sense of the written code we call the alphabet. This begins with discriminating letters from one another (*b, d, p, q*) and also with knowing the letter-sound relationships (*c* = /k/ or /s/). As readers mature, they will be called upon to use a variety of strategies to figure out new words and to recognize familiar words. These strategies may include finding parts of words they know to help them figure out the whole of the word; using familiar prefixes, suffixes, and roots of words to figure out new words; and syllabicating words from left to right, all while using the context and picture (if there is one) to check if the word they read makes sense.

As proficient readers, the strategies that we know are almost always underground. We have developed automaticity in dealing with print that makes it difficult to realize the amount of processing it takes a beginning reader to "crack the code." One exercise I lead teachers through to help them uncover the strategies that have gone underground is to look at text that is very challenging. Usually, I select an excerpt from a scientific journal that has many unfamiliar words. Try to read the following excerpt aloud, and notice what you do when you encounter difficulty:

> *A new hypothesis of the phylogenetic position of the angel sharks, Squatina, is proposed based on a cladistic character analysis of skeletal, mycological, and external morphologies. Squatina is compared with squaloids, pristiophorids, Chlamydoselachus, hexanchoids, and all major rajiform taxa. Squatina is concluded to be the sister group of pristiophorids plus rajiforms; a pristiophorid-rajiform relationship is evidenced by four synapomorphies. (Shirai 1992, 505)*

Most elementary school teachers would have a great deal of difficulty with that excerpt; it would probably take an advanced degree in biology to read that passage with automaticity. So, because there were challenges, it helps us to be aware of our print work strategies. Here are just a few strategies I use when I encounter difficulty in reading that excerpt:

❑ find parts of words I recognize to help me to read unfamiliar words (i.e., *phylo* in *phylogenic*)

❑ read new words based on how I know letter combinations act in familiar words (i.e., *Chl* will probably sound like how it does in a word I know, *chloroform*)

❑ read words syllable-by-syllable when I don't recognize parts (i.e., *pristiophorids = pris-ti-o-phor-ids*)

In the upcoming sections, I recommend two different ways to figure out what strategies young readers are using as they encounter difficulties in a text: running records and one-on-one conferences. In both examples, I take down information about a reader's errors and self-corrections and systematically analyze the data gathered using Marie Clay's advice for miscue analysis.

Running Records

Running records offer numerous opportunities to assess children's use of meaning, syntax, and visual cueing systems as they read. Marie Clay (1993) writes that the purpose of taking these records is to "determine what is already known" so that we can "provide the learner with a useful context within which to embed new learning" (20). When looking at a running record, I ask myself questions to determine the cueing systems that a child is using and not using when making an error and when self-correcting mistakes. I ask myself:

❑ Does that mistake/self-correction make sense (meaning)?

❑ Does that mistake/self-correction sound right (syntax)?

❑ Does that mistake/self-correction look right (visual)?

Running records can be taken to determine a child's independent level— where she can read the words with 97 to 98 percent accuracy, with fluency, and with comprehension. When attempting to analyze a child's print work skills, however, it is often more helpful to do a running record at her instructional level—where she can read the words at or slightly below 95 percent accuracy. The reading of instructional-level texts gives more information because errors are more plentiful.

When children are reading at levels A–I and are expected to move from level to level about once a month, I do running records every few weeks. When children are reading at levels J–Q, I do a formal running record about four times a year. Beyond that, I do running records about two or three times a year.

After I've taken a running record, I return to it to analyze the child's errors and self-corrections that I recorded. After looking across an entire text for patterns, I determine what the child relies on. I'm even more interested in analyzing inside of one of these three cueing systems. For example, if a student usually uses visual cues, making the following miscues: *snack/snake, belt/built, feel/fell*, I know more than just the fact that the child was able to read words that looked like the word in the text. I might guess that the child uses the beginning and ending letters to read the word, but often has difficulty with the middle. I might go even further to say that the "middle" includes vowel sounds that might be posing a challenge to the child.

Likewise, I might look at syntactical errors and realize that the errors are really a problem with part of speech. I might notice instead that the child drops or adds certain endings on words (for example, the child might read *feel* instead of *feels* or *recall* instead of *recalled*).

I might look at meaning errors and realize that when the child gets to a difficult part in the text, she reads any word that makes sense, without regard for whether the word she says looks like the word on the page. For example, a child might read, "The bird had been so gentle, and Harry hadn't been thinking of her," instead of, "The bird had been so *quiet*, and Harry hadn't been thinking of her."

Ideally, children use and integrate all of these cueing systems as they read, and another important lens to use when looking at print work is to see if children are flexible problem solvers, utilizing many sources of information as they read.

From Maggie's running record (Figure 2.11), I can gather some important information about what's happening when she makes an error, and what causes her to

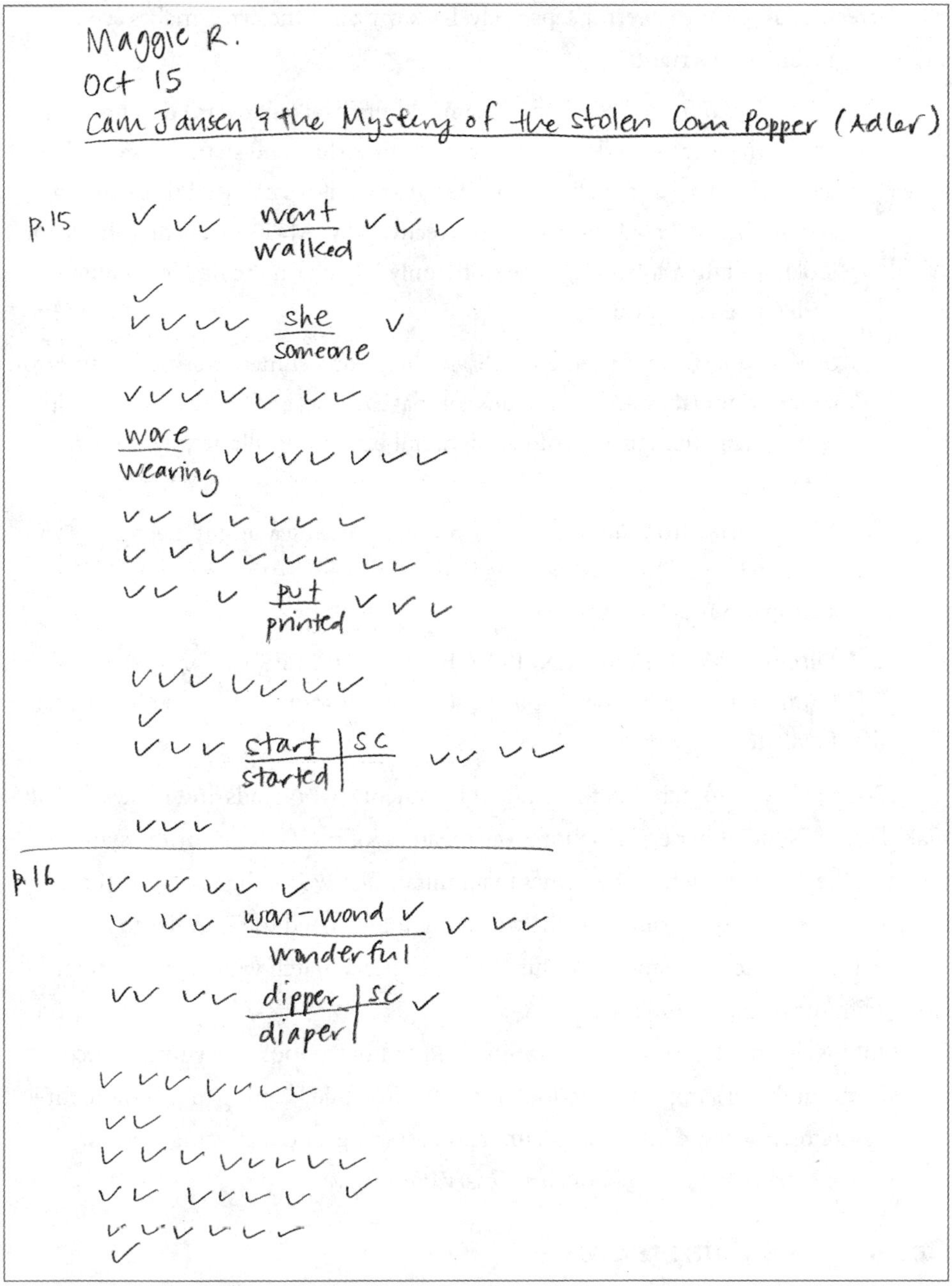

Maggie R.
Oct 15
<u>Cam Jansen & the Mystery of the stolen Corn Popper</u> (Adler)

p. 15 ✓ ✓✓ <u>went</u> ✓✓✓
     walked

  ✓
  ✓✓✓✓ <u>she</u> ✓
     someone

  ✓✓✓✓✓ ✓✓
  <u>ware</u>
  wearing ✓✓✓✓ ✓✓✓

  ✓✓ ✓✓ ✓✓ ✓
  ✓ ✓ ✓✓ ✓✓ ✓✓
  ✓✓ ✓ <u>put</u> ✓✓✓
     printed

  ✓✓✓ ✓✓ ✓✓
  ✓
  ✓✓✓ <u>start</u> | SC ✓✓ ✓✓ ✓
    started |

  ✓✓✓

p 16 ✓✓✓ ✓✓ ✓
  ✓ ✓✓ <u>wan—wond</u> ✓ ✓ ✓✓
     wonderful
  ✓✓ ✓✓ <u>dipper</u> | SC ✓
     diaper |

  ✓ ✓✓ ✓✓✓✓
  ✓✓
  ✓ ✓✓ ✓✓✓✓
  ✓✓ ✓✓✓✓ ✓
  ✓ ✓✓✓✓ ✓
  ✓

Figure 2.11 Maggie's Running Record

self-correct. Looking at each error separately, I ask myself if the error makes sense, sounds right, and looks right.

❑ *Went/walked* from the sentence "Cam and Eric walked toward the shopping bag"—the error sounds right (they are both verbs), and share the same first letter. The error also makes sense. Here, the reader is using all three cueing systems but still reads the word incorrectly. Why? My hunch is that she is not looking all the way through the word, only relying on the first letter along with syntax and meaning.

❑ *She/someone* from the sentence " 'Can I help you?' someone asked"—the error sounds right (they are both nouns), it makes sense, and shares the same first letter. Again, though, the reader might not be looking all the way through the word.

❑ *Wore/wearing* from the sentence, "A woman wearing a bright green dress with a large white button was standing in front of them"—the error follows the same pattern as the last two.

❑ *Put/printed* for the sentence, "I'M A BINKY'S HELPER was printed on the button"—this error does not make sense, but it sounds right and has the same first letter.

So far, I have a hunch that this student is someone who reads and makes sure it makes sense. None of her errors ignores the meaning of the sentence or the syntax of the sentence. However, when she comes to an unfamiliar word, she uses only the initial letter to help her to figure out what the word might be. I need to teach her to look all the way through the word and make sure that the letters match what she's reading, along with the meaning and syntax.

In this section, I gave a very beginning idea of how to look at a running record with the point that it's important to look for patterns while keeping in mind the three cueing systems. For more information on taking, scoring, and analyzing running records, see Marie Clay's 1993 book, *An Observation Survey*.

One-on-One Conferences

One-on-one conferences can be a place to do a more informal record of reading. As a child reads his books, I might ask him to read aloud for a portion of the conference. Usually, I do this only for children in lower levels (A–J). I also usually do this only on a first read-through of a text, because the child should be able to read a high percentage of the words without utilizing any print work strategies. When it is a first read, I will often take a quick running record in my notes, much like the full-page running record in Figure 2.10.

Assessing Comprehension

Comprehension is at the heart of what it means to really read. Reading is thinking and understanding and getting at the meaning behind a text. Comprehension instruction begins in TCRWP's schools before children can even conventionally read. As children are read to during read-aloud, they are asked to think about characters, make predictions about what will come next, question and wonder what's happening, and consider what lesson they can learn from the book.

Depending on which professional book you look at, you will likely see a different list of "the" reading skills. Keene and Zimmermann in their book *Mosaic of Thought* (1997) synthesized a great deal of research and distilled all of the reading skills mentioned down to the following seven.

- ❏ *Activating prior knowledge before, during, and after reading a text.* Proficient readers think about what they already know about a text's structure or topic before they read; they make connections to their lives, other books, and the world as they read; and they think about these connections after they are finished reading.

- ❏ *Determining the most important ideas and themes in a text.* Proficient readers understand the most significant events in a fiction story and use the significant events to retell, and when reading nonfiction can determine the main idea of a passage, section, or chapter.

- ❏ *Creating visual and sensory images before, during, and after reading a text.* Proficient readers have a "lost-in-a-book" feeling when reading and are able to describe the multisensory experiences they have across the course of reading the text. It is not simply about visualizing, but also hearing, seeing, smelling, and feeling what is described in the text.

- ❏ *Asking questions.* Proficient readers read with curiosity. They question the text, often including the characters' actions or motivations, their own reactions to what's in the book, and even the author's decisions of what to include and what not to include.

❏ *Drawing inferences.* Proficient readers constantly read beyond what's literally in the text. They are able to form judgments, make predictions, and determine the theme or message of a story, and they have their own ideas and critiques about a text.

❏ *Retelling and synthesizing.* Proficient readers can figure out how parts of a text fit together. One way to use that knowledge is to retell a text in sequence, chronicling what happened first, next, and finally. Readers can also put parts of the text together to understand cause and effect, character change, or how all of the nonfiction features on one page fit together under a single main idea.

❏ *Using fix-up strategies when comprehension breaks down.* Proficient readers monitor their own understanding as they read and have strategies to fix confusion as it arises. These strategies include the ability to understand new vocabulary.

It is often so challenging to assess comprehension because it is invisible—without a student writing down what is going through her head, or talking to another about what she is thinking, it becomes challenging to see the reader's processing. Comprehension skill assessment is also so complicated because none of these seven skills is static. The way in which a reader uses each of these skills depends upon so many variables including but not limited to genre, text level/difficulty, the reader's prior experience with the topic, and the text structure. For example, a child may have really thoughtful ideas about a character when reading a realistic fiction story about a child in school because the topic and genre are familiar. However, when that same child encounters a fantasy story for the first time, he might find that there is so much to attend to in terms of the magical elements of the genre that all of a sudden it becomes challenging to think in complex ways about the character; the reader simply tries to keep track of who is who and to visualize the world of the story.

As teachers of reading, it is important to find teaching opportunities that are within a child's zone of proximal development. I teach for depth instead of deficit. That is, when I assess a reader's use of comprehension skills, I don't look to check off what I see, as if to say, "Yup! He can infer." "Yes! He's got the visualizing down." Instead, I look at the quality of the skill being used and think about how I can help the child deepen this skill work.

Two years ago, the TCRWP also started working on taking each of these skills and thinking about them along a continuum. We used a short story and preplanted boxes for the reader to stop and jot in response to prompts intended to assess four different skills. We collected hundreds of student and adult responses to the questions and sorted them in an attempt to determine what made some of the responses more proficient than others. Being part of this research think tank allowed me to see that there is varying depth with which any one of these seven skills can be expressed.

Following are some stop-and-jots from a third-grade class of children at PS 158. I read *The Bat Boy and His Violin*, a historical fiction picture book by Curtis, and prompted students to stop and jot their thinking. The book is about a young boy whose father is a coach for a Negro League team. The father doesn't approve of his son's love of the violin and makes him become a batboy for the baseball team. When the boy fails miserably at his batboy duties, the father tells him to just go into the dugout and fiddle. The music he plays has a positive effect on the team, which begins winning. Eventually, the team receives an invitation to play the top-ranked Negro League team. Although they lose, the father comes to develop a new understanding about his son and his love for music because of the time they've spent together.

The first set of responses (Figure 2.12) is from the children looking only at the front cover of the picture book, and I was assessing their ability to active prior knowledge. What's shown is an illustration of an African American boy playing a violin in a baseball uniform, with baseball players in the background. I asked the students to "jot what you know about how stories like this tend to go." The first child's writing indicates that he thought about the mood of the story, the second jotting shows that the child took into account the historical time period, and the third jotting shows that the child thought on a more inferential level about a possible big idea or interpretation from the whole of the book. In thinking about the skill of activating prior knowledge, the first child's sticky note shows a more basic ability and the third child's is more sophisticated.

In Figure 2.13, there are a few collected sticky notes in response to a prompt asking the children to "describe this scene using all of your senses." Here, I was

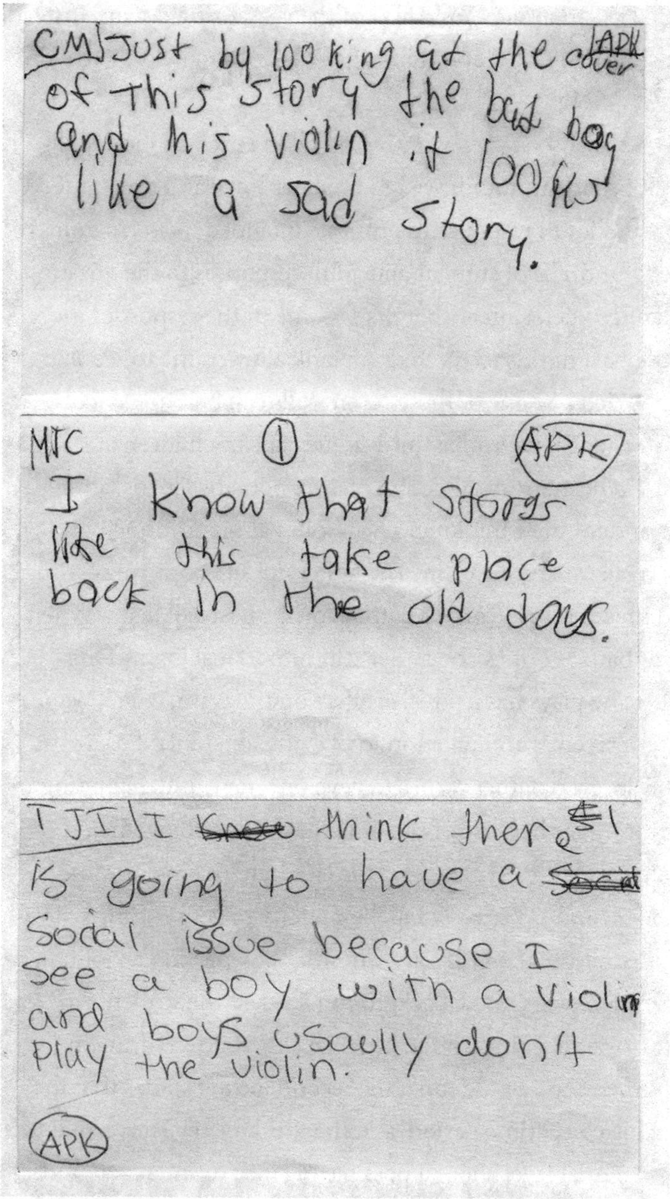

CM) Just by looking at the cover
of This story the bad boy
and his violin it looks
like a sad story.

MTC   ①   APK
I know that stores
like this take place
back in the old days.

TJI) I ~~know~~ think there $1
is going to have a ~~social~~
social issue because I
see a boy with a violin
and boys usaully don't
play the violin.
APK

Figure 2.12 Activating Prior Knowledge Jots

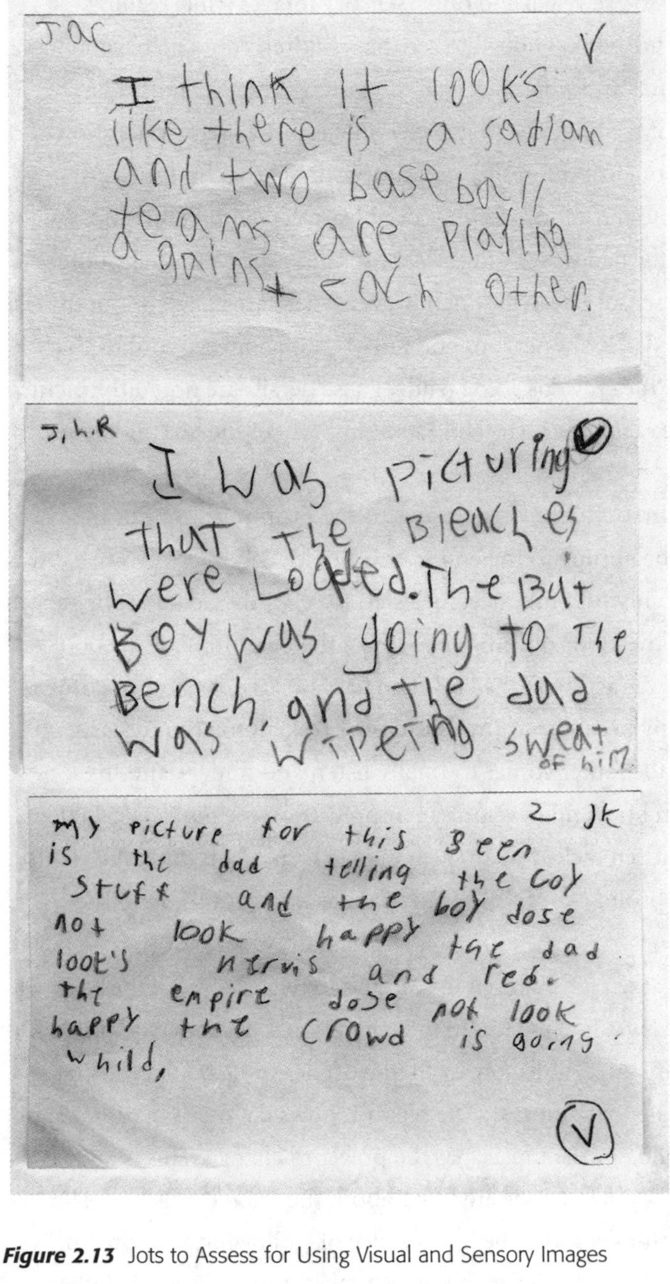

JAC

I think it looks
like there is a sadium
and two baseball
teams are playing
agains+ each other.

J.h.R

I was picturing
that The Bleaches
were Looped. The Bat
Boy was going to The
Bench, and The dad
was wipeing sweat
of him

my picture for this been
is the dad telling the coy
stuff and the boy dose
not look happy the dad
look's nirvis and red.
the empire dose not look
happy the crowd is going
whild,

Z JK

Figure 2.13 Jots to Assess for Using Visual and Sensory Images

assessing children's ability to use visual and other sensory images while reading. Because the book is a picture book, I hoped to see that children could go beyond just what they saw in the pictures and what they read in words of the text and add to the multisensory experience of reading. The first sticky note is just a literal reiteration of what's in the picture. Although accurate, it's very simplistic. The second sticky note shows a bit of inference into the father's feelings or at least the temperature of the day when the student writes "the dad was wiping sweat off him." The third sticky note shows the most complete sensory description, however. There are details about the character's feelings—"the dad looks nervous and red"—and about the sounds that might have been heard—"the crowd is going wild." These details are not in the picture or the words, but are instead inferred. The child took in more of the text and used more sensory images.

Figure 2.14 shows three children's responses to the prompt "How has the father changed from the beginning to the end of this book?" With this prompt, I was assessing the children's ability to synthesize. I wanted to see if they could think about how the father acted and the kinds of things he said in the beginning of the book, and the kinds of ways he was acting at the end. The first sticky note simply states a change in feeling—grumpy to not grumpy. This doesn't take into account large chunks of the text where the father comes to finally listen and understand his son, who was so different from him, and develops an appreciation for his musical talent. The second and third children picked up on a change in attitude in the father—his becomes more caring, or proud—and this idea is a fuller understanding of the whole book.

The final question I asked the children to respond to regarded what the story was *really* about (Figure 2.15). I was looking for an interpretation—an understanding on an inferential level of the message, or lesson, or theme of the whole book. The first child's response is simply a poor summary. The second shows an interpretation about how "the sound of the violin," or the music, has the power to change. This is an insightful response, but it doesn't include anything about the main characters. The third child wrote that the story is about the importance of "following your dream." This response seems the most sophisticated because it takes into account the father, who follows his dream to take his baseball team to championships, and the boy, who follows his dream of being a violinist despite resistance at first from his father.

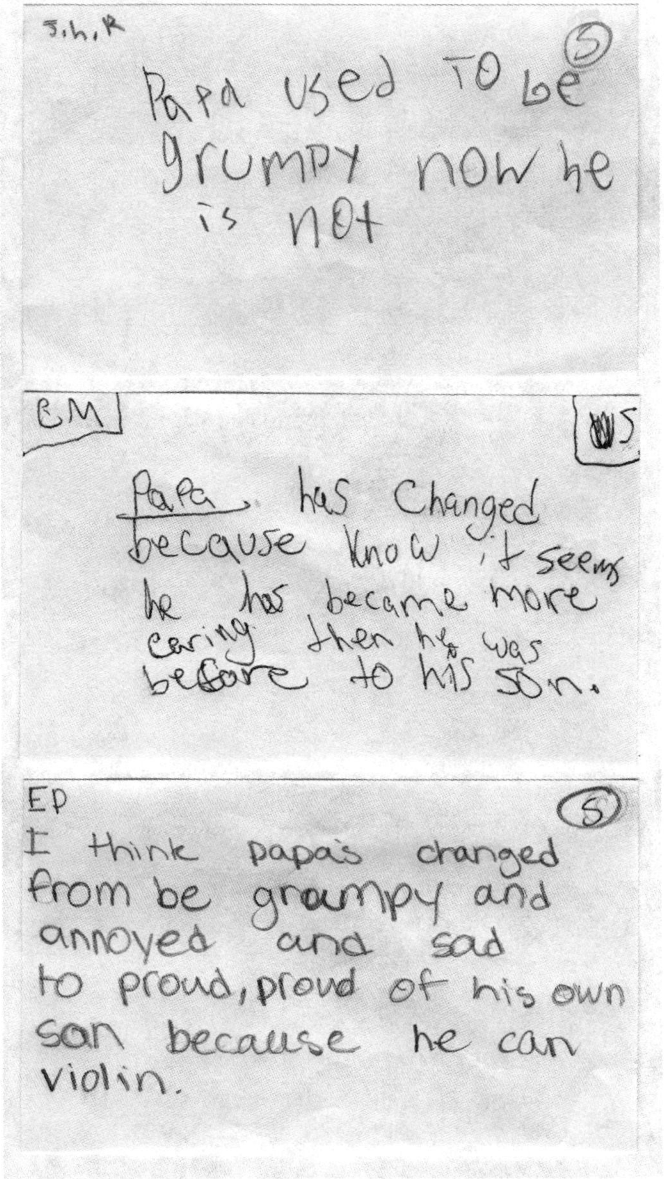

J,h,R

Papa used TO be ⑤
grumpy now he
is not

BM   ⑤

Papa has changed
because know ,it seems
he has became more
caring then he was
before to his son.

EP   ⑤
I think papa's changed
from be grumpy and
annoyed and sad
to proud, proud of his own
son because he can
violin.

Figure 2.14 Stop-and-Jots in Response to a Synthesis Prompt

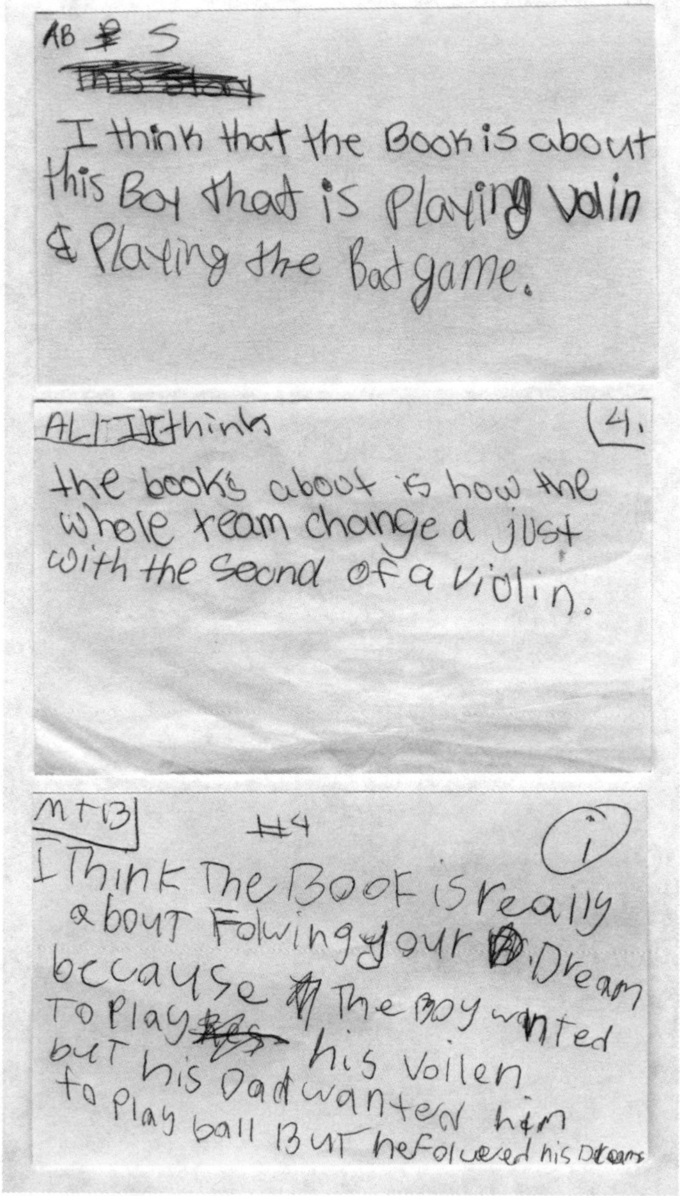

AB ~~$~~ S

~~THIS Story~~

I think that the Book is about this Boy that is playing Volin & Playing the Bad game.

ALL I think   (4.

the books about is how the whole team changed just with the Seond of a violin.

M + 13   #4   (i)

I Think The BOOK is really about Folwing your Dream because The Boy wanted To Play ~~his~~ his Voilen but his Dad wanted him to Play ball BUT he folweed his Dream

Figure 2.15 Inference and Interpretation Sticky Notes

When looking at your own students' comprehension skills and the depth with which each of them can use a skill, I recommend beginning with a read-aloud. Collect sample responses from each child in your class, and then sort and organize them into piles (think, perhaps, "deep"/"deeper"/"deepest"). Next, see what the more sophisticated skill looks like and use those samples as a model for the other children. At the Reading and Writing Project, we call these "mentor stickies." Children who have similar ways of responding in a text can be grouped together and moved toward deeper thinking in small-group conferences. These groups are again flexible and change across the course of time based on formative assessments. More advice for how long readers stay in a group and how to manage flexible grouping can be found in Chapters 4 and 8.

Reading Portfolios

Some of the teachers with whom I work find it helpful to maintain reading portfolios for the students in their classes. These reading portfolios are simply a packet of paper held in a folder. Each page is dedicated to its own skill or own month, with space for the child to jot a response from an open-ended response. For example, one portfolio might say "Retelling" across the top of the page and have eight boxes, one for each month of the school year. The teacher might write or say a prompt like, "Write the most important events in the beginning, middle, and end of your chapter," and have the student respond to the prompt in whatever book she is reading at the time.

Another teacher I work with uses one page per month, with six boxes. Each box is dedicated to a different skill. The child responds to a prompt said out loud by the teacher on whatever book he is reading at the time. Figure 2.16 is an example of such a portfolio. This teacher has one portfolio for independent reading and one for read-aloud.

Still another teacher decided she'd have the pages made up, but planned to have the children stop and jot on sticky notes, then collect and file the sticky notes herself. No matter how it's organized, the important thing to keep in mind is that it's helpful to assess each skill each month to get a picture for how skill work deepens and develops across time, and how it changes from unit of study to unit of study, genre to genre.

We can analyze student responses to the questions in the same ways we just looked at student responses from *The Bat Boy and His Violin*. For example, we can look at Brian's portfolio from October and see that in the Determining the Most

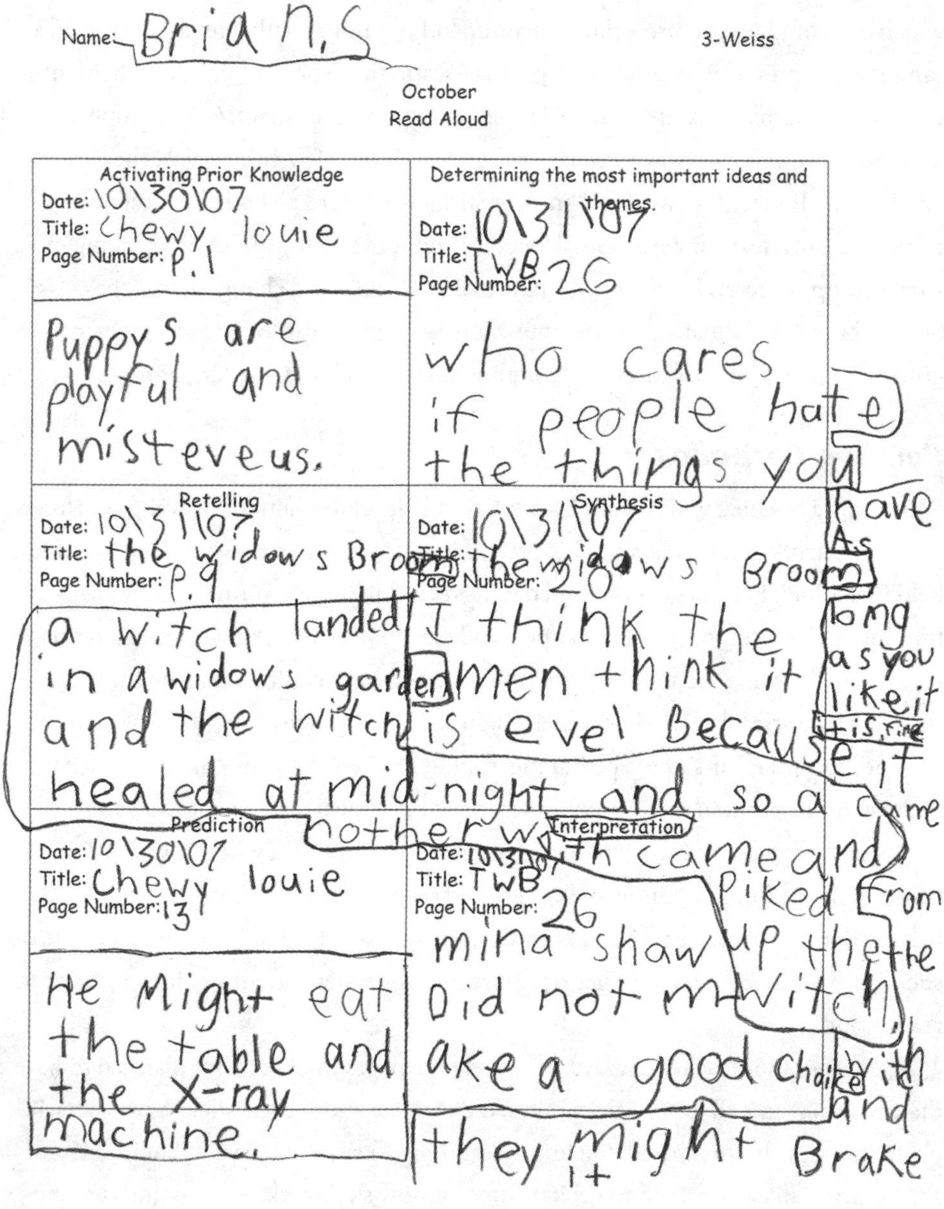

Name: Brian, S   3-Weiss

October
Read Aloud

Activating Prior Knowledge	Determining the most important ideas and themes.
Date: 10\30\07 Title: Chewy louie Page Number: p.1	Date: 10\31\07 Title: TWB 26 Page Number: 26
Puppys are playful and misteveus.	who cares if people hate the things you have

Retelling	Synthesis
Date: 10\31\07 Title: the widows Broom Page Number: p.9	Date: 10\31\07 Title: the widows Broom Page Number: 26
a witch landed in a widows garden and the witch healed at mid-night	I think the men think it is evel because it and so a came

As long as you like it it is fine

Prediction	Interpretation
Date: 10\30\07 Title: Chewy louie Page Number: 13	Date: 10\31\07 Title: TWB Page Number: 26
He Might eat the table and the X-ray machine.	Did not make a good chair they might Brake it

other with came and Piked From mina shaw up the the witch, with and

Figure 2.16 Sample Page from a Third Grader's Reading Portfolio

Important Ideas and Themes box, he wrote, "Who cares if people hate the things you have. As long as you like it, it's fine," about *The Widow's Broom* by Chris Van Allsburg (1992). This interpretation takes into account the characters and conveys an understanding of the whole of the text, not just one part, and it is an inference, not something stated in the text. This shows that Brian is able to demonstrate a strong control of determining a theme, or interpreting the text.

Reading Notebooks

Writing about reading is an important way for students to hold onto their ideas and to grow new thoughts about their books through the act of writing (Angelillo 2003; Calkins 2000). Sometimes, thoughts are so fleeting that without writing them down, they are lost. When readers write about their thinking, they can go back and look at it later. This written record of ideas can become a springboard for more writing, more thinking, or quality conversations about books.

Writing about reading is also important for our assessment. As students collect their ideas and write longer entries, we get a glimpse into their thinking about their books. We can see the kinds of thinking students tend to do, what kinds of reading skills they use, how deeply they use the skills, and what reading skills they shy away from.

In TCRWP schools, teachers have students in grades three and up keep reader's notebooks. These notebooks are sometimes organized into sections: (1) writing about my independent reading; (2) writing to prepare for conversation with partners or clubs; (3) writing from the read-aloud; and (4) writing to reflect my own reading process goals. Other times, the notebooks are kept in chronological sequence with dates at the top of each page. Teaching children to organize the notebooks with dates and the title and author of the book makes it easier for us to see where the student got his thinking. The notebooks can house sticky notes that have been peeled out of books before they were returned to the classroom library, stop-and-jots during read-alouds, longer written reflections about ideas, graphic organizers, character lists, and on and on.

In Figure 2.17, a child wrote a few short thoughts during her teacher's read aloud of Eve Bunting's *Riding the Tiger* (2001). In looking at the student's responses, we can determine the depth with which she uses reading skills to help her understand the story. For example, the first jotting mentions the character's facial expression ("proud face and gleaming") but nothing about the setting. To teach for depth, it

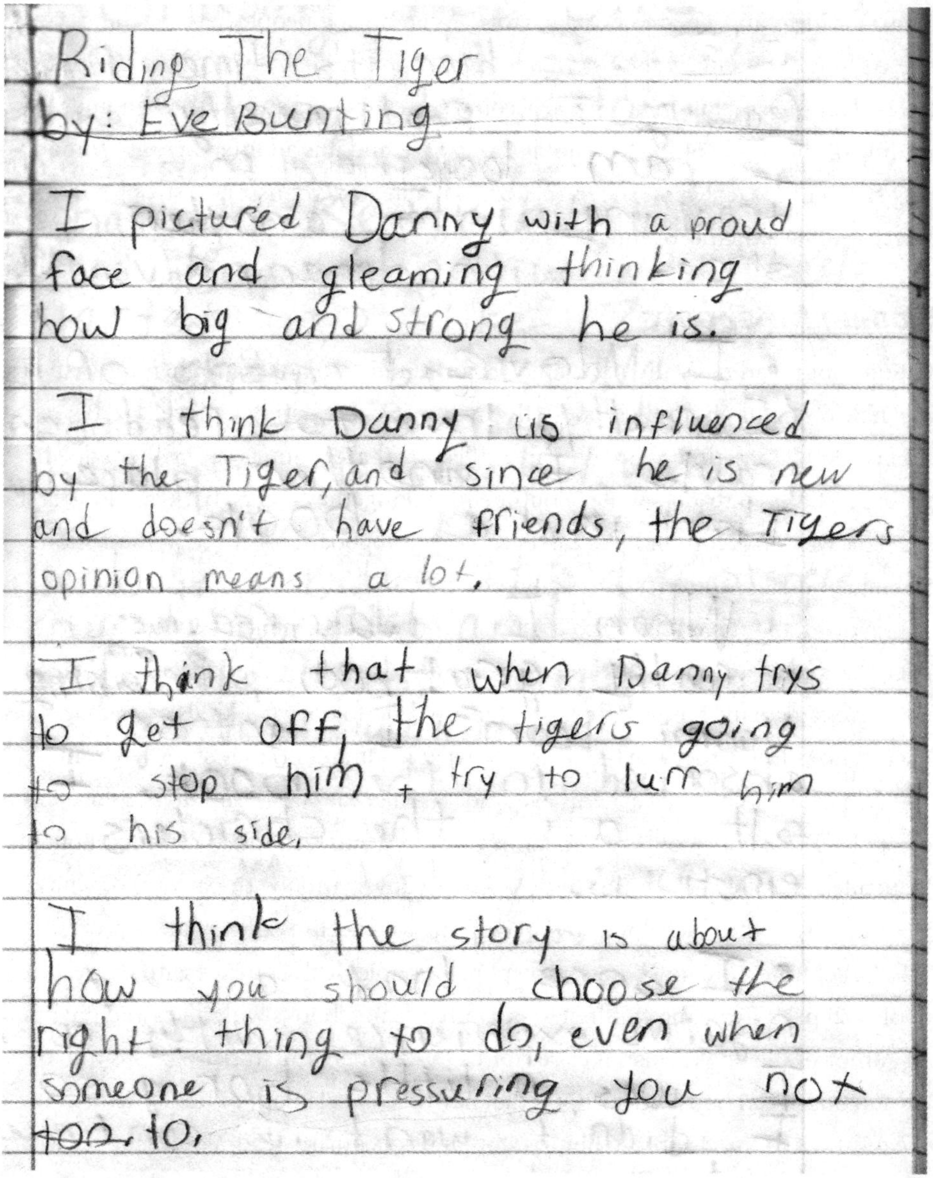

Riding The Tiger
by: Eve Bunting

I pictured Danny with a proud
face and gleaming thinking
how big and strong he is.

I think Danny is influenced
by the Tiger, and since he is new
and doesn't have friends, the Tigers
opinion means a lot.

I think that when Danny trys
to get off, the tigers going
to stop him + try to lurr him
to his side.

I think the story is about
how you should choose the
right thing to do, even when
someone is pressuring you not
too, to.

Figure 2.17 A Fifth Grader's Notebook Entry from Independent Reading

might be helpful to group this student with other children strong at visualizing character, but less apt to imagine setting using all their senses.

Figure 2.18 shows one student's longer written response. The student took one
sticky note from his book and attempted to write a longer response to get ready for a
conversation. His writing shows evidence of interpretation ("money has the power")
and determining importance by his ability to cite relevant parts of the text to go with
his idea.

> ### Organizing a Reader's Notebook
> Section 1: Writing about my independent reading
> Section 2: Writing to prepare for conversation with partners or clubs
> Section 3: Writing from the read-aloud
> Section 4: Writing to reflect my own reading process goals

Clubs and Partnerships

Just as we can look into our students' writing about reading on sticky notes or in their
notebooks to assess their use of reading skills, we can also listen to their conversations.
Partnership and book club conversations can be thought of as an oral text. (For definitions and further discussion of partnerships and clubs, see Chapter 8.) When listening
to a child's discourse for evidence of reading skills, I apply the same criteria as when I
look at her writing about reading. I think about how sophisticated her use of a reading
skill is, and think about how I can work with her to deepen her skill. If we look at the
transcript of three fifth-grade children talking about *Bud, Not Buddy* by Christopher
Paul Curtis (1999), we can analyze the transcript for the skills they're using and get
some ideas about what kind of next steps would push their comprehension even more
(Figure 2.19).

The beginning of the conversation shows evidence that the children were able to
determine importance. Of the entire book, they focused on the idea that what Bud was
meant to understand was beyond his ability as a six-year-old. They then retold parts of
the text that fit with that idea. Later, Kenny talked about the mother loving him so
much that she's preparing him for when she's gone, which is an example of an inference. It doesn't say that directly in the text, but the child inferred it based on the

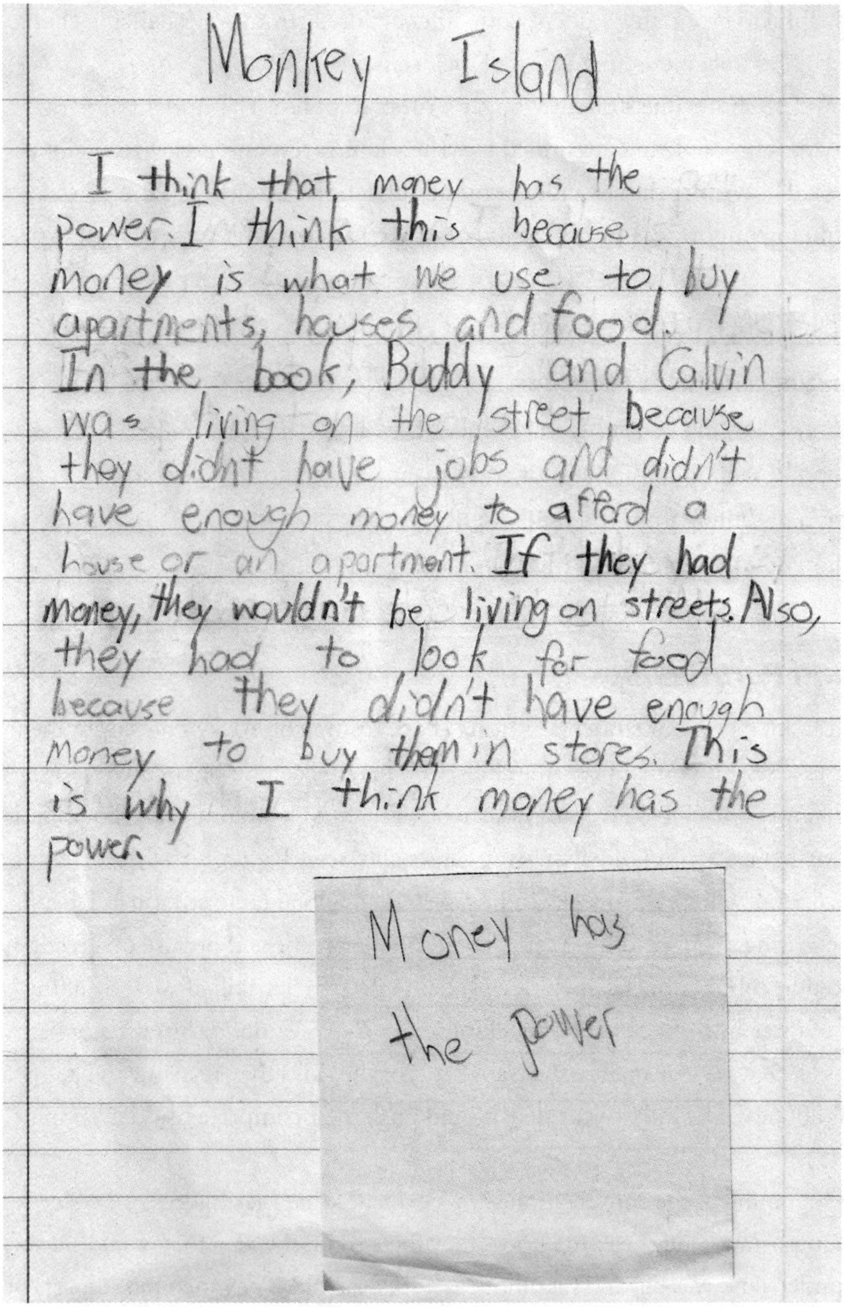

Monkey Island

I think that money has the power. I think this because money is what we use to buy apartments, houses and food. In the book, Buddy and Calvin was living on the street, because they didn't have jobs and didn't have enough money to afford a house or an apartment. If they had money, they wouldn't be living on streets. Also, they had to look for food because they didn't have enough money to buy them in stores. This is why I think money has the power.

Money has the power

Figure 2.18 A Fifth Grader's Notebook Entry from Stop-and-Jots During a Read-Aloud of *Monkey Island*

Kenny: Because Bud had no father, he was on his own and went to this home as a six-year-old. No friends, no mother, no father. Or nothing.

Charlie: Right, but these clues from this mother.

Ella: Right, but at six years old, you don't understand.

Kenny: But now, don't you think he's starting to understand? Like, some of these clues were . . . well, what were some of these clues?

Charlie: His mother says, "When one door closes, another one will open."

Ella: And, but when you're six years old, you don't understand that.

Kenny: Right, so . . . um . . . let's talk about . . . so we've come to the fact that the mother loved him so much, she was preparing him for when she was going to be gone, right? She left him nothing.

Ella: No, she left him this suitcase.

Kenny: Right, and what was in the suitcase that's so special? When he went to the Amos', would he even have stepped out of their door without his suitcase? They even had a gun to guard it and he took that gun and threw it away so nobody could steal his suitcase. He knew everything—the knots of the twine.

Ella: He could take a quick glance at the suitcase and see if anyone had touched it.

Kenny: But why?

Ella: That's the only key to his whole mystery of life. His suitcase is like him. It contains everything about him. It's not just like a physical suitcase, it's kind of a mental suitcase. Because everything kind of represents him. Like who he is. And without those things—

Kenny: Wait, what do you mean, it's a "mental suitcase"?

Figure 2.19 Transcript of Children Talking About *Bud, Not Buddy*

mother's actions. At the tail end of the transcript, Ella got the idea that the suitcase is a "mental" suitcase, with the items representing symbolically who Bud is.

In setting goals for the children in this club, I might choose to support Kenny and Charlie a bit more in using their initial inferences to come up with deeper interpretations about the whole of the text. Kenny only questioned the text at one point in the story; perhaps teaching him to do this at more points across the text would help him with his ideas. Ella came up with a great idea about symbolism in the text, and teaching her to question other details the author includes about other characters as well might deepen her comprehension. Here, as elsewhere, the goals I form for these students are always about finding what work they could manage with some support that is within their zone of proximal development. I try in my goal setting to find what students can do and imagine next steps.

Minilesson Active Involvements

When teaching a minilesson involving a comprehension skill, the active involvement is an important opportunity to determine how well a student can practice the strategy. The active involvement of the minilesson is the part of the minilesson right after the teacher demonstration where every student has an opportunity to practice the strategy with a partner or alone. (For more information on minilessons, see Chapter 8.) Although active involvements are often very supported first tries at a strategy, they provide an important window into who could benefit from immediate follow-up.

When my students turn to their partner to practice off of a shared text, or turn to their own independent reading book to quickly jot, I make my way around the group, listening in or reading over their shoulder. Sometimes I quickly jot down what I see or hear. Other times, I just make a mental note. Another helpful technique is to have the children write their attempt at the strategy on a sticky note that they hand to me before returning to independent reading. This way, I can quickly sort children into groups based on what they've written on the note. When I sort, I use the same way of thinking described at the start of this section—how I can help children go deeper with a skill as opposed to teaching them something they aren't yet doing or ready to practice.

When I decide to teach a group conference based on quickly listening in during a minilesson, I can just keep the children for the group right there in the meeting area and conduct the lesson. These conferences flow seamlessly from the minilesson as I'm just helping the children to have more practice with a strategy I've just taught, often in their own independent books now as opposed to the practice text I used for the mini-lesson. If I choose to have children jot on sticky notes during the minilesson, I can decide to call them back after the few minutes it took me to sort them, or to save the group for another day soon.

Individual Conferences

Individual conferences are an opportunity to monitor and assess student comprehension and to make teaching decisions based on that assessment (Calkins 2000; Collins 2004; Serravallo and Goldberg 2007). Usually, I enter a conference with a sense of the skill or skills that I want to assess for, and I'll ask questions pertaining to those skills. For example, when I knew I was working on retelling with Mehak, a fourth-grade reader, I started off a conference by saying, "So, you're on Chapter 5 of your book, I see. Can you tell me the most important thing that's happened to your character in each of your chapters?" Instead of starting with a broad question like "How's it going?" or "Tell me about what you're working on today" or "What's your book like?" I targeted a specific skill from the very start of our conversation together.

I listened to Mehak's response with an ear for a good retelling, based on the work we'd done together so far. I looked for signs of whether she was able to respond in a way that indicated that she was telling only the important details, not every single thing that happened in every chapter. I also listened to hear if she was retelling in sequence or out of order, and also if the retelling sounded inferential—embedded with her own ideas about the chapter—or literal—simply recounting the events of the characters. As I listened, I recorded all of my impressions. My notes from this and all my conferences end up being quite thorough, as seen in Figure 2.20. I write down several possible compliments and several possible teaching points, and mark the compliment I ended up giving with a *C* and the teaching point I ended up using with a *T*. Then, I

Mehak—

Compliments I could give the reader	What I could teach the reader
9/16 −retells while flipping through book to jog memory ⓒ −has a post-it w/ main event for each chapter—helps w/ retelling −retelling literal	−retell using problem-solution −retell more inferentially — ⓣ what's a big idea about main character? use that to retell *NS: could use more work on developing idea about character

Figure 2.20 Sample Note-Taking Form

record next steps (*NS*) based on how the student did at practicing the strategy with me in the one-on-one conference.

You will develop a system that works for you personally; what's important is that you write down information that will help you look across many possible compliments and teaching points and make a decision not only in this conference, but also to help you to think about next steps and plan for small-group work.

I can go back across my notes from the week and see which children would benefit from the same strategy.

Sources of Information for Comprehension Assessment

- Reading portfolios collect student responses to general prompts, assessing for each skill over time.
- Reading notebooks house children's authentic writing about reading.
- Conversations students have about books are an oral text, allowing us a glimpse into their comprehension skills.
- Active involvements of whole-class minilessons, where children have a quick chance to try a strategy, can lead to small groups right away to give more practice with a strategy.
- Individual conferences are one-on-one opportunities for assessment. Recording notes about next steps lets you look across notes to form groups based on common needs.

The Take-Away: Implications for Grouping

When grouping children for comprehension, it's helpful to make sure that they are working on the same, or about the same, level of proficiency within a skill, not simply that they need support with a skill. For example, I may have a child who infers about character by only thinking about how the character feels. Another child might not think about the character's feelings but make predictions about what will happen in the next chapter. Both children are inferring, but the work that would help them to infer on a deeper level, the *strategy* I would teach, is different. For the child who is focused on characters' feelings only, I might work on being able to name character traits or to look for ways in which the character's feelings change, indicating an important moment in the story. For the child who is inclined toward prediction, I might help make stronger predictions based on information he has about the character to determine how the character will probably act, or to think about narrative structure to make predictions about how the story will unfold, not just the very next event. Because these children would benefit from different strategies, they need to be part of different groups.

Assessing Conversation

I've already discussed the value of listening in on students' conversations about books to determine what reading skills they are and aren't using, and how proficiently they are using those skills. An oral text, these conversations provide a window into what children are thinking about as they read and discuss their books.

It is important to also listen for conversational skills as children talk. Helping children to work not only *in* a group, but also *as* a group helps children develop shared understanding, affiliation, and a "deeper sense of caring" (Johnston 2004). Author/educator/social activists Katherine and Randy Bomer write in their book *For a Better World: Reading and Writing for Social Action* (2001) that "democracy . . . exists only when people deliberate together," and conversations provide a platform for this. Conversation about ideas, in classrooms where TCRWP works, are a daily occurrence. Children talk in whole-class conversations from the class read-aloud, to partnerships, and to book clubs.

At PS 277 in the South Bronx of New York City, first thing in the morning children discuss ideas about their lives and communities during a time called "talk now," in an effort to emulate the kinds of dinner table conversations that the children in this community are often not privy to. They come to the classroom, quickly unpack their bags, and gather in the meeting area to talk about topics like "Why are rents going up in our neighborhood?" and "What time do you think third graders should go to bed?" Children talk during social studies about social justice and history, and in science to hypothesize and develop plans for testing theories. The talk transfers to reading and writing workshops where quality conversation pushes their literacy thinking.

When children discuss their books, I listen and think about ways I can support the quality of their conversation, knowing that it will have huge payoffs in their abilities to share and grow strong ideas. I hold in my mind what good conversation looks like. In particular, I might watch for:

- ❑ whether students' body language indicates they are actively listening (i.e., facing the speaker, nodding, reacting to what's been said)

- ❑ if children ask questions to clarify ideas

- ❑ if readers stick to one idea, adding and building on that idea

- ❑ if readers are open-minded and talk to arrive at new thoughts and ideas, or if they simply share what they already thought

- ❑ if readers are prepared for conversation by using writing on sticky notes or in a reading notebook

- ❑ if children provide textual evidence for what they're talking about

- ❑ whether children stop to reread parts of the text

- ❑ if students offer questions or controversial thoughts to entice more interesting conversation

To listen for both conversational skills and comprehension skills takes an attentive ear. For me, it takes some good note taking. I go back and forth between two types of note taking when listening to conversations. Sometimes I divide my page into two columns. On one side, I write "comprehension skills," and on the other side, I write "conversation skills." As I listen to the conversation, I write down the name of the skill that I hear. I sometimes take notes by microtranscribing the conversation, writing in my own shorthand. I find this easier if I'm having a hard time listening because then I can go back across the transcript and analyze it to identify skills instead of having to do that work in the moment.

Whole-Class Conversations

Interactive read-alouds and whole-class conversations are an important part of supporting readers to think and talk about books (Calkins 2000; Collins 2004; Nichols 2006). In TCRWP classrooms, teachers read aloud to the class at least once each day. During these read-alouds, children have a chance to turn and talk to their partners about their thinking, or to stop and jot what they are thinking in a notebook. Two or three days a week, I open up the discussion to the whole class. At this time, partners share their ongoing discussion with the rest of the class, and individuals share some of their writing from their reading notebook. The class decides on a topic of conversation, and we have a lengthy conversation, growing ideas, questioning, and challenging each other.

These whole-class conversations are a large-scale model for what happens during partnerships and book clubs off of independent reading. Observing and taking careful notes during this time always provides crucial fodder for future conferences. Often, I take notes as a sort of microtranscript as well as keep track of who talks. This way, I can go back to the whole-class document and see each child as an individual. See Figure 2.21 for an example of note taking from one conversation.

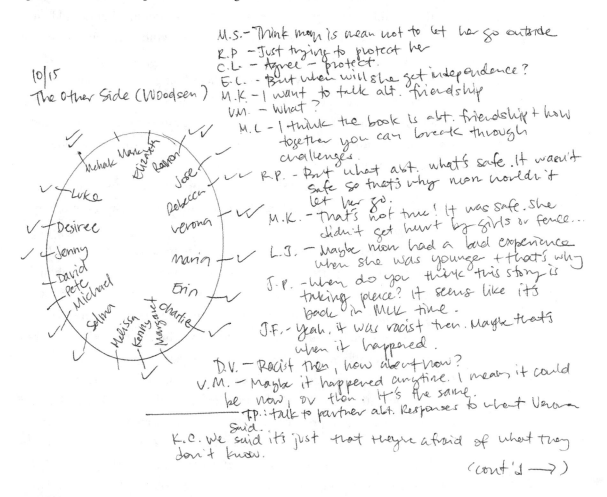

Figure 2.21 Whole-Class Conversation Note-Taking Example

I keep these notes in a binder so I can see each student's progress over time. I also refer back to notes from book club conferences during this whole-group conversation time. This way, I can hold children accountable for those conferences during book clubs.

Partnerships and Book Clubs

Just as with whole-class conversations, partnership conversations and book club conversations offer endless opportunities for assessment.

In order to spend this time assessing, it is important that conditions are established so that my role isn't to put out fires around the classroom. That is, children must be independent enough to carry on conversations without needing me to facilitate. It should be the case that the partners and/or clubs can sustain productive conversation if I leave the room, walk to the teacher's lounge and get a soda, and come back. (Don't worry; I don't really do that!) I make this joke to drive home the point that it is essential to provide opportunities for scaffolded conversations, and to release support over time, so that children have the tools to function independently. In most classrooms, putting children into small groups right away will not yield productive conversation. See Chapter 5 for more support on how to do this. As my children talk, I make my way around the classroom listening in, taking notes, and teaching these groups.

Let's look again at the transcript of the fifth graders talking about *Bud, Not Buddy* (Figure 2.19) as practice for the kinds of things I notice and record about their conversation. I might notice that in terms of strengths, or possible compliments, the students demonstrate the ability to listen to and respect many voices. Also, they do a great job of laying out ideas and responding to each other's thinking. Instead of each child on his own conversational trajectory with his own agenda, the students let one child set an agenda and each comment afterward follows from that initiating comment. They question each other's thinking, asking for clarification when an idea is presented that they don't understand. They reference examples in the text that fit with the conversation. They have such a strong conversation going that it's challenging to think about what I might teach them. One idea is to help them see how one of their members, Kenny, took on a leadership role, and I could support others in taking on that role in subsequent conversations so that he's not the only one in charge.

> **Opportunities to Assess Conversational Skills**
>
> - During whole-class conversations, observe and take notes on children as individuals.
>
> - During conversations when children are grouped in book clubs or paired in partnerships, analyze their conversation for possible follow-up teaching.

Because the social groupings during reading workshop are fixed during partnerships and book clubs, I often meet with the already-formed group for a lesson as opposed to taking one or two children from a couple of different groups. Because of this, I tend to see the group as a unit and make most of my teaching decisions based on what the unit needs.

Preplanned Groups Versus Impromptu Groups

Expert teachers are masters of both planning effectively and efficiently and of responding to needs of their students in the midst of teaching. In a reading workshop, some small-group work will likely be planned out ahead of time, and some groups will likely be pulled together in the moment, based on careful kid-watching, quick assessment, and an ability to be responsive and reflective. The answer to the question "Should I plan out my groups ahead of time or pull them in response to what I see in the classroom?" is a strong "Both."

First, some thoughts about planning. When teachers ask me for support with planning, it is often the case that they ask for support planning the teaching points for the minilessons of the unit of study, or incorporating their state or city standards into whole-class lessons. Although I empathize with this, I also believe that I need to have a balance in my planning time. Although minilessons are best planned in response to what students need and are able to do, I also need to plan how I'll spend the 75 percent of the workshop time individualizing instruction in conferences. For that reason, it's important to spend a considerable amount of time planning one-on-one and small-group conferences. In each chapter to come, you'll get advice on how to plan for these groups across the course of a week.

There will, of course, be times when I recognize a need and do a group conference that I wasn't planning on doing. Perhaps I overhear something during the mini-lesson's active involvement that leads me to believe that a few children could benefit from more coaching. Or perhaps I observe that some of my children aren't engaged during independent reading, so I pull them together for a conference without waiting for tomorrow to come. These impromptu small-group conferences are an important part of being a responsive teacher and are balanced with the planned groups that I do each week.

The Last Word

As you form and plan for group reading instruction, it is helpful to see students as individuals and keep your purpose in mind. Are you listening and observing for engagement? Fluency? Print work strategies? Comprehension? Conversational skills? Remember that you have more than one place to assess for each one of those behaviors and skills. The more information you have about a student, the more precise your assessment of each student will be.

In deciding who will take part in a group conference, it's essential that children need practice not only with the same *skill* but with the same *strategy* for that skill. The more exact and careful you can be with your assessment, note taking, and forming of the groups, the easier it will be to manage the group when it is in front of you, and the more each student will benefit from the conference.

Without Engagement, We've Got Nothing: Helping Children Want to Read

*M*y book club recently decided to read *American Wife* by Curtis Sittenfeld, a novel based loosely on the life of former first lady Laura Bush. When I first glanced at the cover, I was a bit turned off. Both the book and the author came with high praise from readers I trust, though, so I decided to give it a try.

By the second chapter, I was hooked. I read while walking on the sidewalk in New York City, glancing up from time to time to avoid bumping into a stranger. More than once I read it and almost missed my stop on the subway. It was the last thing I looked at every night before bed.

This level of engagement in a book is not always a given with me. I'm a big book abandoner. Life's too short, and there are too many books, to read ones that don't keep my interest. I've abandoned books that are so-called runaway best sellers, books that friends have professed "changed their lives," and professional books that weren't what I thought they'd be. This is significant, I think, because I'm not the kind of reader who is automatically engaged just because she has a highly recommended book in her hands.

If I reflect on the list of books I've stuck with and books I've ditched, I can find some patterns. Often, the books I've stuck with are either memoir or nonfiction, or, when they're fiction, they read like memoir. I know from experience that I tend to like most of the books my close friends recommend to me. I also know that just because a book is a best seller or even Pulitzer Prize winner doesn't mean it's going to be a right fit for me. I like books that are more character-focused than plot-driven, and in non-fiction I like books that have a sociological aspect to them, like *Freakonomics* by Stephen Dubner and Steven Levitt or Malcolm Gladwell's books, *The Outliers* and *The Tipping Point*.

My reading habits might surprise you. I rarely read one book straight through before starting another. I have three to five books or magazines going at once. As I write this, I'm getting ready to give birth to my first child and have a stack on my nightstand of books about childbirth and breast-feeding and sleep-training a baby, and I'm also trying to finish up *A Heartbreaking Work of Staggering Genius* by Dave Eggers. I also have a few magazines—*Rolling Stone* and *Parenting*—in the pile.

With all I've told you—my tendency to abandon books, juggling several books at once—would you call me a reader? I call myself one. I like to read and when I find something I like, I'm very engaged. I read widely for many purposes. I know what I like and I have strategies for choosing good books. I have people with whom I share my reading. Compared with other people whose nose is constantly in a book, who will stay up all night with a page-turner instead of sleeping, or people whose cars don bumper stickers demanding "Kill your TV" or "Fight Prime Time—Open a Book," do you still think I'm a reader? My point is that there is room enough for all of us in the definition of "engaged reader" and as teachers, when we look at our students, it's important to consider that engagement. A love of reading might have more than a few profiles. Each reader might have his or her own reading rhythms, habits, patterns, or tastes, but one nonnegotiable is that each needs to be able to be engaged with print.

> ### ✿ QUESTIONS TO ASK YOURSELF AND TO EXPLORE WITH YOUR COLLEAGUES
>
> ✔ Think about yourself as a reader. What makes you engage with a text? When are times you've been unable to put a book down and when do you find that you abandon what you're reading? What are your habits and routines as a reader?
>
> ✔ What do you look for when you check to see if your students are engaged readers?

As reading workshop teachers, we wear our love of reading on our sleeves for all children. As the mentor readers in our classrooms, we talk about our own reading lives, the books we choose and love and those we abandon, and we read aloud as if every word were gold. For some students, though, it doesn't seem as if it's enough. Just as I use groups in my own life to give me a vision for what it means to be an engaged reader, small-group conferences can be the perfect solution to meet the needs of students in my class with engagement difficulties. I have groups of friends who recommend books to me, who talk with me about my choices and help me set goals, who read with me by the pool or on the couch, and who taught me to refocus when I get distracted. As teachers, we can help create these groups for children. For my students, I found:

- ❏ When my rally cries around reading seemed to still fall flat, I made it a priority to see those students in small groups for some additional support to *mentor them into developing their own reading identity*.

- ❏ When my students felt it was an impossible task to find a book that they'd enjoy, I pulled them in small groups to *talk up books* so they could make better selections.

- ❏ When I noticed students had trouble staying focused, I gathered them in a small group to teach them to *self-monitor and fix up disengagement*.

- ❏ When some of my children seemed like dutiful, but not really engaged readers, or had a hard time keeping up their own reading life, I found that helping them to *establish their own goals* in small groups helped.

In this chapter, I'll show examples of each of these types of small-group conferences and help you get to know some readers who took part in these small groups. As you read, reflect on the networks in your life that help you stay engaged with books and discover new ones. And as you read, pay attention to the students who come to mind, children who have mystified you a bit on the unevenness of their thirst for reading. Reasons for disengagement come in many colors, and this chapter will help you discover how to discern the true nature of the child's resistance and use small-group interactions to get him to that "subway-stop missing" state we want for all our students.

The Urgency of the Engagement Problem

Before we get to the groups, it's important to set the stage for why this deserves our attention. Researchers agree that engagement is essential to helping children become strong readers (Guthrie and Wigfield 1997; Ford 1992; Flippo 2001). When students are engaged in reading, they are able to self-generate learning opportunities (Guthrie and Wigfield 1997). Allington, a researcher concerned with what matters most when working with struggling readers, writes that engagement in reading has been found to be the most powerful instructional activity for fostering reading growth (2000).

Yet, if each of us looks critically at the independent reading time in our classrooms and does some kid-watching, it's likely that we'll find some kids who are not engaged. They might be blatantly staring off out the classroom window, or they might be earnestly faking it, hoping we won't notice (Tovani 2000; Kelley and Clausen-Grace 2007). Every year, I find it essential to conduct an engagement inventory in my classroom, as described in Chapter 2, to get the pulse on the level of engagement in my classroom while children read independently.

Even without the engagement inventory, it's easy to make a case for why this problem so urgently needs our attention. A 2007 National Endowment for the Arts study, *To Read or Not to Read*, found that Americans are reading less, with children ages fifteen to twenty-four spending two hours a day watching TV and less than seven minutes a day reading. The people surveyed *can* read, they just choose not to. Kylene Beers terms these kinds of readers "alliterate" (1996, 2002). The National Endowment for the Arts' 2008 study *Reading on the Rise* gives some hope—it found a 21 percent increase among eighteen- to twenty-four-year-olds in the amount of time spent reading, a cohort that the study notes have been the recipients of some of the largest initiatives in high school literacy. We need to bring initiatives geared toward helping children stay engaged with books into all the grades in an effort to improve this statistic even more in years to come.

In school-aged children, summer reading loss is well documented (Shin and Krashen 2007; Kim 2004; Mraz and Rasinski 2007; Cooper 2003). Children can drop as much as two levels of reading in the two months they are on summer vacation because they aren't reading. Although it's possible to argue that the availability of books is difficult for some children, I would maintain that if they wanted to read books, they would find a way from video games and television to the local library or bookstore. If children saw reading as an important part of their lives, not just something that teachers make them do in school, they would keep it up over summer vacation.

It is our job as teachers to find ways to mentor students into engaged reading lives by creating positive experiences with reading and by helping them plan for their own networks to support reading lives and to develop positive expectations about reading.

Mentoring Readers into Developing a Reading Identity

Small-group instruction can be used to mentor readers into developing a reading identity. To figure out how to form my groups, I start each year asking every child in my class to complete a reading interest inventory, and as they read, I watch them and complete an engagement inventory (both are described in detail in Chapter 2, and an example of one is presented). After these two assessments, I often find that there are some children who would benefit from small groups to help them with some reflection. When it's clear that there are children who have trouble sustaining even ten minutes of reading during a workshop in a book that I am confident is not too hard for them, my first thought is often that they just aren't into it. And by *it*, I like to think that I mean their book, not reading. Children should experience a "lost-in-a-book" feeling, what Nell (1988) refers to as "flow" when they are reading. Stopping every few minutes is clear evidence that a reader isn't experiencing this feeling.

My job now becomes helping them expand their possibilities and concept of what it means to be a reader, to give them permission to abandon books that don't work for them, and to mentor them into reflecting on their own reading tastes so they can better find a book that will keep them engaged. Trelease's (2001) idea of a "home run" book—the first positive experience that will hook a child into becoming a reader—was tested by researchers with exciting results. It turns out that among children who say they like to read, well over half of them could point to a single book or series that got them hooked on reading (Von Spreken, Kim, and Krashen 2000). I need to help some readers find their home run book and that lost-in-a-book feeling.

Which Readers Are Good Candidates for This Small Group?

I chose two students for the group below based on their reading interest inventories and two students based on watching them during an engagement inventory. When Vasilios wrote, "I don't want to read because I find it boring," in response to the question "What do you think about when it's time for reading?" and in response to whether he reads at home, "Yes because I need to, it's my homework," I felt I could work with him a bit on developing his reading identity. He went on to write about how he likes Goosebumps books and books where characters go on journeys—this was a good place to start (Figure 3.1). Another student in the group, Samantha, wrote a reflection about how she's a "very impatient" reader who will give up on a book after the first page if she doesn't like it, and who can take "an hour to read one page" when the book isn't interesting (Figure 3.2). The two students I chose for the group based on their engagement inventory, Mark and Vanessa, showed signs of fake reading. They would look at their book when I glanced at them, but when I looked away, out of the corner of my eye I saw them gazing out the window or playing with things in their desks. If I walked past their desk and peeked over their shoulders, I saw that they had progressed barely a page in five to ten minutes' time.

I followed a specific structure in this small group. I first *told the readers why they were gathered*. I next *taught* them by modeling my own reflections, then I *engaged* them by having them try to reflect in the same ways I've just modeled first alone and then with partners, and I finally *linked* the lesson to their independent work by having them go to the library to choose books alone or with a partner.

CONNECT: TELL THE READERS WHY THEY'VE BEEN GATHERED I began by gathering the children in my group around me to lead them through a reflection much

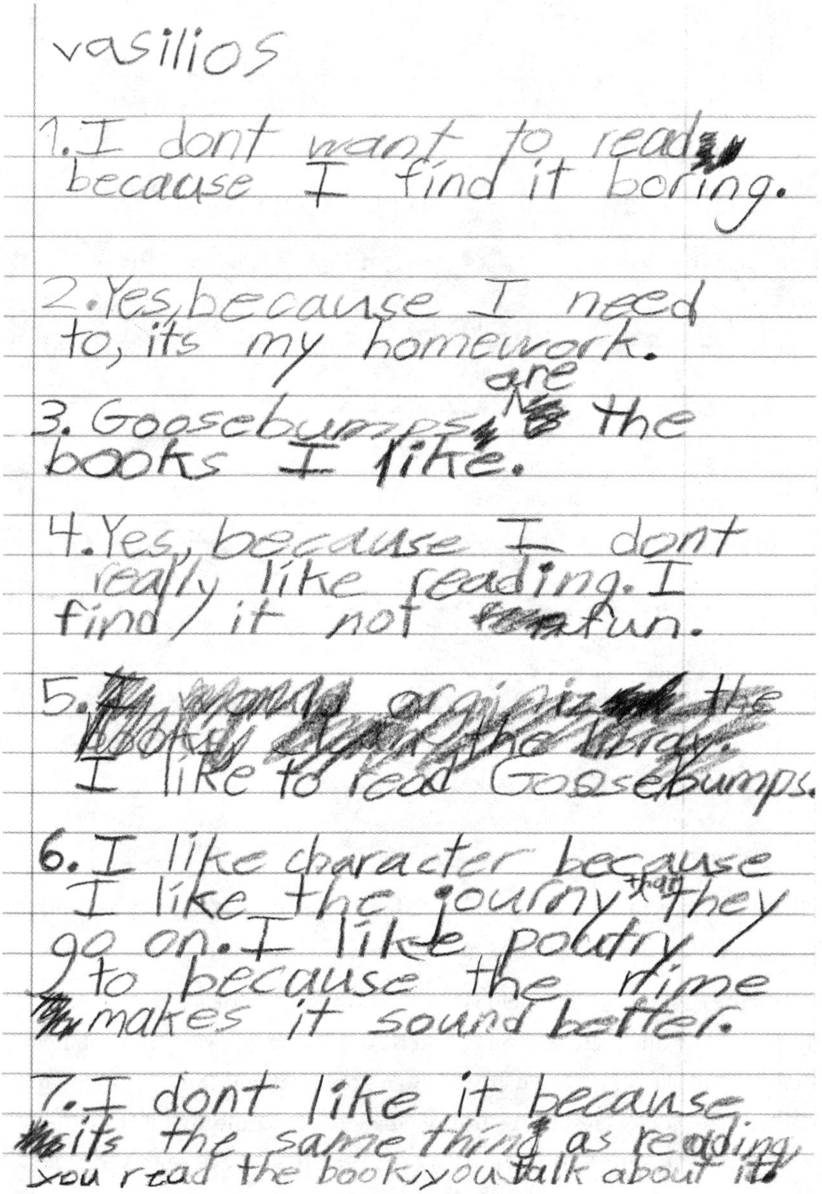

vasilios

1. I dont want to read because I find it boring.

2. Yes, because I need to, its my homework.

3. Goosebumps are the books I like.

4. Yes, because I dont really like reading. I find it not fun.

5. ~~My mom organize the books at the library.~~ I like to read Goosebumps.

6. I like character because I like the journy that they go on. I like poutry to because the rime makes it sound better.

7. I dont like it because its the same thing as reading you read the book, you talk about it.

Figure 3.1 Vasilios' Reading Interest Inventory

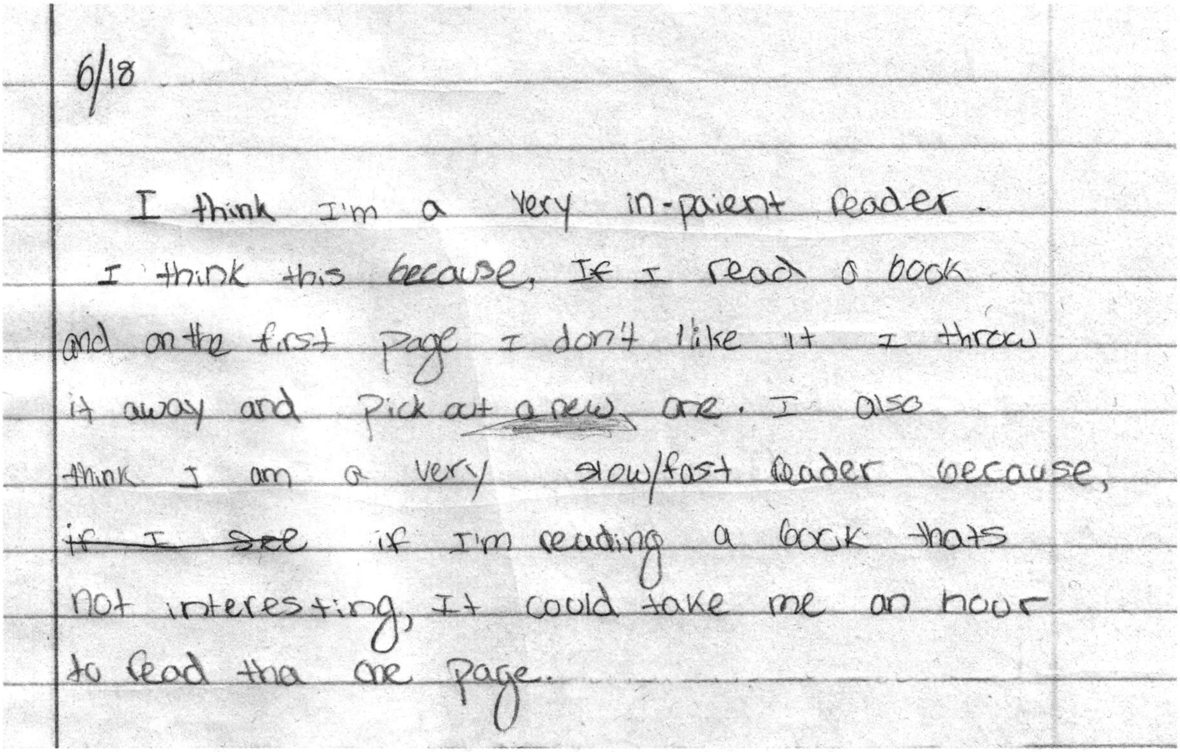

6/18

I think I'm a very in-patient reader. I think this because, If I read a book and on the first page I don't like it I throw it away and pick out a new one. I also think I am a very slow/fast reader because, if I see if I'm reading a book thats not interesting, It could take me an hour to read tha one page.

Figure 3.2 Samantha's Reading Reflection

like the one that I did to begin this chapter. I did this work this past September with a group of disengaged fifth graders. Here's how I opened it:

> Readers, it's my goal this year to help you fall in love with books. I've read your reading inventories and watched you as you read, and today I want to begin helping you get to the place where you are so into a book that you can't put it down. Where it feels like you're almost in a trance when you read and that if someone calls your name, you almost need to shake your head to get back to this world. I want to help you look forward to the time you have to read.
>
> So, I pulled you together to talk to you about figuring out who you are as readers, because I think doing so will help you with this goal. Every person in here has different tastes in books just like you have different tastes in pizza toppings or ice cream flavors or TV shows or sports. Our work together is going to be to have a few meetings to talk about this—what kinds of books we've read, why we read

what we do, when we were bored out of our minds, and when we found that we couldn't put the book down. To get you started thinking, I'm going to talk about myself for a bit and there might be some things I say that surprise you!

TEACH: MODEL YOUR OWN REFLECTIONS Then I pulled out my own bag of books—both books I love and books I hate. Magazines, newspapers, children's books, professional books. I assembled an assorted bag so I had different things to say so that kids felt safe to share their honest thoughts about their books. This part of the lesson took longer than in subsequent meetings with this group, because I wanted to provide a lot of support through modeling. Over time, the "teach" part of the lesson got shorter.

Let me show you what I've been up to for the last few months. Here's what I've read—and what I've tried to read. [*I start by pulling out a copy of the* New York Times.] I have a really good friend, Sarah, who always impresses me with her knowledge of what's going on in the news. I don't know how she finds the time to read it all! I had dinner plans coming up with her and I thought that I might be embarrassed to not know what's going on in case some big news story comes up in our discussion. So I picked up a copy at the newsstand and read it on the train to and from work. There were a lot of articles in here that I just read the title to, like this one about fashion week—I don't care about that—and others where I read the whole article, like this one about Obama's plans for health care reform. I could tell when I wanted to read the article because I felt like there was something in the title that made me go, "Hmm. That's interesting." Other times, I read the title of the article and thought "Who cares?" or "I doubt this will come up in conversation with Sarah" and I just skipped it.

Reading isn't like brussels sprouts—I don't have to force myself to read stuff that I couldn't care less about. And the same is true when you're making choices about what to read in reading workshop. [*I modeled how I made choices about what I decided to read and what I decided to leave based on an initial interest. I thought about my purpose for why I was reading—to be able to keep up conversation with my friend at dinner and be aware of current events—and chose the articles that fit with that purpose.*]

[*Next, I pulled out a children's book.*] This is *Dogs Don't Tell Jokes* by Sachar. I'd been hearing kids talk about this book and I haven't read it yet, so I decided to pick it up. Even though I'm an adult, I don't always read books that are at my "just-right" reading level. I find that I often want to read easier books. I love being able to read the whole thing in a short amount of time, and I love that when the book is easier, I sometimes can focus more on thinking a lot. So sometimes readers—even adult readers—read things that are on the easy side. [*Next, I pulled out* American Wife *by Curtis Sittenfeld and talked about my experience with that book. After that, I pull out a tattered, wrinkled copy of* Life of Pi *by Yan Martel.*]

This one's a little embarrassing. I was reading this book because I had heard so many great things about it. I was reading it and the whole time thinking, "Who cares?" I don't know, maybe I just wasn't getting the point of this book. It's an award winner. It's not too hard for me. Many friends recommended it as an amazing book. I just couldn't care less about the character. It fell behind the radiator in my bedroom and I never even went to get it out! I just left it there. And then after much time passed, I was cleaning and found it and stuck it on my shelf. I never finished it, and I didn't care. [*This story is important because children need to understand that sometimes even proficient readers abandon books. Readers are self-reflective and know when they don't like something and make a conscious decision to stop.*]

[*I decided to end with a positive note. I pulled out four books by Augusten Burroughs.*] These books are ones that I couldn't put down. I started by just reading this one, *Running with Scissors*, and then once I read it and loved it so much, I ran out and got everything else the man wrote. I read every single one of these books straight through and barely talked to people when I was reading! I read in bed, on the train, sometimes even at the dinner table. After I finished reading them, I thought, "What is it about these books that I love so much?" because I wanted to make sure I could find more that were just as great. I realized that I really like that they're a bit funny, in a serious and dark way. I started asking friends if they knew of any other memoir writers like Burroughs who had a funny slant to their writing. I got lucky and my aunt recommended another memoirist, Ruth Reichl. Often, you find that if you like one book by an author, another book by the same author will also grab you.

ENGAGE: INVITE CHILDREN TO TRY WHAT WAS JUST MODELED This five-minute talk ended the "teach" part of my small group, and it was time to turn it over to the children and ask them to try some of what I just did. Before I did that, though, I made very clear to them what I hoped they noticed about my reflection.

In just a minute, I'm going to ask you to do a little jotting by yourself in your reader's notebook. Think about the last few things you've read—it can be magazines, poems, books, comics, newspapers—and think carefully about why you chose it, and what your reaction to it was. Were you into it, or not into it? And, more importantly, why? You might remember some books that you started but didn't finish. Or times when, like me, you just wanted to read something a little on the easy side. Or maybe a time when you had a friend who was waiting to talk to you about something you were reading, like for me with the newspaper.

At this point, the children took a few minutes to write, and I circulated between them. I was on the lookout for children who wrote very vague responses. Vasilios wrote, "I read *Bridge to Terabithia*. I didn't like it." I coached him to think about *why*. I saw that Mark only mentioned one genre—nonfiction—and prompted him to think about what kinds of topics he liked most, and the other things he might have read and enjoyed. Samantha and Vanessa were stuck, unable to remember anything they ever read, so I brought them to the classroom library to see if looking through bins jogged their memories. When Vasilios claimed he had never read anything he liked, I prompted him to think about a time when someone read something to him and he enjoyed listening.

Perhaps the biggest challenge here, especially if it's the start of the year when most are trying to make a good impression, is to get kids to be honest. Children often want to put up a front and act like a "good student" and will not make admissions about book abandonment or feeling disconnected to books.

Next, I had the children share.

We need to support each other in this quest to find books we like so that we can look forward to our reading time each day in school. I want you to listen carefully to what your partner is going to share with you and see if you can notice something about the kind of reader he or she might be. You might listen to see if you notice a pattern in the times they liked books and the times they didn't. Or, you might recognize a title of a book that they say they love, and you might be able to think about a book you've read that seems kind of similar to it in some way. Go ahead and turn and talk.

When children talk to each other, I am an active participant, listening carefully to what they say and coaching as appropriate. Setting up some partnerships where children listen to each other and try to help each other solve their problems with liking books takes a bit of pressure off me as the teacher, and also makes them feel invested in solving their own problem.

LINK TO THEIR OWN INDEPENDENT WORK—CHOOSING BOOKS FROM THE LIBRARY I sent the children off, not to their seats but instead to the classroom library to try to apply some of what they just reflected on about themselves as readers to their book choice.

Subsequent Meetings with This Group

Over the course of the next few weeks, this group and I met several times. I asked the students to keep a reading log to record the title, author, genre, and level of books they read and to rate on a scale of 1–10 how much they enjoyed the book. On subsequent meetings, I asked them to take out their log and look at it with their partner to see if they could find a pattern (Figure 3.3).

Sometimes, we went to the classroom library as a group to look through bins. If one partner knew the other partner tended to like scary books, the pair looked together for books with a scary-seeming plot. Sometimes, students heard that their partner loved a book and decided that they wanted to try it, too. In this way, I mentored them into making book recommendations to each other that I hoped would continue even when we were no longer working in groups together. All the while, my role as the teacher became slighter and slighter, with the hope that eventually these partnerships could carry on a life of their own in my reading workshop. This is always my intention: to release scaffolding over time and work toward independence. As children get to know their partner well and the kinds of books he or she likes, book shopping days become much more interactive and helpful instead of just flipping through covers of books.

Name:		Week of:		
Title	Author	Genre	Level	Rate it 1–10

Figure 3.3 Modified Book Log for "Developing a Reading Identity" Group

> ### ◤ Mentoring Readers into Developing a Reading Identity
>
> - Meeting #1: *Tell readers why they've been gathered.* Next, *teach* by modeling your own reflections on books you've loved, hated, abandoned, and read for a variety of purposes. This part of the lesson takes about five minutes on the first meeting. *Engage* students in writing reflections in their own notebooks and then talking with a partner. *Link* by sending the group to the library to reconsider book choices for the week.
>
> - Meeting #2 and onward: *Tell readers why they've been gathered.* Next, *teach* by modeling for them how to reflect on a reading log, looking for patterns. To do this, you might work together with one child in the group as your partner and have that child look at your sample log, and you look at his. When you recognize a pattern or think of a book that your partner might like, recommend it. This should take just a couple of minutes so most of the time in this group is spent with students practicing their own reflection. *Engage* by having students work with partners to notice patterns and recommend books. *Link* by sending children off to the library to choose books together.

Talking Up Books in Groups

My second year as a classroom teacher, I had the good fortune of dating a production editor at Simon and Schuster Children's Publishing who mailed boxes of books to my classroom every week. Many of them were proofs or copies that were lying around the office. It was especially serendipitous because I taught at a school that had only basal readers and, as you might imagine, that has never been my philosophy. Consequently, I had to build my library myself—with these books, books from book orders, and twenty-five-cent books that were slightly worn but on sale from the local branch of the New York Public Library.

When the books arrived, I always made a huge deal about them. I gathered the class over to the rug, and we sat in a circle as I slowly pulled open the flaps of the box, and gasped dramatically with each book I pulled out of the box. "Oh! I love this author. You all know him. He wrote one of our favorite books in here—*Sideways Stories from Wayside School*. Remember? Oh man. This must be a new book he's written. I can't wait to read this one." With every book that I pulled out of the box, I had something to say. Sometimes, I talked about how the book seemed just like another that the kids were familiar with, and if they liked that book then they would be sure to like this one. Other times, I talked about how the cover made the book look so mysterious, and I flipped it over and read the back cover blurb right away. There were also times when I read the book or a review of the book and talked to the kids about the kinds of characters or storyline they could expect if they wanted to read it. Still other times, I read a snippet from the book to entice them. "Listen to this . . . ," I said, and read it in my best read-aloud voice.

My modeling showed that I treasured each of these books like the gift it was and at the same time enticed the children to open the book. It was so funny to me that sometimes great books would just sit and get dusty in the classroom library and just because these were being highlighted, or they came out of a box, they were the hot item for weeks. I put them on the ledge of the chalkboard and called them the "Hot New Books" and they were gone by lunchtime. The moral of the story? We cannot underestimate how infectious our enthusiasm is. Students need to hear and see our excitement.

In subsequent years, with the boxes no longer coming, I replicated this by talking up books to small groups of children who I thought would respond well. There were two differences on how I approached this. First, I used books that were neglected in the library but that I loved and I knew the children would love. Second, I started to look more closely at the student reading interest inventories and put groups of children together who seemed to have similar tastes in books.

I found that talking up books worked even better in small groups. For instance, I grouped the kids in my class who were avid nonfiction readers, and I introduced a new or favorite or forgotten few nonfiction books that I thought they might like. I pulled together my kids who liked to read books with strong girl characters and introduced a few books that I knew they hadn't yet looked at that might fit that category. I found that it wasn't about the books being new and shiny or arriving in a box, it was about me modeling enthusiasm for the books and generating a bit of interest in the books by recommending them and telling a bit about what was in the book. Also, knowing something about the interests of the readers I pulled together ensured that someone in the group would love the book I was talking up.

After a few meetings like this where I did most of the recommending, I started holding a "book recommending" group and had the children recommend books to each other. After all, they were grouped together because of their similar tastes, and getting a recommendation from a peer is like nothing else. Honestly, it's how I choose most of what I decide to read as an adult. Here again, I tried to hand over the reins to the children, giving them more ownership and independence in the types of readerly behaviors I initially modeled in the small group.

In some classrooms, the problem of children being able to find books they like is a little more complex than just finding the right author or genre. For some readers who read far below grade level, the books that they can read with fluency, accuracy, and comprehension are not intended for their age group. It is very challenging to get a fifth grader interested in books with bright, colorful pictures with pigs and llamas as main characters, like Poppleton. It's a great series, but is intended for six-year-olds. Many schools find it helpful to have a healthy collection of what publishers refer to as "hi-lo" books—books that look like advanced chapter books, with plotlines and characters that appeal to older readers, but that are written at a level of low readability. Most publishers now have a section in their catalogue called "hi-lo" and many booklists can be found online by searching for "hi-lo." See Figure 3.4 for some recommendations from the American Library Association. I have also found really engaging titles from Red Brick Publishing, a division of Stone Arch books (www.stonearchbooks.com).

Small Groups to Self-Monitor and Fix Up Disengagement

For some children, what looks like disengagement in reading is really distractibility. For these children, it's not only about the books they choose, but also about giving them some strategies for staying focused, for setting short-term attainable goals for themselves as they read, and for refocusing themselves when they find that they

Chess Rumble by Greg Neri. Lee and Low, 2007.
Marcus learns, through the guidance of an unconventional mentor and the game of chess, how to cope with tragedy and his inner-city life.

Diary of a Wimpy Kid by Jeff Kinney. Amulet Books, 2009.
A novel in cartoons about Greg Heffley and his introduction to middle school, where undersized weaklings like himself share the hallways with kids who are taller, meaner, and already shaving. (Wimpy Kid series)

Knucklehead: Tall Tales & Mostly True Stories About Growing Up Scieszka by Jon Scieszka. Viking, 2008.
Short chapters with family photos describe this popular author's childhood and the adventures he had growing up with five brothers. It's easy to see how he developed his wacky sense of humor with stories that are laugh-out-loud funny.

The Maze of Bones (The 39 Clues) by Rick Riordan. Scholastic, 2008.
Orphans Amy and Dan have a choice to make when their wealthy grandmother dies; they can inherit one million dollars or they can receive the first of thirty-nine clues that will lead them to discover the secret that has made their family the most powerful one in the world. Clues can be entered on the series website and readers can play along. (The 39 Clues series)

Figure 3.4 Hi-Lo Book Recommendations from www.ala.org

become distracted. These strategies can be taught in small groups, with children providing models for each other and holding each other accountable.

We all get distracted from time to time—our stomach grumbles and we think about what's for dinner, the checklist of all that we need to get accomplished the following day makes it impossible to pay attention to that final chapter before turning off the lights and going to sleep, the upsetting conversation we had with a colleague just keeps playing over and over in our heads and we can't shake it. Some of the kids we teach come from home lives that are beyond our imaginations, which of course would distract them during tasks that are independent, quiet, and in-the-head.

One thing that sets readers apart, though, is the ability to notice when your mind has wandered and to pull it back and refocus on the task at hand. For some children, explicit teaching is necessary to help them to identify when they lose focus and to help them refocus on their books. I find it helpful to pull a small group of readers together to teach them some strategies, and then to sit with them and support them as needed in implementing those strategies. Having all of the students with me and at arm's reach helps me feel like I'm being very efficient with my time—the alternative being that I would either be moving around the room refocusing children, or reminding them of what to do when they get distracted, or that I would catch their wandering attention out of the corner of my eye when I was working with an individual or group and stop my group to refocus their attention on the book.

> ### ▶ Strategies for Staying Focused and to Refocus
>
> - Place a bookmark or sticky note just a few pages ahead in your book. Concentrate on getting to that goal. When you get there, stop and take a break, saying something silently. Perhaps retell what you just read in your head or say to yourself a reaction about what you just read (Beers 1996). Look around the room, take a quick stretch, and then resume reading.
> - Place sticky notes every few pages in your book. When you read to the note, stop and jot a thought you had or a big event that happened that you want to remember. Each time you sit to read, put the sticky notes farther and farther apart.
> - When you catch your mind wandering, stop. Skim in your book to find the last place where you remember reading. Back up a few pages more than that. Reread.
> - Use a personal quiet timer to set a time goal for yourself. When the timer ends, stop and take a break. Try to add more time to the timer each day, constantly increasing time until you reach your goal.
> - Have a book in your baggie that can serve as a "break" read. This might be a below-level chapter book, a magazine, a newspaper, or a favorite poem. Set a goal in your longer book and when you reach your goal, take a break with the other reading.

I begin by assembling a group of readers, some who need help staying focused and refocusing, and others that the class thinks of as being "good readers." My point in doing this is to provide models within the group to help children to see that *all* readers get distracted from time to time; what's important are the strategies we use to get back into our books. I begin by *connecting* with children by asking them to reflect on their own distracters, then I *teach* by stating a strategy, next I *engage* them in trying the strategy, and I end with a *link* to send them off to practice.

CONNECT WITH GUIDED REFLECTION I asked the students to bring their entire baggie to the meeting area and we began with a talk. "What distracts you when you're trying to read?" I asked them all. Students volunteered that when someone came in the room or over the loudspeaker, they lost focus. Other students said that sometimes if they didn't eat a good breakfast, they got distracted because they were hungry. Another student offered that she didn't know, her mind just wandered sometimes. I then said, "The thing is, we all get distracted—and probably not just during reading but also in other times of day. I know I do. I find sometimes that I can't quite keep my mind on what I'm reading. But I've learned ways to cope and I want to teach you some of those strategies to stay focused despite distractions, and to refocus yourselves when you do get distracted."

TEACH BY QUICKLY STATING AND EXPLAINING A STRATEGY I continued, "Today I'm going to help you to recognize when you're losing focus, and we're going to practice a strategy together. We're going to practice that when you lose your focus, you can stop, back up to the last part you remember by skimming over the page, and then go one whole page earlier in your book to begin rereading."

I chose not to model here, because the strategy is pretty self-explanatory. I wanted to move quickly to the engage portion of the lesson so that students could spend the majority of their time practicing the strategy with support. For this strategy, it was important for them to have a sense of what I was talking about.

ENGAGE BY HAVING THE STUDENTS PRACTICE THE STRATEGY At this point, I had the students take out their books and start reading. My role was to watch them carefully and tap them when they started to get distracted. I reminded them using a few words: "Back up, reread" or "Skim to find where you'll start rereading." Nonverbal prompts, or very short prompts, were often the most helpful because I tried to help them develop that lost-in-a-book feeling. Listening to me talk too much would take them out of that. After students had a little practice time with me, I ended with a link.

LINK THIS PRACTICE TO THEIR INDEPENDENT READING "So I'm going to send you back to your seats now, and I'd like you to try to tap yourself when you find that you're getting distracted. Don't be upset with yourself, just be aware. Remember the strategy when you lose your focus: stop, back up to the last part you remember by skimming over the page, and then go one whole page earlier in your book to begin rereading."

> **Structure of the Small Group to Help Children Refocus**
> * *Connect* with students by asking them to think of what their personal distracters are.
> * *Teach* by giving an explicit strategy for what to do when they get distracted.
> * *Engage* them by having them read and use the strategy when appropriate.
> * *Link* by repeating the teaching and sending them off to practice.

On subsequent meetings with the group, I did not give the students my undivided attention. After all, they needed to self-monitor, and the frequency with which they needed to refocus themselves decreased somewhat. Often, in subsequent meetings, I had the group working on refocusing on one side of me, and I called another group to an opposite corner of the meeting area or a nearby table to conduct a small-group conference. That way, I could still keep one eye on the "focus" group, and I could tap and remind them when necessary, but most of my attention was on the new group. Of course, it was important that the second group wasn't conducted too closely to the first or too loudly, as that would have surely distracted the highly distractible! Inside voices only.

Self-Assigning Reading Goals for Purposeful Reading

At the Teachers College Reading and Writing Project (TCRWP), we recommend a final unit of study in June to help readers reflect on their year and set goals for their last month of school. There is tremendous benefit to this whole-class study at the end of

the year. When children have some help with this for a few weeks and then create a
new project before going home over the summer vacation, we've found that children
tend to keep up their reading over the summer when it might otherwise have been an
afterthought.

For some children, though, we can't wait until June to offer some instruction on
how to have an independent reading life. Some children could use more direction with
setting plans that are book based—that is, helping them to create book sets, or lists,
that fit together for some reason to propel them through a period of time. For other
students, goal setting may be about having them reflect on their own process or skill
work and set goals aligned to their work as a reader. Each of these types of goal-setting
groups is described in the upcoming sections.

> ### When Could I Teach Small Groups to Help Students Set Reading Goals?
>
> - to help children keep up their own independent reading life during a
>   class unit of study in a different genre
>
> - before a long vacation, helping children who might not otherwise
>   keep up their reading
>
> - when children seem disengaged during independent reading
>
> - when students have trouble making plans for themselves as readers
>   and simply rely on the day's minilesson for a sense of what work they
>   can do as a reader

Goal-Setting Groups to Create Independent Reading Book Sets

Teaching children to self-select books and set plans for themselves as readers for a
chunk of time helps keep them engaged and motivated. On my nightstand, I have a
stack of books that I'm in the middle of reading or that I plan to read soon. I see the
stack every day and knowing what's waiting for me propels me. For young readers,
setting goals and having books "on deck," as we call it at the TCRWP, helps with this
same engagement.

Children in a reading workshop are expected to keep up their own
independent reading lives alongside class units of study, and some children need
help with doing this. If the class is engaged in a unit of study of nonfiction, for

example, and I have an avid fantasy reader and two children who love humorous fiction, I can help them figure out how to keep up their fantasy and fiction reading simultaneous to the reading they are doing that is aligned to the unit. This way, readers in the class practice the work from the whole-class study while maintaining their own reading agenda.

When students seem, based on the research I've done during my engagement inventory, that they are not engaged during the reading workshop time, I consider them perfect candidates for this type of small group. Also, when there are students who don't typically read over long vacations (such as the winter break or spring break), I might have some small groups with them beforehand to get them ready to read during that time.

If students have already completed reading interest inventories, like those shown in Chapter 2 and Figure 3.1, or I'm confident that they know their tastes in books, I can help them develop a reading list for themselves at the start of their independent project. If not, I might back up and have them complete an inventory or mentor them in doing a little reflection on their own reading identity first.

CONNECT AND COMPLIMENT: STATE THE PURPOSE FOR THE GROUP AND REINFORCE STRENGTHS When I pulled my fourth-grade group together, I set up the group by saying to them that readers make plans and goals for themselves. "Readers, I've been noticing that you do a great job at reading the books for our unit of study. I also want to help you to have a life outside of that. A reading life, that is. You know, I read things for many purposes. I read a lot of professional books to get new ideas on how to be a better teacher. I enjoy reading those books, but I also want to keep up an independent life outside of that. Today I'm going to help you get started with you own reading goals."

TEACH BY GIVING AN EXAMPLE AND EXPLANATION "When I pick independent books, I think, 'What is it that I like to read more than anything?' Then I try to make a little set for myself of books that go together by thinking, 'Can I find a few books that go together that would be interesting to read, one right after the other?' and finally, I go and make a little stack or list for myself." I then gave an example for the group of how I pick a focus (like my humorous memoirs) and create a list. I modeled how I use the library, a trusted bookstore, and friends as resources. I want them to be thinking beyond just the books we have in our classroom library.

ENGAGE BY HAVING CHILDREN TRY Next, the children in the group had a chance to work on their own plans for themselves as readers. They started at the classroom library, looking through bins and solidifying what they wanted to read about. I reminded them that they could pick any genre they wanted. For kids who would say something vague like "I want to read fiction," I nudged them to think about how there are all kinds of fiction—mystery and historical fiction and realistic fiction. I also said that within fiction, you could also pick a kind of character, like children who go on adventures without their parents. Sometimes we went back to their book logs to see the kinds of books they liked most, and I named for them the categories they might fit into.

After a little time at the classroom library, children spent a bit of time talking to each other. They first shared their category and then saw if their friends had any suggestions of other books they'd want to read. A few of the children couldn't find many books in our classroom library that fit within the topic they wanted to read, so they started the list with me and then planned to finish it at home with a parent who would take them to the public library. One student asked to visit the school library for some help from the librarian. There, she found a few titles that we didn't have in our classroom library.

LINK BY SENDING THEM OFF TO PRACTICE INDEPENDENTLY Finally, I ended with a link. "So, readers, I'm going to ask you to keep track of how this reading project is going by logging your reading. You'll write the title, author, level, genre, and whether you liked the book or not by rating it on a scale of one to ten. I've made a book log for you to help you do this. I'm going to check in with you next week to see how it's going, and to help you make revisions to your plan if need be." I gave the readers the reading log shown in Figure 3.3.

After the group ended, the children made booklists based on their interests, including books with strong girl characters, shark books, funny books, and books with magic. See Figure 3.5 for examples of some of the titles they chose.

The list they created for themselves was about a week's or week and a half's worth of reading. When I saw them for the next meeting about a week later, I did

Sports Stories
Three books by Matt Christopher
The Story of Jackie Robinson: The Bravest Man in Baseball by Margaret Davidson
Baseball's Best: Five True Stories by Andrew Gutelle

Shark Books
Shark Lady: True Adventures of Eugenie Clark by Ann McGovern
The Best Book of Sharks by Claire Llewellyn
Amazing Sharks! by Sarah L. Thomson
Time for Kids: Sharks! by Editors of *Time for Kids*

Funny Books
Franny K. Stein series by Jim Benton (two books)
Sideways Stories from Wayside School by Louis Sachar
The Adventures of Captain Underpants by Dav Pilky

Books with Magic
Zack Files: My Great Grandpa's in the Litterbox by Dan Greenburg
Deltora Quest: Enter the World of Deltora by Emily Rodda
Secrets of Droon by Tony Abbot

Figure 3.5 Booklists from Setting Reading Goals Small Group

no modeling, just reminded them of the process we went through to make reading goals for ourselves.

Helping Readers Set Process and Skill-Based Reading Goals

It is my goal to help children be metacognitive about the kind of work they do as readers. I teach children that in a conference, they should be ready to share their process and skill work when I ask the question, "What kind of work are you doing as a reader today?" When children are still learning to be aware of what they are doing, they may answer with "I'm reading about Cam Jansen."

When a student responds by telling me what her book is about, as opposed to what work she is doing as a reader, I find that I need to redirect by saying something like "That's what you're reading about, but I'm asking what you're *doing* as a reader. Let's look together at some of the charts in the room and see if you can talk about some of the strategies you're working on today, or some that you'd like me to help you work on." I model this kind of thinking—articulating our process and strategy work—during read-alouds, minilessons, and individual and small-group conferences. The charts hanging on the walls in the classroom support this kind of thinking.

At PS 158, as with other reading workshop schools, children as early as first grade learn to code their sticky notes with symbols indicating they are thinking about a question, or have a reaction, or have an idea. In the upper grades, children are familiar with words like *inference* and *prediction* and *synthesis* and can articulate what they are doing. Their sticky notes will often be marked with an *S* or *I* or *P* alongside their thought.

Goal-setting small groups can help children reflect on the kinds of work they do as readers and set goals for trying new work or to deepen work they've already begun. In these groups, I help children be metacognitive, articulate their process, and set goals in which they are invested.

WHO ARE THE CANDIDATES FOR THIS KIND OF SMALL GROUP? I often choose to teach this type of small group when children view my minilesson as their "assignment for the day" and don't make it a practice to reflect on their own plans or goals for themselves; they simply wait for me to tell them what to do each day. Children who set timers when they are assigned to read for twenty minutes at home and slam the book shut midchapter as soon as the buzzer rings might also be candidates for this group. It is clear to me that these children are dutiful and read when they are told, but they don't have their own reading drive.

When setting reading goals that are process or skill based, it's helpful to have children begin by looking back at reading logs they keep and the writing about reading in their reading notebooks or on sticky notes. They might look for patterns in the kinds of writing they do (e.g., "I notice that I'm the kind of reader who always predicts" or "I notice that I retell what's happening in the story a lot, but not much else" or "I notice that when I read at home, I read a lot less than when I read at school"). They can use these observations about their own skill work or their own reading habits to set goals for themselves. They might decide that because they usually predict, they're going to try a different kind of thinking about the book to see if they get a new perspective. Or, they might decide that because they don't get a lot of reading done in school, they are going to set some page number goals to see if they can make themselves read at the same rate as they do at home.

These small groups can follow the same structure as the ones described in the previous section. First, I tell children why they've been gathered and state the agenda for the group. Next, I teach by modeling how to reflect on what they've written on sticky notes, in their reading notebook entries, and on their reading logs. I do this teaching quickly to allow most of the time to be used to support their practice. Remember, the students in my group were selected because they had trouble self-reflecting and naming their work, so they needed some support from me in the first meeting. In the *engage* portion of the lesson, I help them look at their book logs, sticky notes, and reading notebooks. I coach them to code their sticky notes with the skill work they've tried to help them notice patterns. I next coach them to look at their book logs to see if they can tell their page-per-minute rate, or to see if there are certain books that they are able to read with more vigor, sustaining their reading for longer periods of time. By the end of the engage portion, I have the students write a brief reflection, like the ones shown in Figures 3.6 and 3.7, to set some plans for themselves.

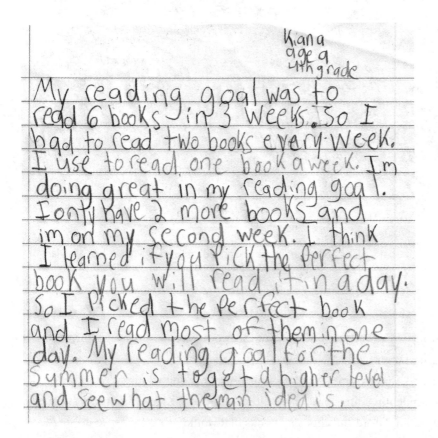

Kiana
age 9
4th grade

My reading goal was to read 6 books in 3 weeks. So I had to read two books every week. I use to read one book a week. Im doing great in my reading goal. I only have 2 more books and im on my second week. I think I learned if you pick the perfect book you will read it in a day. So I picked the perfect book and I read most of them in one day. My reading goal for the summer is to get a higher level and see what the main idea is.

Figure 3.6 Fourth Grader Kiana's Reading Reflection After an Independent Reading Project

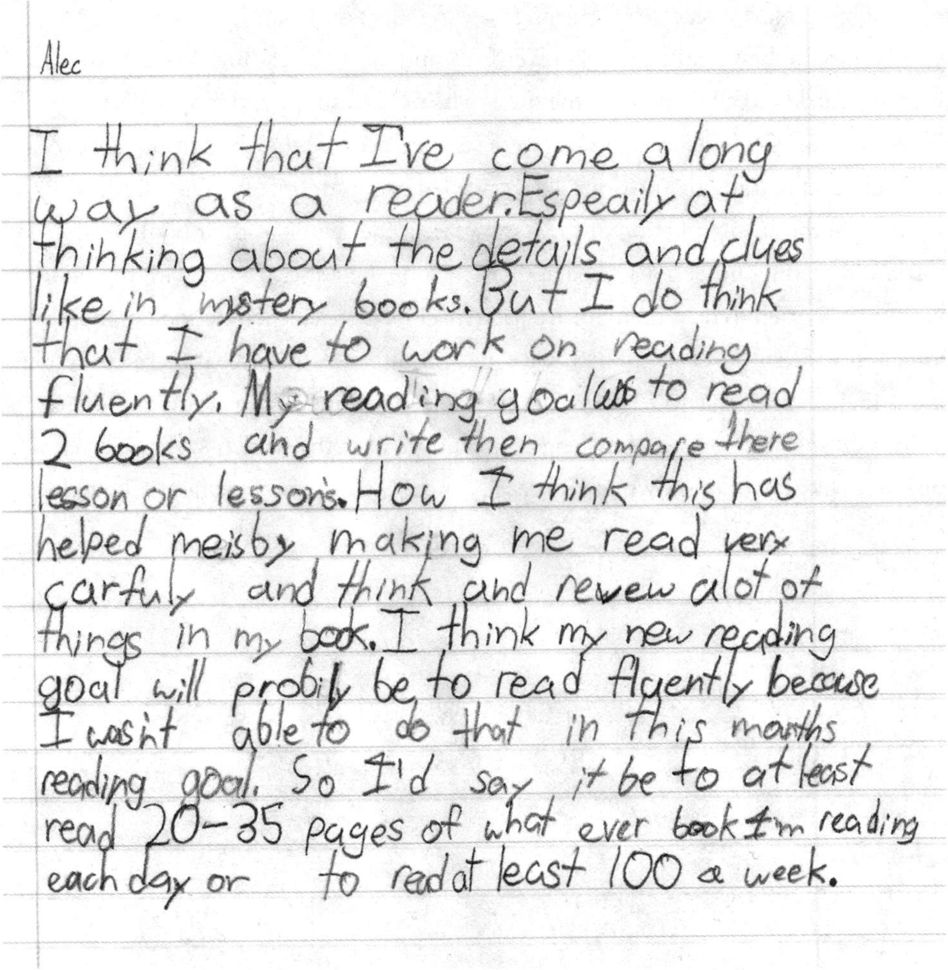

Alec

I think that I've come a long way as a reader. Espeaily at thinking about the details and clues like in mstery books. But I do think that I have to work on reading fluently. My reading goal was to read 2 books and write then compare there lesson or lessons. How I think this has helped me is by making me read very carfuly and think and revew alot of things in my book. I think my new reading goal will probily be to read flyently because I wasn't able to do that in This months reading goal. So I'd say it be to at least read 20-35 pages of what ever book I'm reading each day or to read at least 100 a week.

Figure 3.7 Fourth Grader Alec's Reflection After an Independent Reading Project, and His Plan for the Future

I end the group with a *link*, remind them of the process we went through and send them off to start their work.

Kiana and Alec, two members of a fourth-grade group who were working on setting independent reading goals, chose different focuses. Kiana (Figure 3.6) wanted to work on reading more and choosing books that would motivate her to do so. Alec (Figure 3.7) worked on a goal of thinking about lessons and making connections between texts. Alec said he was making a new plan for himself to "read fluently" but really he meant that he wanted to read more pages.

These groups follow a similar structure to the one described earlier, where I ask the children to reflect, watch me model, make a plan while I support them, and then send them off with a link to continue working independently with a promise to follow up again with them soon.

QUESTIONS TO ASK YOURSELF AND TO EXPLORE WITH YOUR COLLEAGUES

✔ Which students in your class do you think would benefit from one of these types of small groups to set reading plans?

✔ What structures do you already have in place to help children be self-reflective? When do children look at, evaluate, and reflect on their own reading logs, notebooks, and sticky notes to think about their skill work and process?

Sign-Up Seminars to Energize Learners

As a workshop teacher, I believe strongly in the importance and value of choice. Children are given constant opportunities to choose what books they want to read and which strategies from minilessons are appropriate for them at a given time.

It's important, too, to allow children some opportunities to choose the types of things they want support with. This choice relies on their ability to self-reflect and self-monitor, important skills for all learners. To some, this ability to set their own goals affects their emotional state, resulting in an "energization" of behavior, in essence making the learner more motivated, and affecting what is learned and what is remembered (Ford 1992).

I got the idea to do seminars, and to call them that, from a book about independent writing projects (Cruz 2004). I like calling them this because it sounds very collegial and special, especially to young children. To establish these sign-up seminars, I sometimes have topics posted with spots to sign up, and other times have open topics with slots to sign up. In my classroom, these topics came from my unit of study goals, from what I noticed my children might need during conferring or other small-group sessions, from looking at book logs, and often from reading notebook entries in which children reflected on their own reading processes and set goals for themselves. The seminars might be on anything from book choice to understanding a new genre to working on a particular reading skill to learning how to better participate in book talks.

The group itself might follow any of the structures and utilize any of the methods described in this or the other chapters of this book. This suggestion differs from what's proposed elsewhere in the book in that students self-select to be part of the group, instead of teachers choosing who belongs in the group. Groups might meet only once, or there may be a sequence of lessons over the course of a week or two.

> ### ▶ Sign-Up Seminar Topic Ideas
>
> - "I want to learn how to write better sticky notes."
> - "I want to learn how to get ideas about characters."
> - "I want to learn how to carry on a longer conversation in my book club."
> - "I want to be able to read aloud in a smoother voice."
> - "I want help choosing better books."
> - "I need work on my reader's notebook."
> - "I could use some extra help with what the class is learning in the unit of study."
> - "I get stuck on tricky words a lot."
> - "There are a lot of words in my book that I don't know the meaning of."

Because a student chooses to be part of a group, the kinds of accountability measures I usually put in place aren't always as necessary. The children seem to feel a bit privileged to be in the group, and therefore work as hard as they can toward whatever goal they've set for themselves. Still, I take notes on what we worked on in the group and plan to follow up with them during later small-group or individual conferences to offer support and to make sure that students remain focused on their plans for themselves, holding them accountable.

> ▶ **Key Elements of the Sign-Up Seminar**
>
> - Students choose to be part of the group; they are not assigned the group by the teacher. (Students might be gently nudged toward choosing one, though, by a teacher or a reading partner.)
>
> - The teacher might determine possible seminar topics, or the student might suggest a topic. Topics can come from unit of study goals, conferring, analyzing book logs, or ideas from reflective reading notebook entries.
>
> - Seminars can follow any of the structures or methods described in this book.
>
> - By self-selecting the seminar, students commit to a goal and can expect follow-up from the teacher.
>
> - Groups might meet once or there might be a sequence of lessons spread out over time.

The Last Word

Without engagement, we've got nothing. This chapter comes so early in the book because without readers who are actively, excitedly engaged with reading, no amount of teaching strategies and skills and habits and tips will help them. My very first job as a classroom teacher is to get children to feel that reading is for them and to help them identify themselves as "readers." It is essential that children choose books to read that they'll be successful with and to have the ability self-monitor their engagement and refocus when necessary. Watch your readers carefully during the formative days of school and at other points across the year, to make sure that this most basic foundation for a successful reading life is in place. Then, across the year, make sure that children are able to articulate and self-reflect on their process and work as a reader and that they are able to self-assign work to stay energized during the reading workshop.

Groups go a long way to helping you to accomplish these goals. Groups give children other peers with whom to work through challenges in finding books or staying focused. Groups help you target instruction to the exact structure and teaching point that would be beneficial to each reader. Group conferences to work toward engagement also help children move toward independence—from support from you, then peers, and finally by themselves. In Chapter 5, you'll read about other group structures that help with engagement: book clubs and partnerships. Having support and accountability from peers also helps readers stay invested in their reading lives and set and keep plans for themselves.

Revisiting the Tenets

Let's consider together how some of the ideas from this chapter align with the tenets established in the first chapter. We agreed that reading instruction should . . .

❏ *match the individual reader.* This chapter acknowledges that it's important to respond to readers' needs, not simply to plow ahead with unit of study goals. Looking carefully at whether students actually care to read, and doing something about it when they don't, is fundamental to their reading success.

❏ *teach toward independence.* A strong emphasis on all of the groups described in this chapter is to help children become independent at recognizing when they become disengaged, and do something about it when they do. There is also an emphasis on helping students mentor other students in their book choice, goal setting, and project follow-through.

❏ *teach strategies explicitly so that readers become proficient and skilled.* Strategies discussed in this chapter help students access the skills of working with engagement—making good book choices, self-selecting goals, and reading critically.

❏ *value time spent, volume, and variety of reading.* The small-group work suggestions described in this chapter are all in service of helping children to develop into engaged readers so they read more (volume). The more satisfying reading experiences readers have, the more they will use their time to read. When we ask kids to reflect on the kinds of choices they make, it allows them to pursue their own independent reading projects outside of the current reading workshop unit of study. This ensures a good balanced reading diet.

❏ *follow predictable structures and routines.* This chapter suggests ways to mentor children into the kinds of predictable routines that engaged, entranced readers do automatically.

Guided Practice Toward Independence: Strategy Lessons for Comprehension, Print Work, and Fluency

*I*n high school, despite my horrendous singing voice, I was always involved in our spring musical. My drama teacher, Mr. Cantor, deftly cast me as part of a chorus or background dancers or, in the case of my junior-year musical *Barnum*, a clown.

Mr. Cantor must have been well connected—or at the very least resourceful—because he somehow managed to convince actual clowns from the Ringling Bros. and Barnum & Bailey Circus to come to tiny Montgomery High School to teach us how to be part of a circus. Every day for a week we spent our after-school practices learning our trick of choice. Juggling, the devil sticks, plate spinning.

I chose to be a plate-spinning clown.

I learned, in a few days, how to get a plate going on the end of stick. But that's not the hard part. The hard part is that when you get one plate spinning, you place the end of that stick into a stand. Then, you get another plate spinning. And then that one goes in the stand. The wow factor in plate spinning is when you have many plates going at once. Plate spinning is hard because by the time you get the third plate spinning, the first one starts to get a little wobbly and you need to get back to it to give it another twirl. Then you get the fourth one going and the second one starts to wobble. And so on.

My plate-spinning background comes in handy when I work with a group of children in a strategy lesson. The challenge in a strategy lesson is to keep all kids in that one group "spinning"—actively working, actively engaged, actively practicing. Because the students in this kind of lesson are pulled together because they need some support, it's likely that once you get a few up and going, one will start to wobble. As a teacher in a strategy lesson, I find myself bopping and weaving in between them, coach, coach, coaching—moving quickly to offer support when each child might start to wobble.

Why Strategy Lessons?

Strategy lessons are times for students to practice new strategies or review strategies they've learned before, or I can preteach strategies before they're introduced to the whole class. Sometimes, the strategies are ones I've taught the whole class at other times of day, such as during minilessons, shared reading, read-aloud, or word work. Other times, I support readers with strategies that they've just begun to noodle with from an individual conference with me or that they've begun to practice while working independently in their own reading.

In these small groups, children have the opportunity for supported practice with a strategy—either something previously taught that they still need work on, or a new strategy—bringing them step-by-step to independence. I love the versatility of strategy lessons. You can use them to coach students with comprehension, fluency, print work—whatever it is you see several kids need support with.

Too often, we rush through or skip the guided practice phase of instruction—the *with* phase of the *to*, *with*, *by* model I mentioned in Chapter 1. Perhaps it is because of the pressure to cover the curriculum or it is an underestimation of how much support students may need, but it's one of the chief reasons we give up on using a workshop model. Students flounder and struggle in their independent reading and we lose confidence. We may jump to the wrong conclusion that it was the demonstration that failed. This guided practice provides an important way to gradually release responsibility and move readers to become independent (Pearson and Gallagher 1983).

In this chapter, I offer concrete advice for how to effectively provide guided practice to move readers toward independence:

❏   by maintaining a clear *structure* to your group

❏   by providing learners with *explicit strategies*, *effective demonstrations*, and *just-right prompts* during coaching

❏   by *being flexible and responsive* in your teaching as a you release scaffolding across multiple days

Strategy Lessons at a Glance: Structure

Like all workshop components, strategy lessons follow a predictable structure.

❏   *Connect and Compliment:* Tell the children why they've been pulled together, reinforce a strength, and state a strategy for today's lesson.

❏   *Teach:* Provide a brief demonstration, shared practice, example, or explanation.

❏   *Engage:* Coach the students in their own self-selected independent reading books, or, when you're not sure their book will provide an opportunity to practice the strategy, prepare a text for them.

❏   *Link:* Invite students to continue working independently, applying and reapplying the strategy practiced in new contexts.

This structure helps us plan, helps children know their job across all parts of the lesson, and helps keep the work in the group precise and efficient.

While the rest of the class is reading independently, I begin the group by telling the students why they've been gathered. I state a strategy that they will all work on together. Next, I give a brief demonstration, an opportunity for the children to all practice the strategy in a short shared text, and/or a give a brief explanation or example of the strategy. By this point, the students have been with me for about a minute or two.

The next part is the most important, and the longest, portion of the strategy lesson as all students practice right away in their own independent book. As the students practice, I make my way to each of them individually, coaching and supporting their practice. In general, I attempt to see each student a couple of times during this portion of the lesson to increase the potential for success. I keep in mind the amount of support my coaching gives to each reader—heavy, medium, or lean—to ensure that students are able to work independently on the strategy as soon as possible. The *engage* portion, when I coach, lasts about three to six minutes, depending on how many children are in the group.

I conclude the lesson by restating the purpose and encouraging students to continue to practice on their own. In total, the group will last about ten to twelve minutes.

CONNECT: LET STUDENTS KNOW WHY THEY'VE BEEN GATHERED AND OFFER A COMPLIMENT The strategy lesson begins with a very brief connection. In the connection, it's helpful to provide an orientation to the students to let them know what they've been doing well and why they've been gathered.

When possible, I give the children a brief, specific compliment to reinforce something they've done well. This is what Peter Johnston refers to as "noticing and naming" in his book *Choice Words* (2004). It's important that the compliment isn't general, like "Great job reading!" but instead gives a specific insight into what they're doing well, like "I noticed that when you're reading, you're getting your own ideas about the book, not just retelling what happened."

Compliments are especially helpful when they in some way relate to what will be taught: the compliment should complement the teaching point. For example, if I've gathered a group of fourth graders during a nonfiction study because I noticed they need some practice determining the main idea, I might first compliment them on how they can state the main *topic* of a section. That is, if the students are learning facts about what whales eat, the group of children who are able to determine the topic might say "food" or "food for whales." This acknowledges their ability to determine importance. I can then turn my attention to the teaching point: to identify the main idea. Calling attention to their strength increases their confidence to learn something new. The compliment is a clear segue into my teaching (see Figure 4.1).

If I Notice a Student . . .	Then I Could Compliment . . .	And I Could Teach . . .
. . . is using the beginning letter along with the meaning on the page to figure out what a word means, but often doesn't read the correct word.	"I notice that when you get to a word you don't know, you think 'What would make sense here?' and check the beginning of the word."	"Sometimes it's helpful to not only use the beginning letter or letters of a word, but also the ending to help you figure out what the word might be, still always thinking 'What would make sense here?'"
. . . approaches a new word by trying to "sound it out" letter by letter.	"It's great that you know how to look all the way through the word to help you to figure it out."	"Often, it's more helpful to look at words in chunks, not letter by letter. In English, letters act differently in different chunks. Putting them together by syllables might help you figure out the word."
. . . is able to use both consonants and vowels when trying to attack a word, but the child overrelies on one sound for a letter (i.e., always saying /k/ for *c* or long *a* for *a*).	"It's so helpful that you are looking at all of the letters to help you figure out what that new word might be."	"Sometimes, readers need to play around with sounds in their mouth before they're able to figure out what the word might be. When you get to a new word and reading it one way doesn't sound like a word you know, try other sounds that those same letters can make until you come to a word that you've heard before."

Figure 4.1 Compliments That Complement Teaching: Print Work Examples

I next let the children know why I thought they would be perfect for this group. Perhaps I tell them that I looked at all of their sticky notes the night before, or I listened in on the conversations they had with their reading partner, or I noticed their practice during the active engagement portion of the minilesson. By giving the children a sense of where and how I'm learning about them as readers, I'm also holding them accountable for what I'm teaching. Being explicit in this way sends a clear message that their ongoing work matters to me.

TEACH THROUGH DEMONSTRATION, SHARED PRACTICE, EXAMPLE, OR EXPLANATION After stating the purpose for the lesson, I present a clear strategy. A strategy should be a procedure to help the children know *how to* accomplish a specific goal (see Chapter 1). This strategy should set up precise steps for children to take. Of course, because each child in the group is reading a different book, it's important that the strategy transfers to any of their books.

Before getting back to the small group, let's take a moment to understand a critical aspect to the strategy lesson: the strategy.

The strategy should match the reader, and, to some extent, should also match the book. For example, if I teach a group of children how to come up with the main idea of a nonfiction text, which requires skills of synthesis and determining importance, I could use the strategy "Read each sentence on the page. Think, 'What are most of these sentences talking about?' Finally, state the main idea that is not only about what but also about so what." If, however, some students in my group have the kind of book with only one line of text per page, those children will need a different strategy. If I teach about main idea and the children have headings on each page, I'm better off teaching how to use the heading to get the main idea.

For example, I had a student who was reading *Bugs! Bugs! Bugs!* by Jennifer Dussling (1998). The first two pages read, "Yikes! Bugs look scary up close. But *you* don't need to worry. Most bugs are a danger only to other insects. They are the bugs that really bug other bugs" (4–5). When I came to that student and said, "State the main idea as a sentence," and the student replied, "Bugs," I knew that he was only giving a *topic* and not the main *idea* of the pages. Because the book was organized in such a way that there were the sentences spread across two pages with some color photographs, it didn't make sense to teach about headings, but instead I taught about synthesizing the sentences to determine the main idea.

So, when I pull a group of children together for a lesson, I usually ask them to bring their entire baggie of books with them, which serves two purposes. First, it allows me to make sure that the children will have a book that matches the strategy I've chosen. This isn't always about the exact title, but sometimes about where the reader is in the course of the book—the beginning, middle, or end (see Figure 4.2 for examples). Second, it allows the children to move to a different book to practice the same strategy while they're still in the group if that's appropriate for what I'm teaching.

Strategy	What Books Will Probably Work?	What Books Might Not Work?
One way to make predictions is based on a pattern of character behavior. First, look back across the chapters you've read to see how your character has acted in a few situations so far, and then make a guess about how she'll act in the chapters coming up.	• Most books with characters including realistic fiction, historical fiction, and fantasy • Any books in which the reader has already read a few chapters and has some information about the character	• Most mystery, especially those below level P/Q, such as *A to Z Mysteries* (Roy 1997) as they tend to be more plot-driven than character-driven • Books that the child has already finished • Books that the child has only just started
Nonfiction readers need to synthesize information on a page. One way to do this is to look at the heading, the picture, and the main text and think, "What are all of these parts of the page mostly about?"	• Expository nonfiction books that have a heading, pictures, and main text	• Narrative nonfiction (such as biographies) • Fiction • Books that don't have headings and pictures
Readers take away lessons and messages from texts. One way to do this is to recall what a main character has learned and think, "What can I learn from this character?" and "How will I live life differently because of this book?"	• Most fiction books, including historical fiction, realistic fiction, fantasy, and higher-level adventure books like *Hatchet* by Gary Paulsen (1987) • When the child has finished, or is almost finished with, a book	• Books that are more plot-driven, like the Magic Tree House series by Mary Pope Osborne • When a child has just started a book

Figure 4.2 Examples of When Books Will and Won't Work for Strategy Lessons

> ### ◢ Book Bags
>
> Children's book baggies—literally a gallon-size zip-top baggie or home-made cloth bag of the same size—hold the books they've chosen from their once-a-week visit to the classroom library. The number of books children have depends on their reading level: lower-level readers need more books to sustain a week's worth of home and school reading because their books are shorter and can be read more quickly; children who are reading higher levels need fewer books to sustain them for the week. Refer to the reading rates chart in Figure 2.5 to get a sense for about how many books each reader in your class will need based on the level of book he is reading.

When we first started using strategy lessons at the Teachers College Reading and Writing Project, we often led them like minilessons with long demonstrations. But Kathleen Tolan, deputy director of the Project, pushed us all to think more carefully about the method we choose. She asserts that because this is a small group, we should get the children practicing as quickly as possible and keep the teacher talk time as short as possible.

What Kathleen says makes a good deal of sense if we think about the *with* phase on the bridge to independence. Too much time spent in the *to* phase means it's farther from the goal. For this reason, after I state the strategy in clear steps, I decide if I will get the children started immediately, give an example or explanation, give them a chance to practice on a shared text with me, or give a demonstration. The answer depends on how much support I want to give, always keeping in mind that I try to keep this part of the lesson as short as possible, while still providing adequate scaffolding. In order for children to get started immediately, chances are I've worked with them before on this same strategy. Perhaps we worked on this strategy in a conference or in another small group. Or perhaps they just had a minilesson but I noticed that they struggled during the engage portion and I want to help with transference in their own book.

On the opposite end of the support spectrum is a demonstration. I choose demonstration for my group when students need the most support. This might be because it's a strategy that I've never taught before or because I know it's a strategy that I've demonstrated before but they need a demonstration in a different text that is more similar to their own. Demonstrations are opportunities for students to watch me practice the steps of the strategy as I make them visible in both my actions and my thinking process. See Figure 4.3 for advice on when to use which method.

If I get children started right away, providing lean support, it might sound something like this: "So readers, I just showed you how to think about the *what* and the *so what* in the minilesson. Get started trying this in a book you have chosen from the library, and I'll be around to help you out." The children would then pull a book out of their baggie and get started. I make sure all kids are engaged in reading before I begin moving from child to child to offer support. If this group is meeting to practice a strategy for the second or third time, I might instead say, "All week we've been working on main idea. You practiced with me on Monday and Wednesday. Now that it's Friday, I bet you'll be able to figure out the *what* and the *so what* without much help at all! Get started and I'll be right over to listen to your thinking."

If I choose to give an example or explanation, providing medium support, I might say, "Remember when I read this book called *Whales*, and I got to the first section, I read the sentences. I said I knew I couldn't just say that the page is mostly about *whales* because the whole book is about whales! I need to figure out what these two pages alone are about. So I thought the *what* is *whales* and the *so what* is that *whales need to hunt to get their food.*" In this example, I simply reference the past teaching where I first demonstrated the strategy. The key here is to be brief to allow most of my time for coaching.

If I want to give my students shared practice, also offering medium support, I might make an enlarged copy of a section from my whale book. Of course, this shared text must be at or below the level of all of the readers in the group. I might say, "Read this to yourself and be thinking about the *what* and the *so what* of this page." The children would take a moment to read. Then I'd say, "Turn to your partner and talk about *what* this page is about and *so what* about that topic?" As the kids turn and talk, I listen in. We could have a thirty-second discussion of the main idea of the page to help the children understand not only possible "correct answers" but also the thinking behind the answers.

	Degree of Support	**When I'd Choose This Method**
State strategy only	Lean	• We've practiced this strategy before together. • I just demonstrated the strategy in a minilesson; the group immediately follows the lesson. • I know my learners and they are ready to start with extra support beforehand.
Provide explanation/ example of the strategy	Medium	• Students need a quick reminder of the strategy, but don't need to see another demonstration. • I want to allow more time for coaching but don't think students will understand if I simply state the strategy. • I know my learners and I've found from past experience that an explanation or example is enough to get them trying on their own.
Practice strategy together on shared text	Medium/heavy	• The students had success in a minilesson during an engage portion (shared text) but need practice transferring; I want to start with where they were last successful. • I know my learners and they do well after having a shared experience.
Offer a demonstration of the strategy with think-aloud	Heavy	• I'm teaching a new strategy. • I've demonstrated the strategy before, but in a text that looks very different from the ones the students are reading, perhaps because it was a drastically different reading level. • I believe the students could benefit from seeing my thought process/think-alouds again. • I know my learners and they often do well after demonstrations.

Figure 4.3 Deciding How Much Support to Give a Reader Prior to Practice with Coaching

In a demonstration, offering heavy support, I need to model my process. I help the children see how I work step-by-step through the strategy, tackling difficulty. I start by giving children a heads-up on what they should watch for, demonstrate by thinking aloud, and concluding with a summary of what they should have seen. See the section "Explicit Strategies, Effective Demonstrations, Just-Right Prompts," in this chapter for detailed help on demonstrations.

ENGAGE: STUDENTS PRACTICE WHILE THE TEACHER COACHES This portion of a strategy lesson constitutes the majority of the time. I spend, on average, two minutes per student. I do not linger for two minutes with each student, though. Instead, I move among them with the urgency of a plate spinner, giving them just the right support as they practice the strategy in their own book.

Because I want to make sure that all children understand the expectations of this part, I say something to them like, "Now you're all going to get started with trying this in your own book. As you work, you can read, think about your reading, or write about your reading. Keep working on your own even when I'm talking to someone else." When I start strategy lessons in my classroom in September, my children are usually all trained by the end of the month and I no longer will need to say this to set them up before independent practice. In order for the coaching to go smoothly, I can't have children deciding that they're done practicing and just closing their books, or interrupting me when I'm coaching another student.

One of the hardest things to get good at is the pace at which we hand over the reins to students to take over responsibility for the task at hand—whatever that task might be. Whether we call it gradually releasing responsibility, moving students from the *we do it* phase to the *you do it* phase, the point is to support children so they *don't struggle*.

The challenge is in the "gradual" part. The release is generally smooth when we teach well, support the student as she learns, offer feedback and coaching as needed, and *then* watch the student's skilled performance.

During these strategy lessons, the secret for sensing the right pace for each child is to coach mindfully, to get better and better at being aware of what signals the child is sending. What is the child saying? How is he sounding? What's his expression and body language like? What is he asking me? In turn, coaching mindfully means I remain very aware of how much support I give the reader with the words and gestures I use to get him to practice. For more information on how to be aware of this release of responsibility, see the section later in this chapter called "Explicit Strategies, Effective Demonstrations, Just-Right Prompts."

I sometimes end this portion of the group by sharing what one or two students practiced or realized. This helps children because it provides more models for the strategy being practiced. When I do this, I make sure that I keep it very brief because I'm eager to send the children back to their seats with the final part of the lesson, the link, and move on to other students. I also tend to be the one sharing, not the student, because I want to make sure that I highlight clearly what he's done.

> ### ▶ Key Ideas About Coaching
> - Spend about two minutes per student, in short forty-five-second to one-minute bursts.
> - Have all children work on their own, not listening in to another student being coached.
> - Listen carefully to students and only provide the amount of coaching support needed (see Figure 4.3).

LINK: SEND CHILDREN BACK TO CONTINUE INDEPENDENTLY WITHOUT THE TEACHER The small group ends with making the link between the brief time we've spent together and what I expect students to continue back at their own seats. I make it clear in this part of the lesson that I expect them to continue the work we've started with the book they are currently reading, and I remind them to practice as they choose the next book.

In the link, I might ask older children to write down something on a sticky note or in their reading notebook so that when I see them again for the next group or in a one-on-one conference, I'll have a sense of how it's going for them. Sometimes, these tangible artifacts of their thinking make them more accountable in using what I've taught. It also reminds them to practice their new learning between this and the next visit. For younger children, or children who benefit from visual reminders of what I've taught, I give them a three-by-five-inch index card with the strategy written on it or a sticky on which they've written the strategy in their own words. Finally, the link ends when I repeat the strategy in clear steps.

A link would go something like this: "As you go back to your own seat, I expect that you'll keep up this great work. You should keep practicing trying to determine the main idea of each part of your nonfiction book by reading all of the sentences on a page, asking yourself, 'What is the *what* and what is the *so what* of this page?' and by stating the main idea as a sentence. Remember that this is a strategy that can help you any time you're attempting to determine the main idea of a part of a nonfiction book. When you are able to figure out the main idea, please jot it quickly on a sticky note and stick it on your page. That way, when I see you again I'll know how you've been doing with this strategy. See you all soon."

In some cases, I find that certain children demonstrate they're able to work independently before others. In these instances, I might do a "staggered link" where I send children back as they become ready. When I stagger the link, I use the same language I would use with the group to each child individually.

Explicit Strategies, Effective Demonstrations, Just-Right Prompts

I clearly remember learning from the Barnum & Bailey Circus clowns how to spin plates. My lessons began with watching them demonstrate their success, while they'd talk about what they were doing. One clown set up the demonstration by saying, "So I'm going to move the stick in a circular motion, underneath the lip of the plate. As I move it faster and faster in a circle, my circle will get smaller and smaller until the stick is in the central groove of the plate and the plate is making that circular motion all on its own—watch me."

The clown then demonstrated. As she demonstrated, she repeated the parts of what she just told me I'd see: "See this? My circles are getting smaller and smaller" and "I can feel the tip of the stick slip into the grove in the middle of the plate" and "There it is! Spinning all on its own." She then put the plate back on the end of the stick to show me what not to do. She jerked the stick back and forth and the plate went flying. As she did this she said, "This is what a lot of people might do, but you should know, this back-and-forth motion with the stick will end with a broken plate!"

Within minutes, each clown-in-training had his or her own stick and plastic practice plate. We tried spinning, and the plates dropped to the ground; some of us who were a little luckier got them going on the first or second try. As we practiced, the clown moved to each of us, individually coaching us with quick prompts. She said, "Faster with the stick" or "Make sure it's a circle, not back and forth" and "That's it!" Sometimes, the clown didn't talk, but instead put her hand over our hand and like a joystick on a video game made our hand move in the correct way to achieve plate-spinning success. The clown didn't stop us and do a whole extra demonstration when our plates fell; she simply said, "OK, pick it up. Try again!" and offered little running bits of advice as we tried again. As soon as most of what I heard from the clown was "That's it!" and "Keep it going!" I knew I could be on my own and be successful.

Three keys to leading an effective small-group strategy lesson are to use an explicit strategy, do an effective demonstration (if needed), and provide just-right support before and during coaching.

Just like the clown explained how to get the plate to spin step-by-step, so too do I explain a strategy as a process. When the strategy was new, the clown showed me first with some talk to demonstrate before letting me try it. In her demonstration, she included not only a good example of what to do, but also showed common mistakes and how to fix them myself. And just like the clown gave me little tips as I was trying, so too do I need to give prompts to readers as they try new strategies.

Explicit Strategies

For small-group strategy lessons to function well—with the teacher able to provide individualized support to each learner—it is critical that the learners have a clear, explicit strategy to support their practice. This explicit strategy is stated up-front for the group at the beginning of the lesson.

As explained in Chapter 1, a strategy is like a how-to. It's a step-by-step deliberate and carefully selected procedure to achieve a specific end. It's not enough in plate spinning, or in reading, to simply state the end goal—"Get your plate to spin!"—and expect the learner to be able to achieve it. Instead, it is crucial that learners *see* the process and hear the thinking involved in achieving a goal (Afflerbach, Pearson, and

Paris 2008; Serravallo and Goldberg 2007). At first, when learning is new, strategies are explicitly taught, but eventually, a reader internalizes the process and needs only to be metacognitive at points of difficulty. The strategy goes underground and the skill is what's evident.

Our carefully planned and thoughtful teaching is so important. When students understand an explicit strategy, experience solid demonstrations, and receive ample supported and coached practice with responsive feedback, they are more likely to have the agency to go within themselves for help when their reading breaks down.

QUESTIONS TO ASK YOURSELF AND TO EXPLORE WITH YOUR COLLEAGUES

✔ Think about a recent successful learning experience you've had—something outside of reading. What were the steps your teacher used to help you understand? What were the qualities of his or her demonstration? How did he or she support you as you practiced?

✔ When have you recently felt the need to use an otherwise underground reading strategy? What was the challenge and what did you do?

Think about yourself reading something challenging like a legal brief. Most likely, you chug along reading fluently, and all of a sudden you realize that you've lost track of what's been written. At that point, a point of difficulty, you need to select a strategy for reengaging with the text. As you consider possible actions, you might go back to the last place you remember really understanding and reread. Then you continue on to the next section and encounter an unfamiliar word. You slow your reading, perhaps looking for part of the word you may know. You may break up the word part by part, and then try rereading word as a whole. If those strategies or deliberate actions are unsuccessful, you read "around the word," looking for context clues that may offer help with the word.

All of these are strategies you've learned well and practiced consciously at one time. Now you resurrect them to use *at points of difficulty*. However, when everything's going fine, the strategies stay underground.

A strategy helps readers break down an enormous concept, like inferring, into steps a reader, new to this thinking, can follow. Inferring depends upon the genre, the text level, the reader's familiarity with the topic, and the reader's own experiences. Therefore, it is important for readers, and us as their teachers, to have a repertoire of possible strategies for each reading skill.

In Chapter 2, I introduced the concept that when a reader is working on a skill, there is a way in which to do that skill with increased sophistication or depth. Thinking of skills along a continuum is one way to come up with appropriate strategies for a reader. For example, if I know that a child's visualization sounds mostly like a retelling, I can place his ability to visualize on the lowest level of the continuum. I can look to the next level to see what would be a next step for the reader. I see that it says that a child next includes some details that are not explicitly stated. To come up with a strategy, I would have to ask myself, "How would I do that?" I might go to a book and see when I'm able to describe beyond what's explicitly there. I might notice that I can:

❏ Read what the text says. Picture a place that I know that is similar to the one described. Use what I know from my own experience to add in extra details.

Or

❏ Read what the text says. Imagine myself to be in the place and tap into my senses. Ask myself, "What do I hear? Smell? Feel? See?" Try to add more detail.

Notice that in each of these examples, to achieve success with the skill, I lead the reader to create increasingly more detailed images to enhance reading of the text and deepen comprehension. Oftentimes, we introduce strategies by simply defining them. As a good test of whether of not what you've offered is a strategy, ask yourself, "Did I explain not only *what* I want the reader to do, but have I shared *how* the reader could use that strategy?" See Figure 4.4 for examples.

Keep in mind that all readers experience confusion from time to time. There are so many factors that influence a reader's comprehension: the ability to decode the words within the text, the capacity to maintain fluent reading, the genre and text structure and the reader's familiarity with them, the difficulty level of text, the reader's prior experience with the topic, the reader's level of engagement, and on and on. It's important not to overgeneralize from this section that a reader needs only learn "the" strategies and will automatically be a star reader who can read anything.

There are a number of different strategies a reader needs in order to become proficient. Some address the ways in which a reader manages text, some speak to the cognition or thinking a reader does, and some concern the influences of context and

Skill	Strategy	*Not* a Strategy
Visualizing	Read what the text says. Imagine yourself to be in the place. Use what you're experiencing, including all of your senses, to add to your mental picture.	Picture the place.
Inferring	Carefully read a dialogue exchange between two characters. Ask yourself, "What does the way they're speaking to each other say about the kind of people they are?"	Name a character trait.
Determining importance	Read a chapter knowing that a significant event is likely to happen to a character. At the end of the chapter, think about what event made your character change, or act differently.	State the most important event in the chapter.
Questioning	Readers can engage with the text by wondering about the characters. They can ask questions about why the characters do what they do, and consider possible answers to those questions.	Think about what questions you have.
Synthesizing	One way to think about the beginning, middle, and end of the book is to consider the journey the character has been on. Think about what the character was like in the beginning of the book, and how he changed and grew across the middle, and what the character finally learned by the end.	Think about character change.
Retelling	One way to retell your book well is to flip through the pages as you're talking, saying one quick sentence for a major event from each chapter.	Retell the important parts of your book.

Figure 4.4 Comparing Strategies with Reading Tips

planning. There is no one checklist to use when teaching a child to become a strong reader. However, careful assessment and responsive teaching help us teach each reader the necessary strategies to overcome the inherent challenges the reader will meet. It is in the successful integration and orchestration of many strategies that our students become strong readers.

Ensure that what you teach in a strategy lesson small group is, in fact, a strategy. Doing so will help children become independent more quickly.

Effective Demonstrations

As mentioned earlier, some small-group strategy lessons provide new learning for the group of students. It may be an alternate strategy to what's been taught to the whole class, a strategy that you choose to preteach before the rest of the class learns it, or a strategy to provide enrichment to a group. When learning is new, it is often helpful for students to have an effective demonstration. Doing an effective demonstration allows children to begin approximating what they saw right away, freeing you up to coach.

In an effective demonstration, I make the strategy visible so that it doesn't look like the reader achieved the goal/skill through an act of divine intervention. When I learned to spin plates, the clown did not simply say, "See this? I can make this plate stay up all day! Try to spin plates like me." Instead, she carefully showed me the steps it took to get the plate up and spinning, and keeping it spinning, thinking aloud about her process as she went. One time, she even made a mistake on purpose—wiggling the stick back and forth in a way that would not yield a plate in the air—to show us a common error we might make. It didn't end there, however; she demonstrated *how to fix* the problem.

This demonstration is a good example of showing the declarative, procedural, and conditional knowledge needed for learning. The clown "declared" that she was plate spinning. She then demonstrated the "procedural or strategic actions" she was taking. Finally, she offered the conditional knowledge by explaining why she did what she did. The resulting skilled performance was carefully explained and demonstrated. In an effective and authentic demonstration, I will likely:

- ❏ alert the reader to what will be demonstrated by explicitly stating the strategy
- ❏ think aloud during *each* step of the strategy to illuminate the thinking involved

❏   make errors intentionally or use unintentional ones to show how to troubleshoot and recover from those errors

❏   debrief the demonstration to highlight the important parts of the strategy

An effective demonstration in a small-group strategy lesson for reading might sound like this: "I want you to watch me as I read this section in my nonfiction book and try to figure out the main idea. I'm going to first think about what the *what* is. I ask myself, 'What's the topic? What's the *so what* of that topic? What's the big idea here?' I'm going to reread a page of Melvin Berger's *Discovering Jupiter* [1995] that I've been reading aloud to you. Watch as I go paragraph by paragraph trying to figure out the *what* and the *so what*. *Jupiter is not surrounded with air like the Earth. The air around Earth makes plant and animal life possible. While no one is sure, most astronomers believe there is no life on Jupiter. If there is any form of life, it is probably some kind of microscopic being* [21]. Hmmm. This is hard. A lot of the sentences talk about life on Earth and life on Jupiter. But the paragraph starts out talking about the air. So I think that the *what* of this page is either Jupiter's air or life on Jupiter. Let me keep reading to see what the next paragraph talks about. *Instead of air, a thick layer of clouds covers Jupiter. The clouds wrap the entire planet like a blanket. Astronomers guess these clouds may be 11,000 miles deep* [21].

Ensure that what you teach in a strategy lesson small group is, in fact, a strategy.

"OK, well that paragraph was certainly not about life on Jupiter so I'm not thinking that is the *what* of the page. But I also learned that there isn't air around Jupiter, there are only clouds. So now I'm thinking the *what* might be clouds on Jupiter or maybe Jupiter's atmosphere. Let me read one more paragraph to be sure. *Jupiter's clouds are not fluffy and white like the clouds on Earth. They are formed into brightly colored bands—orange, red, white, and tan. The bands are like belts that completely circle the planet* [21]. OK, now I can confirm that the *what* of the page is Jupiter's clouds. That is what most of the sentences are about. But *so what* about the clouds? What's the author's point about them? I could say that the author's saying that the clouds on Jupiter are unlike the clouds on Earth. Or Jupiter's clouds are there in place of air. So, the page is about Jupiter's clouds. So what about Jupiter's clouds? Clouds take the place of air on Jupiter. Did you see how I read chunk by chunk, thinking first what the page was about? Thinking what are most of the sentences teaching? And then I thought about the *so what* of that topic, trying to understand what the author's point was. Also, notice that there is not one perfect answer, but instead a few possibilities based on what patterns we notice on the page."

In this demonstration, I set the children up to listen and watch, I showed them some struggle, I thought aloud as I went, and I capped it off with one more breakdown of the strategy. By doing a demonstration like this for a small group of readers learning a new strategy, I have given them a clear vision for what to practice. They can now begin to attempt this same strategy in their own books. This allows me as the teacher of the small group to move between them, providing differentiated support in the next phase of the lesson.

✿ QUESTIONS TO ASK YOURSELF AND TO EXPLORE WITH YOUR COLLEAGUES

✔ Think of a goal you have for a reader in your class. How can you take that goal and break it down into the steps of a strategy?

✔ What did you notice about the demonstration example that was just given that you already do when demonstrating? What new things will you try?

Just-Right Prompts

Perhaps the most important aspect of the small-group strategy lesson is the portion when you engage the students to try the strategy, providing support in the form of coaching. This coaching is differentiated and individualized based on each student's approximated practice. When you notice the student's attempt, you make an in-the-moment decision about how much support to give.

Finding just-right prompts means that you give as little support as possible for students to be successful and not struggle. Too much support leads to an overreliance on you. Too much reliance on the teacher means the student is farther away from being independent.

Because the strategy is explained as a series of possible steps, the prompts that are given can be reminders of each of these steps. Generally speaking, the more we say in a prompt, the more supportive it is. The less that is said, the leaner the prompt is. The prompts are the scaffolds that we put in place temporarily to help a reader transition toward independence (Wood, Bruner, and Ross 1976; Pearson and Gallagher 1983). How lean my prompts are as a teacher depends on how close the student is to independently practicing that strategy. In a strategy lesson, it is up to us to make decisions for each reader as an individual.

Take, for example, this strategy for improving fluency: "First notice when punctuation marks indicate that someone is speaking, then think, 'What character is this and how does he or she sound?' and finally make your character voice different from your narrator voice."

Heavily supportive prompts might be to say things like "Check to see when you first see quotation marks" or "Make your voice ready to sound like the character" or "Now drop back down to your narrator voice." Leaner prompts might be to just say, "Character voice!" or to use a nonverbal prompt by tapping that page where the quotation marks are to remind the student to change her voice. It's important to know the difference because students who struggle with a strategy may initially need very supportive prompts, but eventually they will benefit from leaner and leaner prompts until they are able to practice the strategy on their own. (See Figure 4.5.)

It is likely that even within one ten-minute strategy lesson, the amount of support you give a particular student varies. You may initially use heavier prompts, but by the end of the lesson, leaner prompts. For another student in that same group, you may find that you need to use only lean prompts the entire time. Flexibility with prompts—finding prompts that are just right for each reader—is at the heart of leading effective strategy lessons.

Releasing Scaffolding over Time

Just like in individual conferring, strategy lessons focused on a particular strategy rarely occur just once. Instead, I work with a child or group on multiple occasions, toward the goal of independent application of that strategy. I work with the child in different genres, to ensure transfer of the skill to new contexts. With each group meeting, I offer less help and encourage and support the child to work more independently.

For example, I saw a group of second graders on Monday to remind them of a strategy for decoding polysyllabic words. I had taught the strategy in a minilesson the previous week, but I noticed during the active involvement portion of the minilesson, or during conferring, that the students were all still practicing the strategy

Strategy	More Supportive Prompts	Leaner, Less Supportive Prompts
	Gradual Release →	
"As you read, put together your own knowledge of places like the one described with the details the author provides. Tap all of your senses to describe the setting."	• "Think about places you've been that are like the one described." • "Use all of your senses. What do you see? Hear? Taste? Smell? Feel?"	• "Picture the place." • "Use your senses." • Teacher points to eyes, ears, nose to signal senses. • "Say more about the setting."
"When you get information about the character's situation, it should change the picture you have of her in your mind. Think about how her body might look, or what her facial expression is like."	• "Think about what just happened to the character. How might she look?" • "Describe what just happened. Now describe how you would look in that situation. How does the character look?"	• "Describe the character's face." • "Describe the character's body." • "Make your face like the character's."
"As you read, your picture should change. The character should be moving through space, to new settings. The character's facial expressions change with new situations. Be on the lookout for words that signal change of time, or change of circumstance (for example, *later, in the next room*)."	• "Where is your character in this chapter? Describe the place. Now in this chapter? Describe the place." • "Look! That's a signal word. The character is in a new place. Tell me how your picture changes." • "How is your character feeling here? What does that look like? How is your character feeling now? How does that look?"	• "Describe what you see here. And here?" • Teacher points to a signal word or phrase. • "Describe your character's face here. Now here." • "Think about what you'll use to help you visualize here."

Figure 4.5 Sample Menu of Strategies with Supportive and Lean Coaching Prompts: Visualizing in Fiction

independently. Even though they read at different levels and they all read different books that they had chosen for independent reading, they all needed practice with reading an unfamiliar word part by part, and then putting the word together as a whole.

When I pulled the group together and supported them through coaching, I noticed that they each needed a different level of support from me. By watching closely and thinking about how close their approximations were to the goal, I decided on how best to support each student. Those children whose approximations were close (they could syllabicate shorter words, or words with familiar beginnings, but struggled with longer words) needed lean support. Those who were farther from the goal came to a long word and froze, often just repeating the first sound, and were uncertain about how to go on. They required heavy scaffolding.

On Monday, it happened that three of the children needed heavy support with this strategy, and one child needed lean support. The three children who needed heavy support needed my help to see the syllable breaks by putting an index card over part of the word, then the next part, so they could read part by part, adding one syllable to the next as in the word *anticipation*: "an- anti- antici- anticipa- anticipation." The one child who needed less support often responded if I were to offer quick, lean prompts like, "Add the next chunk" and "You know that last chunk" and "Put it together." Often, I coached with specific compliments, reinforcing what he was doing, saying things like, "That's it! Nice job changing your voice."

I decided to see them all again on Wednesday after they had time for independent practice on Monday and Tuesday. On Wednesday, I used lean prompts for the three children who initially needed heavier prompting, and also for the fourth student. However, this time I encouraged the fourth student to practice in a new book. This was an important move to make sure that the child was able to have the same success not only with the one book with the few characters he was familiar with, but in other books with other characters as well. For the three children that I first coached by offering greater support, using almost complete sentence-length prompts, I could now give leaner support. I could say things like, "Chunk it" and "Good job reading the word part by part," or "That sounded like a word you know!"

At this point, I felt confident that the fourth student was able to continue on without me. The following Monday I saw only three of the students, and scaffolded them as they read in a new book. Over time, I gave the children multiple experiences and then I decreased support. The group was flexible—one student didn't come to the third meeting—and it addressed individual needs though they were in a group. See Figure 4.6 for a tabular representation of the three meetings at a glance.

	Monday 11/4	**Wednesday 11/6**	**Monday 11/11**
Lin	Heavy support	Medium support	Lean support—new book
Shanique	Heavy support	Medium support	Lean support—new book
Julia	Heavy support	Medium support	Lean support—new book
Marcus	Lean support	Lean support—new book	Not in group

Figure 4.6 Releasing Scaffolding over Time

The Last Word

In this chapter, I explored the idea that there are multiple ways to release responsibility, or scaffolding, as children practice and use strategies to move toward independence.

The first decision I make as a teacher is about the amount of support to give prior to the student practicing in the engage portion of the small group. Before a child practices, I have a choice of four different ways to set children up: demonstration, shared practice, example and explanation, or stating the strategy.

The next way in which I vary the amount of scaffolding given is when the children are practicing. I can vary support by using different prompts as I coach. I can offer heavy, medium, or lean support.

The third decision I have to make is based on my constant assessment as children practice the strategy, and I consider how many times I'll see each person within a group. Once children get to the point of being able to practice with only naming the strategy and are successful with little prompting, I know that I can offer the child experiences with this strategy in other books. This repeated practice over time in varied contexts helps children develop proficiency.

Working in small groups, with a clearly predictable structure, allows me to work more efficiently than teaching the same strategy to multiple students in individual conferences, while still having the benefit of giving children one-on-one attention

Three Levels of Decision Making to Support Children Toward Independence		
Before Coached Practice	**During Coached Practice**	**Over Time**
What method will you use? • Demonstration • Shared practice • Example/explanation • State strategy	How supportive will your prompts be? • Heavy • Medium • Lean	• How many times will you see the readers in the group? • How will you use leaner supports over time? • How will you support transference to new books?

Figure 4.7

through the engage portion of the lesson. As I move from student to student, I respond appropriately by varying the degree of support based on what they write or say as they practice the strategy. Also, because of the plate-spinning nature of a small group, each student also has built-in wait time to allow him to process and practice the strategy before being coached again.

Revisiting the Tenets

Let's consider together how some of the ideas from this chapter align with the tenets established in the first chapter. We agreed that reading instruction should . . .

❏ *match the individual reader.* Instruction that is assessment based matches a reader. When we make decisions about how much support to give to a reader before, during, and after practice with a strategy during a small group, we are matching individual needs. Also, careful consideration about which strategy to use to help the reader to access a skill takes into account the individual.

❏ *teach toward independence.* Each small-group option presented in this chapter can be done in a sequence of sessions. On each subsequent meeting, I offer less and less scaffolding in the form of teaching and coaching.

❏ *teach strategies explicitly so that readers become proficient and skilled.* This chapter offered concrete advice and examples of how strategies are procedural to give readers access to skills that would otherwise be a struggle.

❏ *value time spent, volume, and variety of reading.* Getting students started on practice, with teacher support in the form of coaching, sends the message that reading is improved when a reader practices. Instead of coming to a small group to listen to a teacher go on and on about what to do, the children get to work quickly. This allows for more time during the small group for reading. In addition, following the lesson structure and pacing identified in this chapter allows students to return to their independent reading within a short period of time to continue reading.

❏ *follow predictable structures and routines.* The predictable structures for strategy lessons presented in this chapter will help readers access new content (strategies). When structures remain consistent, students know what is expected of them in a group. I don't need to explain how the group will go—the children already know their role and their job—they need only focus on learning the strategy.

Talking About Books:
Improving Partnerships and Clubs

I took part in my first book club a little late in life. It was just the two of us—Ed and me. He was a bartender, I was a waitress, and I was home on summer vacation trying to earn some spending money for the following year at school. At that time, aside from the books I had to read for classes at Vassar, I didn't really read much literature or many best sellers or interesting current nonfiction, and Ed was appalled. He decided we'd start reading together and we'd talk about the books after our shift, or in the brief moments when I went to his bar to pick up the daiquiris and martinis to bring to my tables.

That summer, Ed introduced me to more than the value of talking about books. He sparked a love of reading that I carried back to school in the fall, and carry to this day. He also introduced me to some of my favorite authors, like Dorothy Parker and Tom Robbins. He had this way of talking the books up that made me feel like I just had to read them, and he gave me enough support with what I'd find inside that I didn't abandon ship halfway through.

Reading partnerships and book clubs play an important role in reading workshop. Allowing time for talk helps children rehearse and revise their ideas about books, practice behaviors with a peer that they practice when reading alone, and develop communities around common texts. The teachers with whom I work most closely say that having children in conversations around books is perhaps one of the most essential times of day.

Supporting Book Clubs and Partnerships

When children work in partnerships and clubs, small-group instruction can help to make that time richer and more valuable. These small-group gatherings to support book clubs and partnerships can take place before children meet to discuss their books, or during the discussion itself.

Many children need modeling prior to being able to participate productively in a social setting. This is especially important when we are not right next to them. Independently carrying on a conversation or listening and responding to a peer can be a challenge if we don't provide initial instruction. Some clubs have difficulty because they aren't adequately prepared to discuss a book. Some partnerships work together, but do not spend the time in a way that best matches the kind of work they should be doing, based on the level of book they are reading.

Small-group work to support partnerships and clubs can be used as a helpful transition from whole-class minilessons—where we explain and model the expectations of this time—to the very independent work students are called to do with their peers in discussion groups.

Children also need supportive practice *while* in partnerships and clubs. The final portion of this chapter will highlight the kind of teaching that is possible when you listen in to conversation with an ear toward conversation and comprehension, and respond to children by choosing next steps within their zone of proximal development.

What's Ahead

- Introducing *differentiated partnership work for K–2 readers* in small groups will enable children to use most of their partnership time working on skills and strategies based on the work they need most based on the level of book they're reading and what we know about them as readers.

- Having children talk about the *read-aloud* in small groups helps students develop a vision for what to do during their independent book clubs.

- Providing *chapter introductions* to clubs helps students read with depth of skill and with enhanced prior knowledge.

- Teaching while *students talk* helps to transition readers toward independent practice with the skills and strategies important to deeper comprehension and conversational skills.

Differentiated Partnership Work: Kindergarten to Second Grade

In K–2 reading workshop classrooms, children are paired with a peer who reads at the same level (Calkins 2000; Collins 2004). These children meet daily to read and talk about their books together. There are a number of ways that these children might interact during partnership time. Children might work together to read and reread part or all of a book to practice fluency and consider what is happening in the text. They might stop on each page and talk about what a character might be thinking or feeling. They might talk with their partner about words they need help reading.

In many classrooms, these partnership activities are offered to children during whole-class minilessons, and the whole class has the same list of options for their partnership time. Although there are some partnership routines and behaviors I teach to the whole class—such as choosing one book to read together, putting the book between the pair before starting, and spending time with one book instead of jumping from book to book—there are many that are better taught as differentiated partnership activities.

The past few years I've worked in primary classrooms helping teachers differentiate partnership activities according to the level of the book that children are reading. To do this, we first looked closely at the expected behaviors and skills that a reader needs to practice at each given level, and then thought about activities that would support them. Using Fountas and Pinnell's book *Continuum for Literacy Learning* (2007), we studied the grade-appropriate level. We looked at the authors' descriptions of the difficulties of the book and then at the kinds of behaviors and skills a reader at this level should be practicing.

At level D, we saw that children should use beginning and ending letters in a word along with word meaning to figure out new words, integrate sources of information (making sure it looks right, sounds right, and makes sense), analyze the story and comment on events and/or characters, read known words (sight words) in a text automatically, and retell in sequence.

With the above goals in mind, we imagined what readers might do as they work with a partner to reinforce these skills and habits. For example, if the goal was to analyze the story content, we might teach partnerships to read the beginning few pages of the book together, pause to reflect, and then talk about the text and their response to what they read. Or, we might teach children the importance of character development by suggesting they stop on each page to check the picture and think, "What would my character be saying here if she were talking?" Figure 5.1 lists suggestions for possible partnership activities to support skills, routines, and behaviors according to what a reader needs most at level D.

We next made easy-to-read labels with a word or phrase describing the activity and a picture to illustrate the activity. We created a separate sheet of labels for each level with differentiated activities so that the we could easily introduce an activity and stick the label on the five-by-seven-inch index card that became a partnership's menu (Figure 5.2).

All of this prep work improved my efficiency during the workshop because I was able to do several small groups during independent reading time to introduce the differentiated activities. I could pull together not only one partnership, but sometimes two or three partnerships (four to six children) that would benefit from the same activity. By the end of the thirty-minute independent reading time, I could see five different groups and introduce partnership activities tailored to each of them.

Level D	
Skills/Routines/Behaviors	**Possible Partnership Activities to Support the Skills/Routines/Behaviors**
Using some of the letters of the word, along with the meaning, to figure out new words	• Teach children to prompt each other with "What would make sense?" or "Check the letters!" • Have children write on a sticky note words they couldn't figure out when reading alone and talk with a partner about the words during partner time.
Integrating sources of information	• Teach children to prompt each other with "Does that make sense?" "Does that look right?" "Does that sound right?"
Analyzing and commenting on the story content	• Have students read the first few pages, stop and say what they think. Read the next few pages, stop and say what they think. Read the end of the book, stop and say what they think. • Have partners prompt each other, "What did you think about that part?"
Analyzing, commenting on, and inferring about the characters	• On each page, have children say how the character might be feeling. • On each page, have children say what the character might be saying. • Have children talk about the way a character changes over time by considering the main character at the beginning and at the end of the book.
Reading known words in a text automatically	• Have students warm up before reading by reading the words on the word wall. • Teach children to prompt each other with "Check the word wall" if it's a word that is familiar.
Retelling in sequence	• Have students tell the story across three fingers at the end of the reading: at first, and then, until finally . . . • Have partners flip back through the pages together and use the pictures to retell the story. • Teach the children to say, "Wait, you missed something" if the retelling skips over an important part.

Figure 5.1 Sample Menu of Level-Based Activities for Reading Partnerships

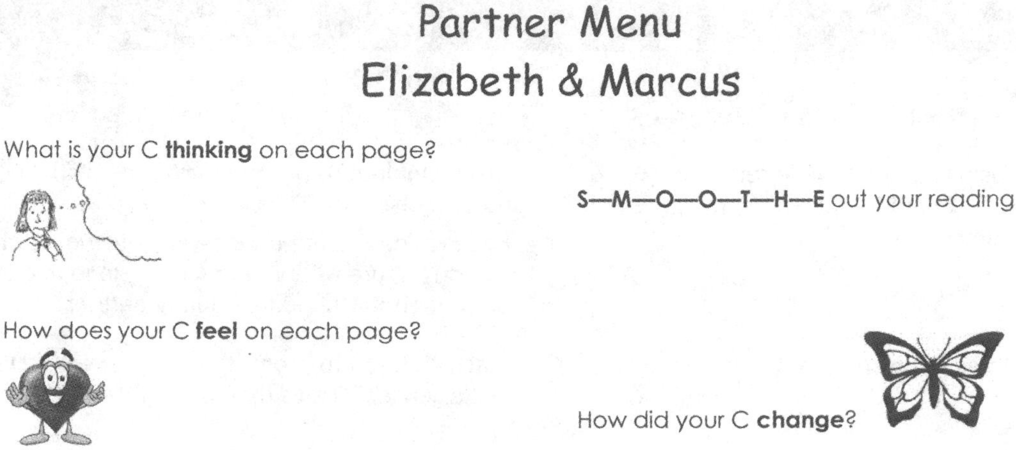

Partner Menu
Elizabeth & Marcus

What is your C **thinking** on each page?

S—M—O—O—T—H—E out your reading

How does your C **feel** on each page?

How did your C **change**?

Figure 5.2 Sample Partnership Menu

I structured these groups as follows. I first told the children why they were gathered; I next explained the activity and showed them the label by putting it on their menu card; and finally I had the children practice the activity in partnerships while I coached. After I was sure the children had enough practice to replicate the activity when they worked independently with their partner, I sent them off to continue reading alone and reminded them that when I said it was partner time, they were to take out their menu and pick an activity to do with their partner. To give an example, I describe a group I gathered to work on the skill of inferring about character.

For example, with one group I used an enjoyable activity I learned from my colleague Marjorie Martinelli, who was inspired by the talking Elmo doll. In this activity, readers were asked to "push the belly" of a picture of a character to make the character talk. This helped the children infer what the character *might* be saying as the dialogue hadn't been included. This worked really well with children who were reading texts with simplistic amounts of words because it made them linger on each page to think about what was happening in the story.

Two partnerships came together to form this group—one partnership read at level E and one read at level F. I pulled both of these partnerships together because when I watched their typical partnership routine, I noticed that they tended to just put the book between them and read together. Although I wanted them to continue that as *one* of the activities, because it helped with fluency and they supported each other with print work skills, it was also important that they spent some time doing some comprehension work. I felt that this activity would be highly engaging and it would help them to think more about their characters and what was happening in their book. If making meaning continued to take a backseat to print work and fluency, these students' progress might stall, which could adversely affect their engagement with the books they read.

QUESTIONS TO ASK YOURSELF AND TO EXPLORE WITH YOUR COLLEAGUES

✔ What do your students currently understand about behaviors, routines, and activities to do during partnership time?

✔ How long can your children sustain their partnership time? How productive is it?

✔ What skills are your students practicing when they work in partnerships?

CONNECT AND COMPLIMENT: TELL THE CHILDREN WHY THEY'RE GATHERED AND REINFORCE A STRENGTH As you read through the following example, you'll see that I began the small group by telling children why they were gathered and oriented them. Notice that I gave them a compliment, which named and reinforced their previous work, and I let them know *how* I knew that they could benefit from what I was teaching them today. This is important because it reinforced my expectations and accountability—that I watch them, listen to them working together, and notice who they are as readers.

I began by saying, "Readers, I was watching your partnership time yesterday and I saw that you did a really nice job of reading with each other—you put the book between you, took turns reading aloud, and supported each other if you ran into difficulty. I want to teach you today that partners can do so much more than just read to each other. I'm going to start a menu with you today. Just like a menu in a restaurant where you get to pick what food you want, this menu is one where you'll get to pick which activity you want to do with your partner. Each activity on this list is going to help you to become a stronger reader, with your partner's help. I already put 'read out loud to each other' because you already know how to do that and it is one choice. Today I'm going to add a new activity, which is to make your characters talk."

TEACH: EXPLAIN AND DEMONSTRATE TO INTRODUCE THE ACTIVITY "The first activity I want to teach you today is going to help you think about the characters in the books you're reading. You can use this any time the book you're reading is a story that has characters—people or animals. The activity is to stop on each page and push the belly of the character and make it talk. Here's the label to remind you." I stuck a label on each partnership's menu. The label read "Talk!" with a picture of a person with a speech bubble.

This first portion of the "teach" section of the lesson set them up to be ready to hear what I would encourage them to do. However, they still needed an example from me. I then segued into some modeling with a familiar text. I chose a familiar text so that they could focus on the strategy I modeled, not the content of the book. I kept my demonstration brief to allow ample time for them to practice with coaching in the next portion of the lesson.

"Let me give you an example." I opened a familiar book they'd read with me, the level C book, *Worm Paints* (Caple 2000) and read, "Worm paints a picture" (1). Then I pressed the belly of the worm in the picture, "Hmm. What might my character have said here? I bet he said, 'Look at my picture! I'm so proud of what I've done. I can't wait to show my friends!'

"Did you see how I read the words and then pressed the character's belly to make him talk? Now you all try," I said. I ended the lesson with a recap of what had been taught to make sure they knew what the point of my demonstration was. This whole explanation, including the set-up and recap, took only a minute or two.

ENGAGE: CHILDREN PRACTICE WHILE THE TEACHER COACHES At this point, each partnership chose one book and put the book between them. One partner read a page and then pressed the belly to make the character talk. When I noticed that a child read without stopping, I whispered into the partner's ear, "Wait! Go back and make the character talk," and that child repeated what I said to her partner. This helped one child get into the habit of coaching the other. Another time, I pointed to the label on the table in front of them as a way to nonverbally coach them, reminding them to use the menu when they worked alone. After about one to two minutes of practice, I called their attention back to me.

LINK: SEND THEM OFF BY ENCOURAGING THEM TO TRY THE ACTIVITY DURING PARTNER TIME During the link of the lesson, I reminded the students that they could practice this activity during partnership time, not during independent reading time. I reiterated one more time what the strategy was and when they should use it: "Nice job practicing, everyone. So now you know that one fun thing you can do with your partner during partnership time is to make your character talk by pushing the belly of the character on each page. Today, when I say it's partnership time, I'd like you to take out this menu, find the activity, and practice it. Do you think you can all try this? OK, have fun!"

> **Introducing Partnership Activities in Small Groups**
> - Plan out activities that correlate with the behaviors, skills, and habits that students would benefit from practicing at each level.
> - Create menus for each partnership that can be added to as children learn new activities.
> - Introduce the activity to groups of two to six students during independent reading time. Tell them why they've been gathered, explain and give an example or demonstration of what they'll do, support them in the practice of the activity, and send them off, encouraging them to practice the strategy during partnership time.

Read-Aloud Book Clubs: First Grade and Up

Read-aloud clubs are small groups of three to five students who get together to discuss something that has been read aloud to them. This type of small group allows students to be supported because instead of the children reading a book independently and coming to a club prepared to discuss, I provide support while the book is being read to them. The second layer of support in this type of small group is that *while* students discuss the book, I listen in and coach the students. In this section, I first lay the foundation for this type of small group by discussing interactive read-alouds and whole-class conversations—two structures that support read-aloud clubs—and then I discuss read-aloud clubs.

Interactive Read-Aloud

Researchers have long regarded read-aloud as an indispensable part of the school day, with some recommending several opportunities each day for teachers to read aloud to students from a variety of genres (Calkins 2000; Collins 2004; Laminack and Wadsworth 2006; Nichols 2006). Many have innovated a bit on the traditional "story time" read-aloud to create an "interactive read-aloud."

In the Teachers College Reading and Writing Project (TCRWP)'s definition, the purpose of the interactive read-aloud is to help children interact with the text, with the teacher, and with each other. These interactions provide support for the kind of work that children do when they are thinking about their books independently during independent reading, and for the kinds of talking children do when they meet with a partner or club during talk time.

During an interactive read-aloud, I preplan, with clear goals in mind, places to stop and model my thinking, or think aloud, as well as places for the children to talk to a permanent partner, or "turn and talk"; write about their ideas, or "stop and jot"; dramatize an important part, or "stop and act"; or sketch to aid with visualizing, or

---

Read-Aloud Prompts

- *Stop and jot:* Stop and write in a reading notebook, on a sticky note, or on a notecard in response to a teacher prompt.
- *Stop and sketch:* Stop and sketch what you visualize in one part of the book.
- *Stop and act:* With a partner, dramatize a scene that was just read, or your prediction of what will come.
- *Turn and talk:* Talk to a partner about a prompt given by the teacher.
- *Think aloud:* The teacher models his thinking aloud to give the students an image of the kind of thinking one person has in a particular part of the book.

Figure 5.3 Read-Aloud Prompts

"stop and sketch" (see definitions in Figure 5.3). For example, one teacher recently read *Becoming Naomi Leon* by Pam Muñoz Ryan (2005) to her class of fourth graders. She decided that her class would benefit from more practice synthesizing the text on a literal and inferential level because they were very detail-oriented, but often didn't think about the big picture. She planned think-aloud, turn-and-talk, and stop-and-jot prompts strategically across one chapter in the middle of the book to support students with these skills.

- ❏ *Turn and talk:* "How does what happened right here fit with what came before?"

- ❏ *Stop and jot:* "You all thought one way about this character earlier in the book. How does your thinking now match up with that?"

- ❏ *Think-aloud:* "We've learned a lot so far about this grandmother. I'm going to just remind myself quickly of what I learned. She often uses humor when things are hard to say, she seems to be a good role model, and she's very responsible. That's all adding up to quite a strong woman."

- ❏ *Stop and jot:* "If you think about the whole text, what do you think the author is trying to teach us?"

Whole-Class Conversations

A helpful common practice in scaffolding children toward read-aloud clubs is the whole-class conversation (Calkins 2000). These whole-class conversations are not in small groups but rather, as the name would suggest, with the entire class. Before discussing ways to use small groups from the read-aloud, it is important to understand this foundational component of balanced literacy.

In TCRWP classrooms, whole-class conversations happen several times a week. The entire class sits in one circle and has a discussion about the book after the whole or a significant part of the book is finished being read aloud to them. This is highly supportive because the children have the help of the carefully planned prompts to guide their thinking along the way, and they have the assistance of the teacher, when necessary, to guide or steer the conversation, to enforce active listening, or to coach children when they are having difficulty.

The children can learn very quickly to respond to an initial request from the teacher: "OK, whoever wants to start the conversation, go ahead and start us off."

One child will likely share an idea he had when he was turning and talking to a partner, or will talk about something he had jotted down. The other children then need to listen to what the first child has said, and then formulate their own response.

While children talk, I listen and take notes and think about ways to ratchet up the work they're doing. I keep in mind the conversational skills and comprehension skills the children exhibit. I make a decision about what to teach and which method to use. More detail on methods for teaching into talk are presented later in this chapter. I also keep track of who talks and who is quiet, to ensure a balance of voices. When it feels like the conversation is a bit stilted, or when there is an explosion of many children who want to talk at once, I might have the class turn and talk to a partner about what they'd say next if it were their turn to speak to get everyone talking, and then reconvene children to whole-class conversation again. At other times, I might choose to fishbowl a few children to provide a model for how a good conversation looks, while other children watch and research and prepare to state what they've noticed.

The way that I listen during a whole-class conversation, and the way that I teach, are the same as when I'm working with a club. For many teachers, it's helpful to learn to do this first when the whole class is engaged in one conversation, and then move that same way of teaching to small-group conversations.

Perhaps, for example, I'm listening to a conversation and notice that the children who are speaking have great ideas, but they really aren't listening to each other or sticking to one topic. I may decide to interrupt, saying, "I notice that so far we've had about four different ideas laid out. This is a great way to start a conversation, but now we need to pick one and really listen to what that person's said, thinking, 'How would I respond to that idea?' Janie, why don't you repeat the idea you just had and everyone else's job is to listen and think, 'What would I say back to Janie's idea?' " This is a teaching point and a method that I would use with the whole class or with a small group having a conversation.

I keep notes over time, set goals for the class' conversations, and tailor read-aloud plans to support better conversations. These whole-class conversations occur once or twice every week from September on.

Read-Aloud Clubs

When independent book clubs are on the horizon, I recommend teachers begin grouping their children into clubs to discuss the read-aloud. About a month before independent book clubs, I take two sets of read-aloud partners and put them together for a group of four. During the actual read-aloud, children will still independently sketch or jot, will still turn and talk to or act out a part with a partner, and will still witness my thinking during think-alouds. What changes, though, is that time will be devoted to having children sit with their club and attempt a sustained conversation independent of my guidance.

Sometimes I use the time originally earmarked for whole-class conversations to instead have read-aloud club time. The instructional methods during this time stay the same as during whole-class conversations, except that I now need to move quickly between the multiple groups occurring simultaneously in the room instead of listening to only one conversation. Because these clubs were scaffolded with prompts during the read-aloud, children can usually sustain conversation longer than they would have been able to from their independent reading alone.

Read-aloud clubs not only benefit the students, but also the teacher. If I am new to conferring into conversation, knowing the book well allows me to jump into the midst of a conversation and have a sense of what's going on. Later, when the children are in independent book clubs, I may not know every book that every club is reading, making the listening in for teaching opportunities even more challenging.

Chapter Introductions for Clubs:
Second Grade and Up

One of the biggest obstacles to children having productive, independent conversations during book clubs is their ability to come to the club with ideas that are conversation-worthy. Many children often think about the text very literally. They are able, for example, to recount the facts of the text. They are able to tell you who the characters are and what they've done and how they're related to other characters. These students struggle, however, with coming up with ideas. Without ideas, it's impossible to have a conversation.

Book introductions can be used to help students read with a lens of inference, interpretation, visualizing, making connections (activating prior knowledge), or determining importance. Reading with a specific lens helps the children enter the text with attention toward that skill. Front-loading the information for readers so that they read with attention allows them to actively think as they read.

There are other instances when students may be inexperienced with the genre of the book they've chosen, a setting in the book, a concept integral to the meaning, or a book format. In these instances, I can decide to provide a chapter introduction to support prior knowledge. These introductions are especially helpful with genres like historical fiction, when a reader might not know anything about the historical time period, and knowing about the time period has a tremendous impact on the ability to get ideas and the ability to monitor for sense. I am reminded of a classroom I recently visited where a club was three-quarters of the way through *Anne Frank: Diary of a Young Girl* (Frank 1953) and was discussing the book with no mention of the Holocaust! Helping readers establish prior knowledge before and during the reading of the text will positively affect their ability to think and talk about the book more deeply.

In the case of either type of introduction, I have learned I need to be very familiar with the text. Speaking to readers in generalities is not as helpful as speaking in specifics. It is also the case that I will probably introduce a small portion of the text, not the whole book. This is to ensure that children will remember the introduction.

I prepare introductions for a chapter or two at a time. I often find that once I have introduced a few chapters, the club can continue without me. In other cases, children will need chapters introduced to them throughout the course of the book. When I find myself providing this much support, I am careful to make sure that I give less and less support in subsequent books with the eventual goal of having them work independent of me.

Helping Readers Deepen a Reading Skill

I prepare for a book introduction to help readers get ideas by looking back over the past notes I've taken in individual conferences and small groups. Even in a book club, it's essential that I still see the children in the group as individuals. I study what makes each reader unique and I find commonalities. I look at my notes for the kinds of goals we've clarified together in past conferences and I think about how close the students are to meeting those goals. The common goal becomes my small-group teaching point and I keep in mind what I know about each individual for the coaching part of the small-group lesson.

For example, I recently met with a fourth-grade club that was about to begin reading *Fantastic Mr. Fox* by Roald Dahl (1970). I learned from their classroom teacher, and the notes she'd taken on past conferences, that the students used sticky notes profusely, though for different reasons: some of them exclusively marked events that they considered important and used their sticky note to retell (e.g., "The man just went downstairs") and occasionally would write a prediction (e.g., "I think he went downstairs to get breakfast or something"). Their teacher worried about them functioning productively in clubs, because when they shared what they had written on their notes with the hopes of sparking an interesting conversation, it was likely that they got little more than "Yes, I read that part too" in response from another club member. Figure 5.4 shows samples of the kinds of sticky notes that tended to permeate their books; notice how literal the thinking on each of them is.

> *. . . it's essential that I still see the children in the group as individuals.*

This club needed help with inferring so that they would each get some ideas about their characters or the events in their books, not just retell the events. These ideas could then be brought to a club and discussed. When book club members bring ideas that are conversation-worthy, not just notes that retell literally what happened in the book, they are able to debate and consider each other's perspectives. Often, just by coming with more quality ideas, the children's conversational skills improve as well.

CONNECT AND COMPLIMENT: BEGIN BY STATING A PURPOSE FOR THE GROUP I began this group as I begin most: stating a purpose for why I've pulled them together. In this first part of the lesson, I wanted to let them know what strategy we would be working on together, as well as give them a rationale for why I thought this would be a good strategy for them to work on. I couch this new learning inside of

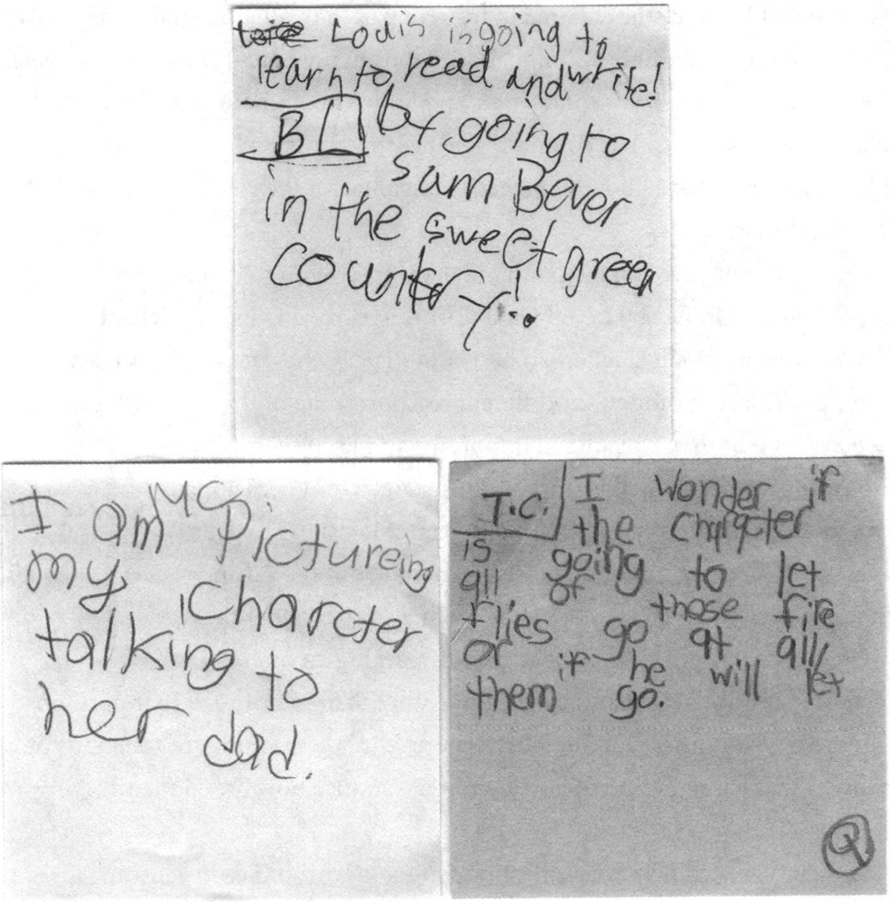

Figure 5.4 Sample Student Sticky Notes in the "Chapter Introductions to Help Readers Deepen a Reading Skill" Group

a strength they've demonstrated. This shows them—and me—that they are ready for this new learning.

"Readers, I pulled you together today because you're about to start this new book, *Fantastic Mr. Fox* by Roald Dahl. It is one of my favorites and I wanted to talk to you a bit before you started. I want to talk to you about how when you read, I've noticed that you're all really focused on the plot. You pay close attention to what characters are doing and saying and are about to do. I noticed because this is what you typically jot on your sticky notes.

"I want to tell you today that you can take this noticing one step further and start thinking critically about the characters. In doing this, you'll be able to bring strong conversation-worthy ideas to your book club. This means that your conversations will start to get a little more exciting.

"One thing you can be thinking is, 'What kind of person is this?' and 'Do I like this character or not?' and 'Would I make the same decisions as the character if I were in his or her shoes?' This kind of thinking will make it more exciting to read, and will also help you have really lively conversations when you meet as a club tomorrow to talk. I'm going to tell you a little about what you'll be reading about in the first few chapters, and some of what you might be thinking about when you get there."

TEACH: INTRODUCE THE PORTION OF THE TEXT THE CHILDREN WILL READ IN THE FIRST SITTING Before this lesson, I read and preplanned what I would say to this group. I had to be very familiar with the details of the text because as I read to plan, I came up with thinking prompts that encouraged them to try the strategy I would propose. In this way, it felt almost like I gave them read-aloud prompts, but for a book that they would read independently.

"The first chapter is called 'Three Farmers' because they are some of the important characters in the book. Roald Dahl writes that they are 'rich' and they are 'nasty' so you should think as you read about them, 'Do I agree or do I have other words to describe their actions?' You're going to read about the kind of food they like to eat, and how they are with other people, and all the while you should think, 'What kind of people are they?' Stop and jot a sticky note describing the kind of person you think each of them is. Think about whether or not you like the characters, and jot why. Let's put a blank sticky note on that page so when you get to it, you'll remember to jot an idea." Notice that I gave them questions to consider as they read, and also embedded a few text details so that when they got to that spot in the text, they could better remember what my prompts were. Planting blank sticky notes in spots is a nice trigger to remind them to stop, think, and write when they get to that spot.

"The second chapter is called 'The Fox' and he's an important character too—you can tell from the title of the book. Roald Dahl writes in this chapter about Mr. Fox, his wife, and his children. You should think about these characters, too. You'll read how Mr. Fox talks to his wife and you should think, 'What kind of person would talk like that?' You'll read that his nightly routine is to steal from the farmers from the first chapter and you'll think, 'Do I agree with what he's done? Would I do the same thing if I were in his shoes?' At the end of the chapter, you'll see the farmers again. At this point, you can remember what you were thinking about them before and see if you have anything to change or add to your first idea based on what you now know from meeting them again. Go ahead and put a sticky note on a spot where you think you'll be jotting."

Across this introduction, the children heard different phrasings of questions asked with the same goal in mind: thinking critically of the character. It was not important to me that they remember each question exactly where I said it. What was important was that they thought about characters and that they stopped and jotted to hold onto those ideas. I again had them place a sticky note in their books, this time giving them a little more freedom about where it went. The next time they placed a sticky note was back at their independent reading spots, entirely on their own, when they were moved to jot something.

ENGAGE: SET THE CHILDREN UP TO PRACTICE, AND GET READY TO COACH

"OK, remember I told you to keep track of your thinking about the characters. You'll be thinking as you read, 'What kind of people are they? Do I like them? Would I do the same things they do if I were in their shoes?' When you find a blank sticky note, that's a reminder to you to stop, think, and jot. Go ahead and get started while you're right here with me and I'll come around and help you out."

At this point, the children began reading, and as in any other small-group conference, I spent time coaching. Every child was working independently at this point—they were not waiting for me to come to them, and they were not listening in to what I said to another reader. As they read, I moved among them, spending just a fraction of a minute with each child and whispering quick coaching prompts like, "Remember, think about what kind of person would do that" and "Would you have done the same thing?" and "Jot—do you like this character? Why or why not?" to scaffold their practice of the work I just described.

LINK: SEND CHILDREN OFF TO CONTINUE WORKING INDEPENDENTLY When I'd gotten to each student once or twice during the engage section, and I was confident that they could keep going without my help, I sent them off to work independently to read the remainder of what I'd introduced.

"Everyone stop reading and look up for a moment. You're going to go back to your reading spots now and I want you to keep reading the rest of Chapters 1 and 2 on your own. Remember what we're practicing here: writing down *ideas* about the characters based on the kind of people you think they are, whether or not you'd make the same decisions if you were them, and whether or not you like the character. Take a quick second to jot down what your work will be when you go back to your seat on this purple sticky note so it can be a reminder to you." I gave them each a sticky note to put on the cover of their book. They wrote their goal for themselves in their own words on the notes. "Great. That can be your bookmark now. Remember, no need to write down what's happening in the book—just your ideas. OK, off you go."

> ▶ **Helping Children Read with a Skill Focus**
> * Keep in mind your (skill) goal for the readers in the group.
> * Introduce a small section of the book that you've read and preplanned.
> * Introduce the section by giving away bits of the plot and the kind of thinking students should be doing at each part of the section being introduced.
> * If part of the goal is to have students jot as they have ideas, you or the students can preplant sticky notes as a reminder to stop, think, and jot.
> * Give students a chance to practice applying the strategy before going off to read independently.

Chapter Introductions to Enhance Prior Knowledge

When children are already grouped in clubs and are reading the same text that they've chosen together as a group, it provides the perfect opportunity to do some small-group work around prior knowledge. One obstacle to some readers is a gap between their own experiences and the historical time period or genre of a new book. Small-group work to enhance prior knowledge helps their reading, and discussion, of the book.

Preparing for a chapter introduction to help readers establish prior knowledge requires that I've read, or at least skimmed, the covers of the book and the chapters I'll introduce. It's also essential that I know the children. What are their strengths as readers? What types of content knowledge do they have, and what would they benefit from having introduced to them?

A club with whom I worked at PS 158 on Manhattan's Upper East Side recently chose to read *Bud, Not Buddy* by Christopher Paul Curtis (1999). This book posed a number of potential challenges for these fifth graders: the book is set during the Great Depression, a time period they had not yet studied in social studies; the book takes place in Michigan and they are New Yorkers; the main character is in the foster care system and they all live with their parents; and there is heavy mention of jazz music and I doubted they had much experience with the musical genre.

I looked closely at the book to see how much support there was for the time period and the concepts for a reader without prior knowledge. It seemed like the city wasn't so essential to the first chapter and because they are city kids, being able to visualize and imagine another city wasn't that hard. Introducing all of this at once would have been overwhelming, so I decided only to introduce the concepts that would help with the first few chapters. Jazz doesn't come up in the first two chapters, so I thought I could introduce that at a later time. The biggest priority seemed to be the fact that the main character, Bud, is in the foster care system, and I also felt it was important to talk a bit about the time period so they'd be able to imagine how the characters looked, and how the place might have looked, from the very beginning of the book.

CONNECT AND COMPLIMENT: BEGIN BY STATING THE PURPOSE FOR THE GROUP AND REINFORCE A STRENGTH I began by pulling the students together to establish the purpose for the group. This is a book they chose for their book club, so they already had some excitement around reading it. They might have even been a little bothered that I was taking up their reading time with a small group! Because of this, I wanted to get them excited about what I had to say, and to convince them that what I was going to teach them would help them with the reading of the book. I established the purpose alongside a related strength.

"I'm pulling this club together today because you're about to start this amazing book, *Bud, Not Buddy*. I remember the first time I read this book I couldn't put it down! The characters really came to life for me and I was so interested in reading about the time period.

"I know that as a group, you are all very detail-oriented readers. I know that you like to know and understand what's in your books or else it becomes frustrating. I want you all to have the same experience with this book that I did: to fall in love with the characters and really be able to envision the setting. One thing that might be tricky is that it's possible that you've never read about the setting or themes that are in the book. So I thought I'd teach you all a little about them before you get started."

TEACH: INTRODUCE ELEMENTS OF THE STORY (THEMES, CONCEPTS, TIME PERIOD) TO HELP WITH PRIOR KNOWLEDGE   In this small group, I employed a very different method than I used in my other small groups. Because the group was focused on establishing prior knowledge, I would not simply give them a little lecture on the content. Instead, I wanted to support them with the things readers do to get prior knowledge for themselves, so the next time they encountered historical fiction and I wasn't there to help, they'd have some experience with working through that challenge on their own. Notice that I chose to use a bit of guided inquiry.

Me: Let's all take a look at the front cover. Tell me what you see.

Annalise: I see a black-and-white photograph of some musicians. It looks old-fashioned.

Gregory: I see a boy sitting on a bench. He's wearing funny clothes. I think I saw short pants like that once in a movie.

Melissa: I see his suitcase, too. It looks old and leather and it's kept together with ropes. He's probably poor.

Gregory: Also, everyone on the cover is African American.

Me: OK, a lot of what you noticed is going to help us to get to know the time period a little bit. This is set in the 1930s in America, so that's probably why you noticed things looked "old-fashioned"—it was almost eighty years ago! Back then, people often wore collared shirts and suspenders like you see this character wearing, and dress shoes every day, not just on special occasions. People didn't really wear jeans, like you do, or T-shirts. Here, I brought a couple of other pictures of people at that time so you can see what I mean. [*I pulled out a few pictures I quickly downloaded from Google Images. I wanted to help them develop a sense of the world of the story. On the cover, you just see a boy with his suitcase, which doesn't help much with what others might have been wearing, or what settings typically looked like.*]

It was also a very poor time. Many people were losing their jobs or were getting paid less. It was a time called the "Great Depression." People sometimes had to line up to get food for free from the government, and they had to take any job they could just to afford their rents. Many people were very sad, and many were very poor.

The main character, Bud, is especially poor. You were right to notice that from the suitcase, Melissa. Bud does not live with his parents. He is in the foster care system. The foster care system is a government agency that finds temporary homes for children whose parents can't keep them. In the first couple of chapters of the book, Bud and his caseworker—that's the person who's in charge of making sure he's taken care of—are discussing where he's going to go live, and we get a little bit of a glimpse of what it was like for him in a foster home. [*As I introduced aspects of the time period, I also tucked in how what I was saying connected to the kinds of things the students noticed when we were looking at the front cover. This helped them connect new learning with what was already known.*]

As you read, you're going to have to do extra work to imagine and picture the time period. Use these images I brought for you, the front cover, and any details the author gives you. You're also going to have to think about what it must be like in foster care. You might jot down thoughts or questions you have to discuss with your club mates when you meet tomorrow.

I ended by making it clear that when they read historical fiction about an unfamiliar time period, they needed to make sense of what they could, and they should also ask questions. Their club is a place to not only announce and discuss ideas, but also a place to help them to fix up confusion and to have questions answered.

ENGAGE: HAVE THE STUDENTS START READING, AND GET READY TO COACH

After this rich introduction discussing concepts and the time period, I wanted to see not only what students understood but also how they applied this new understanding in the midst of reading. Therefore, I didn't send them back to their seats right away, but instead I kept them for a few minutes to allow me to check in and coach as necessary. "Go ahead and start reading, and I'm going to check in with you to make sure the book is making sense to you. We'll read here for a just a couple of minutes and then I'll send you back to read on your own."

All of the children started reading, and I made my way to each of them for just a handful of seconds each. When I was with a reader, the other readers continued to work independently and didn't listen in to my brief conversation. I made my way around, questioning, prompting, and coaching for their ability to visualize the setting and the characters in period dress and to understand the details of the concept of foster care. I said things like, "Tell me what you know so far about foster care" and "What are you thinking about the time period?" and "What are you picturing in this part?"

LINK: SEND STUDENTS OFF TO CONTINUE WORKING INDEPENDENTLY Once I felt secure that the readers could continue on without my help, I sent them back to their seats. "I'm going to send you all back to your seats now to keep reading. Keep doing a great job of visualizing the places that are described in the book, the kinds of dress the characters are in, and the kinds of experiences Bud, who is in the foster care system, is having. When you meet with your club tomorrow, one of the things you'll probably want to do is to come with questions and your own thoughts about the time period and about foster care to make sure you all understand important elements of this book. Off you go."

Helping Readers Establish Prior Knowledge

- Decide on a couple of elements to introduce to the readers in the club. These could be about time period, genre, concepts, or themes that you anticipate will be a struggle for the readers.

- Follow a predictable structure: orient them to why they're there, explicitly teach, have them practice while you coach, and send them off with a link to independent reading.

Teaching During Partnership and Club Talk

When conversations about books go well, they're invigorating. Readers' eyes light up with surprising new ideas, children challenge each other, laugh together, and engage in lively debate. When conversations about books go well, children's comprehension deepens and their motivation to read increases. When children are talking about books, then, I make sure I listen hard and seize the important teaching opportunity. Keeping in mind what I know about conversational skills and comprehension skills, and my individual goals for each reader, I make decisions about what to teach the partnership or group. Using one of four methods—example and explanation, demonstration, ghost partner or proficient partner—I'll support their conversation.

> ✾ **QUESTIONS TO ASK YOURSELF AND TO EXPLORE WITH YOUR COLLEAGUES**
>
> ✔ How often do your students have opportunities to be social around books? Do you currently use structures such as whole-class conversations, book clubs, or partnerships?
> ✔ What is your role when students are talking about books?

Deciding What to Teach

In Chapter 2, I give advice for how to assess conversational skill and comprehension skill. When I'm deciding what to teach to partnerships or book clubs, I carry these ideas with me and listen into students' conversations with these two categories in mind. There are times when I have made a teaching decision prior to the start of their conversation—based on watching the group in the past, based on small-group conferences I've had with them in the past, based on how they function during whole-class conversation, based on the comprehension goals we're working on during individual reading conferences—but often the decision I make about what to teach happens in the moment.

Deciding on a Method

In *Conferring with Readers: Supporting Each Student's Growth and Independence*, Gravity Goldberg and I (2007) wrote at length about different methods of instruction for teaching into talk. The methods that I most commonly use when teaching into conversation are:

- ❏ example and explanation
- ❏ demonstration
- ❏ ghost partner
- ❏ proficient partner

Example and explanation and demonstration are familiar from Chapter 4 and others in this book; ghost and proficient partner are unique to teaching into conversation.

GHOST PARTNER The ghost partner method was originally called "whispering in" by Lucy Calkins (2000). When using this method, I move around the periphery of the club and whisper in quick coaching prompts. At times, I whisper in prompts that get the child to think or talk in a new direction. Other times, I whisper in sentence starters that the child is meant to repeat and finish.

In both partnerships and clubs, the benefit to whispering into a child's ear as opposed to just saying my prompt aloud for all to hear is that it forces children to take on the language of conversation. When I've used ghost partner a few times with a club, the students start naturally using the language that I once whispered in.

Whenever I choose the ghost partner method, I am sure to stick to one specific teaching point so all of my whispering is aligned to that one strategy. I use ghost partner more frequently in clubs than in partnerships because it sometimes feels awkward when there are only two people talking and I'm whispering in one of their ears, though I do find it helpful in partnerships when the conversation is in a lull and neither person is currently speaking. See Figure 5.5 for examples of prompts that are aligned to specific strategies.

PROFICIENT PARTNER In the proficient partner method, I assume the role of one of the members in the club. After listening to the club talk, I decide on one strategy and make comments only pertaining to that one teaching point. At the end of a short

Strategy	Prompts That Help a Child Think	Prompts That Are Meant to Be Repeated as Sentence Starters
"When you hear an idea that is different from one you had, try it on for size. Think about places in the text that fit with, or go against, that idea."	• "Go back into your book and see if you can find some proof." • "Think about how it goes with the idea you just said."	• "One place in the book that goes with that idea..." • "That idea is similar to mine because..." • "What do you mean by that?"
"To get a better idea of characters, think about how they don't act only one way. Find places where the characters act out of character, and talk with your club about how that changes your ideas about who they *really* are."	• "Check your notebook to see if you have any other ideas." • "Flip back through your book to see if you can find a place where the character acts differently."	• "I think the character acted differently when..." • "I think the character changed when..." • "Can anyone find a place where he or she acted differently?"
"Asking questions of each other and of the book is a great way to get conversation going stronger. You can think about things you don't agree with—that the character did or that a friend in your group said—and challenge them!"	• "Think about something the character did that you didn't like." • "Think about something a club mate/your partner said that you disagree with."	• "I disagree because..." • "I wouldn't have done what _____ did when..." • "Why do you think the character did that?"

Figure 5.5 Ghost Partner Prompts

amount of time, I stop the conversation and highlight the role I've just played in the club so that students become aware.

For example, when listening to a third-grade club discuss their A to Z Mystery book, I noticed that they had nice club behaviors like listening to each other and using body language to show they were listening, such as nodding heads and facing the speaker. When I listened to what they were talking about, I noticed a preponderance of predictions. One child laid out a prediction, then the next child laid out another prediction, then another child laid out a different prediction. I wanted them to linger on one prediction for a while, consider what evidence they had from the story that that prediction would come true, and *then* move on to a different idea. I decided to take on the role of a proficient partner and interjected with thoughts and questions focused on that one prediction.

I first said, "Oh! That's an interesting prediction. Let's think about why she's the main suspect. What makes her suspicious?" Once the children talked for a while, I stopped again and said, "Yes, but she's busy driving a taxi all day so how could it have been her? I'm not so sure anymore." After that comment, some children started referencing some other parts of the text and had some things to say back to me. Then, another child shared her prediction and I said less. I just interjected, "What do we think about that idea?" and let the children talk it out.

After a few minutes had passed, I stopped the group and said, "Did you see how when someone has a prediction, it's fun to stop and think about it for a while? We can stop and think about it by considering the reasons that prediction would come true, and the reasons it wouldn't based on what we've read so far."

One important caution in the proficient partner method is that children can become dependent on you to swoop in and save the conversation with some good ideas and questions. Sticking to one teaching point and articulating what you just coached them to do help support them toward independently practicing that strategy again on their own, without you there.

Structure of a Conference to Teach into Talk

The conferences described in this section take only about five minutes each, making them the shortest in this book. While students are talking, I make my way quickly from group to group. In most primary classrooms, children talk for ten to fifteen minutes at a time, and in upper grade classrooms, fifteen to twenty-five minutes. This means that keeping my conferences to five minutes each allows me to see several groups within each period of talking time.

The structure of this conference is most similar to a one-on-one conference. I begin by *researching* the club, looking and listening for evidence of conversational and comprehension skills. Next, I *decide* on a strategy to teach—either comprehension based *or* conversation based—and on a method to use for teaching. Then, I *compliment and teach* the group and *engage* the children in trying the strategy. After a brief period of practice, I *link* what they just did to their independent practice by reminding them of my goal for them.

The Last Word

In this chapter, I wrote about the value of using what I know from students' conversations, and my work with them in independent and other group conferences, to conduct small-group lessons to support their social groupings—partnerships and clubs—before and while they are in the groups.

Some of these small groups, such as read-aloud clubs, can occur at the very beginning of the year to prepare for later units when children are working in independent reading clubs. Others, such as the group to enhance prior knowledge or the group to help children read with a skill lens, occur on days when children are not meeting to talk with their book club, but are instead reading in preparation for their club. A structure mentioned in Chapter 4, the strategy lesson, would also be a helpful structure to use when children are in ready-made groupings during club time.

As always, it is important to keep in mind how much support I give a club with the structure I've chosen, and to have a plan for how I will decrease the support over time as children become more responsible and bridge their way toward independent conversation. See Figure 5.6 for reminders on how the structures mentioned in this and other chapters fit along the continuum of *to*, *with*, and *by*.

Heavy Support	Moderate Support	Independence
• Whole-class conversations off of read-alouds • Read-aloud book clubs	• Chapter introductions • Skill introductions • Strategy lessons • Differentiated partnership work • Conferring with children while they talk about books	• Independent partnership work • Independent book clubs

Figure 5.6 How Much Support Am I Offering Partners and Clubs?

Revisiting the Tenets

Let's consider together how some of the ideas from this chapter align with the tenets established in the first chapter. We agreed that reading instruction should . . .

❏ *match the individual reader.* In this chapter, I discussed how planning conferences to help children with their book discussions and partnership activities must be rooted in what you know about each individual reader. Even when readers are in groups or pairs, it is still essential to view them as individuals. Revisit conference notes from individual and group conferences when making teaching decisions. Also, give each child practice with coaching during the engage phase of the lesson to enable them to have individualized support.

❏ *teach toward independence.* The structures mentioned in this chapter were with the purpose of helping children function productively in the independent club or partnership time. When children have had a few meetings in these types of groups, they get the hang of the kind of prep work that is involved on their part to have a productive conversation. The strategies introduced during these small groups become common practice. When teaching while students talk, it is important to remember that you are not the director of the conversation, questioning and leading the group. Instead, you are there to provide a strategy to enhance their comprehension or conversational skill.

❏ *teach strategies explicitly so that readers become proficient and skilled.* In this chapter, you saw how to help readers get ideas, activate prior knowledge, have experience with conversation with a more supported structure using the read-aloud, and practice partnership activities aligned to the level of book they were reading. Inside of each of these structures, we present clear strategies that are replicable and transferable from book to book.

❏ *value time spent, volume, and variety of reading.* This chapter presents ideas for helping children read, think, and talk about their books more deeply. Knowing that they have support for books that they might not otherwise have felt comfortable tackling (like historical fiction about an unfamiliar time period) helps children with their variety of reading.

❏ *follow predictable structures and routines.* Every conference in this section follows the predictable "connect and compliment–teach–engage–link" structure, although the subtleties inside each portion of the conference are slightly altered depending on the purpose. Still, children learn to follow the predictable flow of conferences: We tell students why they're gathered, they watch and learn, they practice, they go back to their seats and continue on their own.

Reading with Fluency and Expression: Shared Reading, Warm-Up and Transfer Groups, and Performance Clubs

I think most people have a memory like mine. For me, it happened in second grade when Mrs. Nichols read aloud *James and the Giant Peach*. I remember sitting on the carpet squares in front of her large wooden rocking chair, listening intently to Auntie Sponge's and Auntie Spike's voices coming from my teacher's mouth. I can remember having this aha moment, thinking: "Oh. So that's what it's supposed to sound like."

Now, mind you, I was read to a *lot* as a child. I wasn't one of those children who came to school having little experience with books. I had a whole bookshelf of books, and I insisted on my favorites being read to me over and over. My parents were great readers, and I'm sure my kindergarten and first-grade teachers were as well. But there was something about the way Mrs. Nichols read the story aloud that finally clicked for me. I heard and saw the story in my head as if it were right in front of me. She was probably the most fluent and most expressive reader I'd ever encountered and it helped me to better comprehend.

Hearing Mrs. Nichols read changed the way I heard myself read, when I read out loud or when I read in my head. It also changed how I *understood* what I read. It was then that I began to understand that hearing the story fluently and expressively is part and parcel to being able to comprehend the story. For *most* children, the two are inextricably linked. Kuhn (2008) writes that fluency contributes to a reader's comprehension in two ways: "accurate, automatic word recognition and the appropriate use of prosodic, or expressive, features such as stress, pitch, or suitable phrasing" (4).

Fluency instruction has recently gotten a bad name with the No Child Left Behind's Four Pillars mandates, and DIBELs (Dynamic Indicators of Basic Early Literacy Skills) assessment. Some have taught children to read fast, timing them with a stopwatch, which often means comprehension gets the backseat. This is not what I believe about fluency instruction. Instead, I believe it's about helping readers to link their understanding to their fluent reading and vice versa—not just trying to make their reading "sound good."

Fluency is something that is learned in part from models like Mrs. Nichols, but also from guided practice with a fluent reader and from plenty of independent practice. Small groups can go a long way toward helping readers to become more expressive. In this chapter:

- ❏ I take a spin on whole-class *shared reading* and suggest that it can be used as small-group work during reading workshop for great benefit as it's assessment-based and targeted toward the needs of the readers in the group.

- ❏ I offer a structure I call *warm-up and transfer groups*. These groups scaffold children by giving them a chance to practice in a book that is easy for them, and immediately transfer the felt sense of fluent reading to their independent books.

- ❏ I write about one way to engage children in fun and exciting rereading with a purpose by grouping them in *performance clubs*.

> ### ✿ QUESTIONS TO ASK YOURSELF AND TO DISCUSS WITH YOUR COLLEAGUES
>
> ✔ Who have been the models of fluent, expressive reading in your life? Do you have any aha! memories like mine?
>
> ✔ How are you a model of fluent reading in your classroom?
>
> ✔ When do children have a chance to hear one another read aloud to provide models for one another?

Shared Reading: Assessment-Based Support from Teachers and Peers

Shared reading has the potential to be a great small-group intervention during independent reading time. Grouping children allows me to decide to put children together who need similar work with regard to fluency, or children who have different strengths and can support one another. Grouping also allows me to choose a text that is appropriate for the children by keeping the range of reading levels represented in the group narrow. In this section, I'll first define and explain shared reading as it's traditionally done—in whole class—and then discuss how to make the structure work well for small groups.

Defining Shared Reading

Shared reading is a method developed by Donald Holdaway (1984) and written about by Barbara Parkes (2000), Sarah Daunis and Maria Iams (2007), and others. Originally, this method was meant to mimic the experience of a child sitting with a parent while the parent reads aloud. When a child reads with a parent, they look together at the same physical copy of the text, and pause and respond at parts of interest.

In primary elementary classrooms, shared reading is most commonly done as a whole class. I typically have an enlarged copy of a text—a big book, a chart, a poster, or an overhead projection—in front of the class of readers who are gathered together on the rug. The whole class reads the text in unison, chorally, while I point underneath the words or at the start of the line to keep the class together. The children benefit from hearing the other readers—peers or me—around them reading while they do.

When and if the students become disfluent, have difficulty figuring out a word, or stumble through a portion of the text, I may stop and use that teachable moment to provide support with print work or fluency instruction.

I might say, "Hold on, that sounded choppy. Let's see if we can read that again and this time try to sweep our eyes under the line a little more quickly and put our words closer together as we say them." I may also stop during shared reading to ask the children to predict what might come next, to respond to the text, or to retell the text, helping them all the while monitor for comprehension. I will also likely offer words of encouragement as children read correctly, again, noticing and naming (Johnston 2004) what they've done well, saying, "That's it! Nice smooth voices on that last page!"

Shared Reading in Small Groups

Just as in whole-class shared reading lessons, when conducting shared reading in small groups we should gather the children around an enlarged copy of a text—a big book, a chart, or an overhead projection. It is important that children look at the same physical copy instead of having their own personal copy, as children are more likely to be attentive to the text and engaged with the instruction when all eyes are in the same place.

One benefit of doing shared reading as a small group instead of a whole class is that we can control who is in the group and why they are grouped together. Instead of having a first-grade class that ranges from levels C to J, we can pull a small group with a range of only a few levels. The text that is chosen, according to Brenda Parkes (2000), should be slightly above the level of the highest reader. When the range of reading levels is too wide, the lesson is likely to be too hard for some children and easy for others. If we pull students who read levels D, E, and F for a small group and choose an F- or G-level text, then all children benefit from the shared reading practice.

We can choose to pull a group of children with similar needs, and the shared reading lesson can be more focused to meet those needs. For example, I might pull a group of readers at levels D, E, and F who are working on paying attention to punctuation as they read, integrating sources of information, and phrasing across multiple lines of text. I can choose an appropriate shared reading text that will set children up for this kind of practice, and I can anticipate the ways in which I'll respond to children's miscues and errors in fluency when reading.

A third benefit is that when children are in a whole-class lesson, it is likely that a few students' engagement will falter at points. I find that this is often the case with children who most need the lesson in the first place! When children are in a small group, it is easier for them to stay more engaged, and for us to notice and reengage them if their attention wavers.

Benefits of Shared Reading in a Small Group

- We can match the text level to the group (choosing a text that is above their independent level).
- We can match the text challenges to the group.
- We can preview the text and anticipate coaching opportunities.
- We can more closely monitor and support engagement.

Shared Reading Structure

In a small-group shared reading lesson, I gather students and begin by telling them why they have been pulled together. Often, I talk to children about what I've noticed from listening to them read with partners, during whole-class lessons, or in our conferences together. Often, I compliment a strength I've seen in their reading that is a clear complement, or segue, to the teaching I've chosen for the group.

Next, I teach by telling them in clear and explicit language what it is that we'll be working on today, and offer a strategy to accomplish this goal.

Then, the children read in chorus. I might read with the students (if they benefit from a little extra support), or my voice might drop out to decrease scaffolding and to better hear what the children can and can't do without my support. As the children read, I offer coaching tips, suggestions, directives, and compliments. Although I have previewed the text to ensure that it will pose some challenges to the readers for the strategy we're working on, I often choose to interrupt in response to what the children do as they read. That is, I can't script out such a lesson ahead of time because there is a limit to what I can predict children will do. I can, however, plan where some prompts might occur that address the goals that I have selected (see Chapter 4 for help on planning prompts aligned to strategies).

At the end of the lesson, I recap what we worked on together. I again state the strategy clearly and in the same language, and strongly urge the children to continue to practice in their own books back at their seats.

Shared Reading Lesson Example

I pulled together a group of K- and L-level third graders to work on fluency. These readers in October were all reading at or slightly below grade level. I had noticed that these children, who were new to levels K and L, were starting to have some fluency challenges. When I looked at the books they were reading, I noticed that the books had more text density (more words on a page) than what they were used to before. I decided to do some small-group shared reading of a few pages of our read-aloud, *Pinky and Rex and the School Play* (Howe 1999), level L.

I planned to work with these students on smoothing out their reading, but while still monitoring for comprehension. I didn't want to send the message that we were just going to read more speedily—instead, we were going to read in more meaningful phrases, or parse the text meaningfully, thereby preserving the author's syntax (Figure 6.1), to better understand what the text was saying. The children also read in a monotone voice, another indication that they weren't making meaning. One thing I planned to highlight in this group was the switch between the narrator sound and the character-talking sound of reading.

CONNECT AND COMPLIMENT: STATE THE PURPOSE FOR THE GROUP AND REINFORCE STRENGTHS

Me: So, I started this book yesterday as a class read-aloud. I thought we could read the first few pages of the next chapter together as a group because I want to practice reading a little more smoothly when there are a lot of words on the page. I've noticed that the books you're reading have more words on each page than they used to. Also, the words often go all the way across the page instead of being written in short lines. For example, you used to read books like *Mr. Putter and Tabby* and the pages looked like this. . . . [*I held open a copy of a book they all knew.*] When you read these books, you read smoothly and with expression. You made your voice sound like the characters and when you read narration it sounded smooth, like how you talk. But now you're reading books

Understanding Parsing, or Phrasing

In the following excerpt from Horrible Harry in Room 2B *by Suzy Kline (1998), slashes show places where pausing would maintain the author's syntax and phrasing would be meaningful. Although eventually we want to hear that a child can read all the way to a punctuation mark—either a comma or ending punctuation—before pausing, this phrasing is an intermediate step while still indicating that the child is making meaning of the text. Try reading it aloud and pausing where you see a slash.*

Miss Mackle held up / a big glass jar / with the names of everyone / in Room 2B. /
  "Today," / she said, / "we will pick secret pals." /
  Everyone looked around the room / and pointed at somebody. /
  Harry pointed at me. /
  I pointed at Harry. /
  "Just a minute," / Miss Mackle continued, / "when I say, / 'pick a pal,' / I mean pick a pal / out of *this* jar." /
  Everyone stared at the jar / and groaned.
  "For one week," / Miss Mackle continued, / "you will send letters / and little homemade surprises / to your secret pal. / On Friday, / you will bring a letter / to school / saying who you are. / I hope this activity / will promote writing skills / *and* new friendships." (3–4)

This next section is the same excerpt, but this time with slashes in places that do not maintain the author's syntax. A reader who reads and pauses like this is probably not reading with meaning. Notice that it is possible to read in many-word phrases but read in such a way that confuses the meaning even within a sentence. Try reading this aloud to see if you can make sense of what you read when you pause where the slashes appear.

Miss Mackle held / up a big / glass jar with the names of / everyone in Room 2B. /
  "Today," she said, "we / will pick secret pals." /
  Everyone / looked around the room and / pointed at somebody. /
  Harry pointed at me. /
  I pointed at Harry. /
  "Just a minute," Miss / Mackle continued, / "when I say, 'pick / a pal,' I mean / pick a pal out / of *this* jar." /
  Everyone stared at / the jar and groaned. /
  "For one week," / Miss Mackle continued, "you / will send letters and little / homemade surprises to your / secret pal. / On Friday, you will / bring a letter to school / saying who you are. / I hope this / activity will promote writing / skills *and* new friendships." (3–4)

Figure 6.1 Understand Parsing, or Phrasing

that look like this. . . . [*I held open a copy of a book at the new level with a visible change in text density.*] Big difference, huh?

We're going to practice today really thinking about what's happening in the story and how the characters are feeling, and we're going to practice moving our eyes more quickly across the page to read it so it sounds like we're talking. This way, you'll read your new books with the same fluency and expression that you read your old books.

TEACH: EXPLAIN THE STRATEGY AND GIVE A BRIEF EXAMPLE "We will read thinking of what's happening, and whether it's the narrator or a character who is speaking. We want to make sure our voices match what's happening on the page. Before we start, it'll help to remember what's going on.

"For example, if I were to practice reading our read-aloud *Olivia* (Falconer 2000), I would first have to make sure that I knew what was going on. I would remember that Olivia lives with her family and all of the pages so far have been talking about the things she likes to do. Then, I would look to see if it's narration or dialogue and think about who is speaking to make my voice match what's happening. Here, on this page, I see dialogue marks so I know someone is talking. Also, I know that Olivia's mother is trying to get her to go to bed and she seems kind of annoyed, so I'd make my voice sound like that when I read it. (*I'd read aloud the sentence.*) '*Every day Olivia is supposed to take a nap. "It's time for your you-know-what," her mother says.*' Did you see how I made my voice match what was happening?"

ENGAGE: HAVE CHILDREN READ IN UNISON, WITH AND WITHOUT TEACHER SUPPORT

Me: Let's try it. Begin by telling your partner what's happened so far and how the characters are feeling.

[*Amitabh and Lijuan talked at the same time as Allison and Marcus.*]

Amitabh: Pinky and Rex were talking about the school play.

Lijuan: Yeah, and Pinky really wanted to get a part but he was nervous.

Amitabh: I think he asked Rex to come to the tryouts to keep him company.

Lijuan: And Rex didn't want to try out.

Allison: Pinky wanted Rex to try out for the school play with him.

Marcus: But she didn't want to.

Allison: She was worried she'd forget and get stage fright.

Marcus: But in the end I think she said she'd come since Pinky was so nervous.

Allison: Yeah, she did because she didn't want to go to spelling.

Me: OK, you all seem to remember pretty well. So we're going to use what we know has happened and keep thinking about what's happening as we read.

[*I turned on an overhead that was projecting onto the easel and all of the children looked up and got ready to start. All four children read chorally with me: "Pinky's Part. 'A monkey?' Pinky couldn't believe his eyes. It had been two days since the tryouts, and the cast list had just gone up on the bulletin board in the main office." (1) I began by choral reading with the students so they had the support of my voice with theirs.*]

Me: OK, what's happening here?

Amitabh: He just found out he got a part—a monkey.

Me: Yes, and how is he feeling?

Allison: He's probably a little surprised.

Marcus: Maybe he doesn't like the part.

Me: What makes you think that? [*I prompted the children to look closely at the text to reinforce that author's use of punctuation purposefully to help enhance meaning.*]

Lijuan: He says "A monkey?" with a question mark. Like he's confused.

Me: OK, let's read it again and act like he's surprised and disappointed. And look at this [*points to text*]—this whooooole thing is one sentence. You read all the way to the period. Try again.

[*All four children in unison, without me: "Pinky's Part. 'A monkey?'" This time they read it without me because they had already practiced reading once with me. I released scaffolding. Also, by being quiet I could better attend to what I heard them saying as they read, and responded as necessary.*]

Me: That's it! Nice expression.

[*All four children, in unison, without me: "Pinky couldn't believe his eyes. It had been two days since the tryouts, and the cast list had just gone up on the bulletin board in the main office."*]

Me: Better with the smooth reading. Look to where the next sentence ends . . . right here! Read it till the period. [*I almost pretaught. I anticipated that this long sentence might trip them up, so I gave them a "heads-up" of where I expected them to read to before pausing. Notice my voice was still absent as they read this sentence.*]

[*All four children, in unison: "There under 'Monkeys' were six names. One of them was his. He kept closing his eyes and opening them again."*]

Me: Is this him talking or the narrator? [*I interjected when needed, quickly prompted their thinking, and then got them reading again. I don't want to pause and linger too long in discussion because it would break the flow of the reading and might interfere with comprehension.*]

Lijuan and Marcus: Narrator.

Me: Right, let's read it again and make it sound like a narrator.

[*All four children, in unison: "There under 'Monkeys' were six names. One of them was his. He kept closing his eyes and opening them again." We continued in the group like that, reading together for about another five minutes or so. The entire group lasted under ten minutes.*]

LINK: SEND THE CHILDREN TO READ THEIR INDEPENDENT BOOKS, AND REITERATE THE LESSON TO ENCOURAGE TRANSFERENCE

Me: So when you go back to reading your books, they'll have a lot of words on the page just like this one. Practice when you're reading in your head, or out loud with your partner during partner time, smoothing out your reading. Remember to think of what's happening, and whether it's the narrator or a character who is speaking. Make sure your voice matches what's happening on the page.

> **Tips for Shared Reading in Small Groups**
> - Pull together a group of readers who are within a similar range of reading levels.
> - Review why you have pulled these particular readers, and choose a text where the children will have an opportunity to practice the strategies that will benefit them.
> - Open by telling them why they've been pulled together.
> - Plan to be responsive in the group, listening in as children read and teaching as you notice difficulty arising.
> - Repeat the work you've done together at the end of the session, and encourage children to replicate it in their own books back at their seats.

As you attempt these small groups on your own, it might be helpful to reference Figure 6.2, which offers help with predictable challenges students have when trying to read fluently, and the coaching support we might give them in a small group.

If the Reader Is . . .	Then I Might Coach by Saying . . .
Reading choppily, in two- or three-word phrases	• "Try to put more words together." • "Sweep your eyes under the whole line." • "Read to the comma, then pause." • "Read to the period, then pause."
Reading in a monotone voice, without regard for what's happening in the story	• "Think about what's happening, and read that sentence again." • "Think about how the character is feeling here, and read that part again." • "Keep reading, thinking about what's happening."
Reading without regard for punctuation	• "Read that part like dialogue." • "Read that part like narration." • "Look ahead to the ending punctuation. Now read it again." • "Make sure to pause at the comma, try it again." • "Take a breath at the period, try it again."
Reading smoothly and expressively	• "Nice smooth voice!" • "Way to put your words together!" • "The way you're reading that matches what's happening." • "Good job paying attention to punctuation!"

Figure 6.2 Coaching Prompts for Fluency

Warm-Up and Transfer Groups

One familiar challenge with teaching is the child's ability to transfer what he learns in one part of the day to another part, or from whole-class work to independent work. I commonly hear teachers complain, for example, that their children can spell words correctly on a spelling test or during word study, but then they spell the words incorrectly in their writer's notebooks. Or that while children are reading as a whole group, they read smooth and expressively, but later with their partner, they resort to choppy, monotone reading.

A warm-up and transfer is a small-group structure in which children warm up with a group experience in shared reading or in a text that is familiar or easy, and then transfer immediately, with coaching and support, to their just-right independent reading books. In this structure, the children act as models for one another. It is important that this method is used in a small-group or individual conference, because our role in supporting students with coaching while they practice is critical.

Before we get to how to conduct the group, and an example of the group, I want to talk for a moment about the concepts underlying why this works.

First, research suggests that when children practice initially on an easier text and then move to a just-right level, they will be able to more successfully read the just-right text fluently (Rasinski 2003). There is also overwhelming evidence that repeated readings of familiar texts have positive effects on fluency (Rasinski 2003; Kuhn 2008). These both have effects because it's easier for the student to understand the meaning of the text, and it helps to increase confidence, as well as helps readers get into the feel of what it's like to read fluently and expressively.

When a reader attends to a text that is difficult for him, he needs to keep up his fluency, comprehension, and decoding skills. When a text has heavy demands of one of these—say decoding—then it takes a lot of the reader's cognitive energy to attend to the print. Comprehension and fluency, in this example, would suffer. By having a child read a text that would be considered easy or below her just-right reading level, the child can more easily access the meaning (comprehension) because most of the words are known words. This allows the student to shift extra cognitive energy to fluency.

For example, if I know a G-level reader who is struggling a bit with reading fluently, I might give her a level E or even F text to read to warm up on, and then ask her to move quickly to start reading her G-level text. Alternatively, I could have this same reader reread a familiar text at or slightly below her level, and then have her move to a new G-level text.

Warm-Up and Transfer Group Example

In the following example, notice how I began by making a connection for the readers by telling them why I chose them for this group, and giving a compliment to reinforce a strength. Instead of a teach portion of the lesson where I demonstrate, this lesson has two engage sections. If I felt that my readers needed more support, I might have chosen to demonstrate or explain what I meant by fluent reading before having them try it. Since this was common knowledge in this classroom, and students were familiar with what I was describing, I decided to get them started right away.

In the first engage portion of the lesson, students practiced right away with a text that would be considered easy for each of them. Then, I had them read a just-right book from their book baggie. When they read the easy and the just-right texts, I coached them as described in Chapter 4, moving quickly between each child, offering lean prompts.

Finally, I ended the group with a link to let them know that I expected them to continue practicing what we just practiced in the group when they read independently.

CONNECT AND COMPLIMENT: STATE THE PURPOSE FOR THE GROUP AND REINFORCE STRENGTHS "First graders, I pulled you together for this group today so that we could work together on reading smoothly and expressively. We've talked before about how reading should sound. We've talked about how you want to read the words not like a robot, but instead smoothly, like how you talk. You should pause at the end of ideas, but not after each individual word. When something is exciting in the text, your voice should sound excited; when there is something sad happening, your voice should sound sad.

"I know that each of you knows what I mean. When I was listening in yesterday during our shared reading lesson, you all had great expression! You made your voice sound mad at the part of *Three Billy Goats Gruff* when the troll was angry about who was on his bridge. You all made your voice sound angry! 'Who's that tripping over my bridge?' So I know you can do it.

"I've noticed that sometimes when we've read together in conferences, or when you read with a partner during partner time, you pause a lot as you read, instead of reading to make it sound smooth like the way we talk.

"So, I have a secret trick for you that I hope is going to help. I'm going to give each of you a book that has much fewer words on the page, shorter sentences, and easier words. This way, you can be concentrating all of your energy on thinking about what's happening in the story and how to make your voice sound based on what's happening. You'll start by reading that and getting the feel for how you should sound.

Then, you'll take a book that you've chosen that's a just-right level, and you'll try to read that one with the same voice as you read the easier one."

ENGAGE, PART ONE: READ AN EASIER TEXT (OR SHARED READING OR FAMILIAR TEXT) WITH COACHING "OK, here's a book for each of you. Go ahead and read out loud in a quiet voice to yourself, and I'll listen in."

Each child read her own book, not the same title. This was not shared reading, it was still independent reading, but at an easier level. I separated the children a little bit so that the other voices didn't become distracting. As the children read, I listened and assessed. If I needed to intervene, I used quick prompts that didn't interrupt the reading. I was careful not to say a lot because I wanted to make sure that the majority of the time was spent with them practicing and getting the feel for fluent, expressive reading.

Most of my coaching during this phase of the lesson was to positively mark appropriate expressive reading. I had many opportunities to do this since children were reading books that were easy for them. I would say, "That sounds smooth!" or "Good job matching the feeling with your voice." These positive coaching prompts help children to become self-aware and metacognitive about their own fluent reading. I want this awareness to transfer into the next phase of the lesson.

ENGAGE, PART TWO: READ A JUST-RIGHT TEXT WITH COACHING After a few minutes of practice, I moved the children who demonstrated fluent and expressive reading in the easier books into their just-right books. If a reader was still struggling to read fluently in a book a few levels below what he usually read, this would have been an indication that extended practice in the lower-level book would better help him than moving into harder texts.

For the children ready to transition, I said, "OK, now take out whatever just-right book you're reading and try to read that book in the same smooth, expressive voice as you read the last one. I'll be around to help out. Don't forget that not only are you reading expressively, you are also reading to understand the text."

As the children began reading their just-right books, I used the same coaching prompts from the first phase of this lesson to encourage them to read smoothly and with expression. See Figure 6.2 for some examples of coaching prompts to respond to predictable situations that might arise in the group.

LINK: ENCOURAGE TRANSFERENCE TO INDEPENDENT READING After about seven to ten minutes altogether, I sent the children back to their seats to continue independently. I had been able to coach each reader with prompts that either supported or enhanced her performance. I then said to the group: "You all did an excellent job practicing that. When you go back to your seats, I'm going to ask you to keep an ear out for how you're reading. If it starts to sound choppy, or if it starts to sound like you're no longer paying attention to what's happening, I want you to pretend like you have me whispering in your ear, telling you to go back and try it again! If you feel like you need a break from your just-right book, you can take out the easier book I just gave you and warm up a little on your own before jumping back into your just-right book. OK, off you go!"

Warm-Up and Transfer Small Groups

- Set the purpose for the group.
- Have the children practice in a text that is one or two levels below their just-right reading level (while you coach).
- Have the children practice in their just-right book (while you coach).
- Link their work in the book to independent practice.

Performance Clubs

Last year, I listened to a teacher inservice workshop at Teachers College with visiting lecturer Timothy Rasinski. Rasinski is widely published in the field of reading instruction, particularly in the area of reading fluency. He had the audience singing songs with the lyrics posted on an overhead projector and chorally reading poetry and nursery rhymes from an overhead projector. The audience members laughed and clapped and had a wonderful time.

Rasinski's point in his presentation is that singing and reading poetry and nursery rhymes are fun and engaging. Not only that, he quipped, but short predictable texts when read repeatedly are shown to drastically affect a child's ability to read fluently. He cited research that showed that middle school children who did shared reading of poems and songs for thirty minutes a day, three days a week, for twelve weeks made one year of progress in fluency. One year of progress in just three months (Biggs and Homan 2005)!

This experience and the research sold it for me. Kids need to be singing and reading poetry in school, even in upper elementary school and middle school, and especially readers who struggle with fluency. I began thinking that this would be an engaging way to help children who are often disengaged with reading and/or those who struggle with fluency, to work together in small groups. Other researchers have found success with adolescents as well. Ash (2002) and Kuhn (2008) frequently use daily oral and shared reading as part of their intervention plan for readers who struggle in middle school. (See Figure 6.3.)

I worked in a third-grade inclusion classroom at PS 63 in the East Village of Manhattan. In the classroom, there were many children who read below grade level, and when I asked their teachers what was holding the students back, they said that when they tried to assess the children in higher levels, their fluency was drastically stilted.

I pulled one group of students together and told them that they were specially chosen because their teachers told me that they were kind of the actors of the classroom. I had heard that they liked to put on shows for their classmates, and that perhaps they'd like to be part of a club with me: a performance club. This club would meet a few times a week and they'd have work to do in between our meetings. Then, at the end of the week, they could perform what they'd been working on for the rest of the class. My proposal was met with cheers.

- Humorous poetry by favorite children's poets like Shel Silverstein and Jack Prelutsky or Paul Janeczko (whose latest is *A Foot in the Mouth: Poems to Speak, Sing, and Shout*)
- Classic nursery rhymes
- Reader's theatre scripts (many of which you can find for free from websites such as www.aaronshep.com/rt/, www.teachingheart.net/readerstheater.htm, and www.storiestogrowby.com/script.html)
- Songs

Figure 6.3 Sources for Texts to Use in Performance Clubs

> ### QUESTIONS TO ASK YOURSELF AND TO EXPLORE WITH YOUR COLLEAGUES
>
> ✔ Think of your students. Can you imagine any that would enjoy being part of such a club? Perhaps there are some that are otherwise reluctant rereaders but would enjoy the incentive of performing in front of others?
>
> ✔ What are some of your favorite songs, poems, and plays that could be used in this type of small group?

Performance Club Example

On the first day, I had prepared an enlarged copy of a silly Shel Silverstein poem, "Peanut Butter Sandwich," from *Where the Sidewalk Ends* (1974). I chose this poem because it was full of innuendo, the tone varied from stanza to stanza, and it was laugh-out-loud funny. It also happened to be narrative—it had characters and dialogue and action—and I thought that reading this would be good practice to transfer back to their fiction reading.

We began by reading the poem together. On the first reading, we practiced reading how we thought the author might have meant it to be read. We talked about what was happening and what the poem was about, and practiced matching our voice to that meaning. We practiced reading it smoothly—trying to sweep our eyes underneath the entire short line, pausing, and then moving on to the next line. The goal for this first meeting was to get them excited and to work together on providing a model for how the poem should sound.

At the end of our first meeting, I gave each reader her own personal copy of the poem. I told them, "You have this poem now and I expect you'll want to practice it a lot. You might decide during reading workshop that you need a break from your chapter book, and take this out to read. Or you might say to yourself, 'I want to warm up before I read my chapter book today' and start off workshop with this poem. You might pick some people at home to read the poem to. You could have them autograph the paper in the margin here after they hear you read it. All week, you'll be practicing and practicing because on Friday—it's showtime!"

All week, the children did just as we'd planned. Sometimes, if I noticed their attention was drifting during reading workshop, I walked over and said, "Remember, you have that poem you could practice if you need a break for a minute!"

By Wednesday, one of the girls in the group ran up to me and said, "Guess what! We made up hand motions to go with each line!" and she pantomimed the first few lines of the poem for me. They were really taking this seriously!

On Thursday, we met for one more quick meeting to make sure they were ready for the next day's performance. We practiced reading it fluently and expressively—and with hand gestures!—how they wanted to perform it the following day. They self-assigned some homework to read it to a few more people at home to get ready.

On Friday, their performance was celebrated by the whole class, which motivated them to try a new poem for the following week. The effects it had far surpassed fluency, in my opinion. The children started to experience the power and celebrate the success of reading in ways that they hadn't in perhaps some time. As struggling readers, reading for them was often intimidating or a challenge. They sometimes checked out, or got tired, or gave up. But having an end goal—with their peers as an audience, no less—really helped motivate them to practice and practice and reread, something they were often reluctant to do. In just a few weeks, their teachers reassessed them, and each moved to the next higher-level book for independent reading.

> ### Tips for Performance Clubs
> - Choose a highly engaging text—a song or poem—that will motivate the children to want to read, reread, practice, and perform.
> - "Sell" the club to the group members in a way that makes it feel exclusive and special.
> - Start the week with a shared reading club and give each reader his own individual copy.
> - Encourage the children to practice all week: to warm up before independent reading, to take a break from independent reading, and to practice at home with an audience of family.
> - End the week with a brief performance, allow the other children in class to celebrate the group's hard work.

The ideas in this section could also easily be applied to reader's theatre. Many scripts of popular children's books are available on the Internet and at bookstores, or children could make their own. Poems, songs, or scripts, when the promise of performance is at just at the end of the week, all have the ability to engage children's excitement and motivate them to read and reread to get ready to share with others.

The Last Word

This chapter discussed several options for supporting student fluency development: small-group shared reading, warm-up and transfer small groups, and performance clubs.

One important thing to keep in mind when teaching children with the goal of improving fluency is that comprehension and fluency are linked. It is hard to read fluently if you don't understand what you're reading, and it is hard to understand what you're reading if you don't read it smoothly. Oftentimes, when children are very disfluent, I recommend that they read more books at a level that they can read fluently. One of Allington's principles is that children spend lots of time reading easy books (2000).

Finding a just-right reading level means that the student can read the text fluently, accurately, and with comprehension. Then, I can use some of the small-group structures discussed in this chapter to give the child experience with the next level higher (as long as the child can comprehend and read the next level higher and read with accuracy).

The three small-group structures described in this chapter allow me to support the student through coaching while the child works toward independent fluent and expressive reading. Unlike whole-class fluency practice, being in small groups allows me to more easily control the members of the group. This leads to a better focus in terms of the teaching point and text selection, as well as differentiated coaching while children practice.

Revisiting the Tenets

Let's consider together how some of the ideas from this chapter align with the tenets established in the first chapter. We agreed that reading instruction should . . .

❑ *match the individual reader.* You learned in this chapter about a few different structures that can be used for the purpose of supporting children's fluency development. The trick here is not only to match a teaching point to a reader or group of readers, but also to match a structure. Can you think of children in your class who would love to perform? Can you think of others you'd like to try in a shared reading small group?

- ❏   *teach toward independence.* Within each of the different structures presented in this chapter, I showed how I released support across the course of one lesson and over time. In the shared reading group, I let my voice fade out and only interjected briefly when needed. With the warm-up and transfer group, I gave students a model for how they can warm up on their own during independent reading when they notice their fluency is starting to falter. In the performance club group, I set them up to independently practice their poem multiple times across the week without me.

- ❏   *teach strategies explicitly so that readers become proficient and skilled.* The groups presented in this chapter differ a bit from the groups in other chapters of this book in that I expect that children will synchronize a few strategies as they attempt to read a book fluently. In every case, though, I said up-front at the start of the group what my goals for them were, and I stayed focused on the blend of goals as I coached them, offering support.

- ❏   *value time spent, volume, and variety of reading.* Reading easier books to warm up to harder ones or reading poems, songs, or scripts intermittently throughout workshop to practice fluency helps children read a variety of materials and read more. When children get discouraged or disengaged, they might drift off or lose attention to their reading. These groups help children to reengage with purpose.

- ❏   *follow predictable structures and routines.* In this chapter, I presented three clear structures for helping children with fluency. Remember, also, that the structure of strategy lessons, as presented in Chapter 4, can be used for this goal. Regardless of what structure you choose, children will know what is expected of them in that kind of group as they return to the same kind of group again over time.

Moving Readers to the Next Level: Text-Level Introduction Groups

*M*y brother, sister, and I had a Nintendo system in our basement when we were kids. We went downstairs, sat in beanbag chairs, and played Super Mario Brothers. There were only two controllers, so we had to take turns. When it was Nick's or Melissa's turn, they passed from level to level. When it was my turn, I kept playing through level one, trying desperately to get past the stage where I jumped from toadstool to toadstool and onto the levels with the moodier music, the mazes, and the dragons shooting flames. Unfortunately, I ran out of "lives" and my turn ended. I could only take so much redundancy before my patience wore out and I stopped going down to the basement to play.

Constantly repeating the same level in Super Mario Brothers caused me to become disengaged and disheartened, and to just give up. This could likely happen with the readers in our classrooms, too, if they have to return month after month to the same few baskets of books in the classroom library that are at their independent reading level.

What also begins to happen is that for children who don't make adequate progress in their reading levels, the books that are available to them begin to be largely inappropriate for their age and maturity level. Sure, there are "hi-lo" books that I wrote about in Chapter 3, but most children's literature is written with the intent to match the age of the child reading the book—that is, a "second-grade" book typically has characters that are around seven years old who encounter problems seven-year-olds would encounter. It's hard to convince a middle school student reading on a third-grade level that reading about two eight-year-olds who get into a magic tree house and go on adventures is enticing.

"Children do not have levels; books have levels."

Reading below level also has implications for the amount of access children have to grade-level content materials. Richard Allington (2000) reminds us that for children to maintain their progress, they need several hours a day reading just-right material. When children spend time with printed material in science, social studies, or math that is above their reading level, not only does this time not help them become stronger readers, but they also won't be able to learn the content.

Keeping an eye on children's reading levels and supporting their movement through these levels are essential to their success with reading, with other school subjects, and with life. We need to make sure we are supporting readers to have a strong start at reading in kindergarten and first grade, and that they continue making adequate progress. At the same time, it's important that we don't overemphasize this concern with levels to children.

As the assistant principal of PS 158, Dina Ercolano says, "Children do not have levels; books have levels." Levels are one tool that we as teachers use to help children work within their zone of proximal development (ZPD) and that children can use to quickly find books that they'll be able to read. Creating in children an overawareness of what level they read on can have detrimental effects to the kind of culture we try to create in a reading workshop.

In the video gaming world, you can buy video game strategy guides or, colloquially, "cheat books." One of the bigger publishers of these guides has the tagline, "Get the strategy you need when you need it" scrolled across its Web site masthead. In our classrooms, there are many children who, like my brother Nick and sister Melissa, can progress through levels at a fine pace. Then there will be other students, like me, who need some strategies. These children need us to give them the strategy guides through targeted small-group conferences to help them to move with independence to the next level. In this chapter, I talk about how to get to know book levels and children's skill within a book level to help you group them appropriately, and then I introduce a small-group structure. Specifically, I will:

❏ help you to understand how to look at a child's progression through reading levels to determine whether or not the individual is making *adequate progress*

❏ give advice for how to *get to know leveled books* so that you can develop your own strategy guides for the levels to use during group conferences

❏ show how to *get to know each reader within a level* so that you can determine which difficulties, of all the potential challenges a new level poses, this particular reader could use support with

❏ introduce a small-group structure called *text-level introduction groups* that can be used to help support children to the next level, as an alternative to guided reading

What Is Adequate Progress?

Before launching into the how-to of these types of small groups, it's important to consider who the candidates for the group would be. To figure this out, I need to look beyond the assessments described in Chapter 2. What I am looking at is a portrait of how the reader is progressing over time.

How quickly children should move through guided reading, developmental reading assessment, or any other leveled book system is hard to pin down exactly. There are so many variables that go into determining how fast a child can move:

❏ How much time does the child spend reading in school each day?

❏ How much time does the child spend reading at home each day?

❏ Does the child read on the weekends?

❏ Does the child read over the summer?

❏ Does the child have access to books at home?

❏ Is the child able to stay engaged when reading a book?

❏ Does the child choose books that are on or near his just-right reading level?

❏ Does the child receive explicit instruction that is helpful and targeted toward strengthening strengths and compensating for challenges?

❏ Is the child an English language learner?

❏ Does the child have any learning disabilities that affect decoding, comprehension, or fluency?

Each of these variables can be seen in any combination, which makes pinning down the number of months a reader should spend in each level challenging. Fountas and Pinnell, in their book *Guided Reading* (1996), offer benchmarks to correlate reading levels to grade levels. The number of books a child needs to read before progressing to the next level varies from level to level. Children at lower levels typically move more quickly. Books at lower levels are short and frequently reread, whereas it can take a week to read books at levels W, X, Y, or Z. See Figure 7.1 for a chart of reading levels ranges aligned to grade level across four months of the year created by TCRWP. What you will notice is that there is much more movement when children are reading lower levels, as in, say first grade, than in higher reading levels, such as in fifth grade.

Grade	September	November	March	June
K	Preemergent	Early emergent	A/B/C	B/C/D
1	C/D/E	E/F/G	G/H/I	I/J/K
2	I/J/K	J/K/L	K/L/M	L/M/N
3	L/M/N	M/N/O	N/O/P	O/P/Q
4	O/P/Q	P/Q/R	Q/R/S	R/S/T
5	R/S/T	S/T/U	S/T/U	T/U/V
6	T/U/V	U/V/W	U/V/W	V/W/X

Figure 7.1 Independent Reading Level Benchmarks (Teachers College Reading and Writing Project)

When I look at a class set of reading levels, I keep in mind what I know from Fountas and Pinnell, from Richard Allington, and from my own experience. I go through and highlight any children who are of concern because they haven't progressed at an expected rate, because they are far below grade level and just eking their way slowly from level to level, or because their current level is far away from the grade-level benchmarks. Figure 7.2 shows one third-grade class' year's worth of reading levels. (The data are real but the names have been changed to protect the students'

Student	September	November	March	June
Mamotaz	L	M	N	N
David	L	M	M	N
Patti	L	M	N	O
Rabbil	J	K	M	N
Jamel	M	N	O	O
Natalia	N	N	O	P
Michael	O	P	Q	R
Kayleen	I	L	M	M
Malik	L	M	M	M
Jonathan	H	J	K	L
Sarah	L	L	M	M
Nelson	M	N	O	P
Jill	J	K	L	M
Drew	M	N	P	Q
Cesar	M	N	O	P
Dora	O	P	Q	R
Christian	M	N	N	P
Kristian	P	Q	Q	Q
Rick	L	M	M	M
Lateek	H	J	L	M

Figure 7.2 One Third-Grade Class' Year's Worth of Reading Levels

privacy.) As I look at the data, I ask myself, Whom am I worried about? Whom do I have questions about? Who do I think is making adequate progress?

Knowing that a third grader should start the year around level L and end the year around level O, there are a few children whose profile raises some red flags. Malik, Sarah, and Rick are concerns because it seems as though they all hit a slump. They made progress, but not enough progress. They are leaving third grade at almost the same level they started. And, in a lower-income community like this one, summer slippage is a particular concern. It is likely that they'll start fourth grade at the same reading level they started third grade. Mamotaz and David are concerns because they entered third grade on-level and are leaving slightly below. They also have not made adequate progress. Rabbil and Lateek have made some nice gains and need to have as strong of a year next year to catch up. Many students, including Patti, Nelson, Drew, and Cesar, are making beautiful progress and leave the year strongly on or above grade level.

> ### QUESTIONS TO ASK YOURSELF AND TO EXPLORE WITH YOUR COLLEAGUES
>
> ✔ Do you have a systematic way of collecting data about your readers, including ways to keep track of their reading levels across the year?
>
> ✔ When you look at your class' reading level data, whom are you concerned about? Who is making adequate progress?

Getting to Know Leveled Books

After deciding on the candidates for the small group, the next step to doing these small groups successfully is to get to know text levels well. This will require a bit of a time commitment and a bit of dedication. To begin, it's helpful to choose at least one book at each level in your class and get to know that book well. Perhaps choose a book from the series Poppleton (Rylant) for level J, Frog and Toad (Lobel) for K, Pinky and Rex (Howe) for L, Magic Tree House (Osborne) for M, Julian (Cameron) for level N, a Ramona (Cleary) series book for level O, a Time Warp Trio (Scieszka) for level P, and so on. I recommend choosing one book in a series that you have many copies of in your classroom so that by reading one book you'll not only get to know the level, but you'll be familiar with a series, which will help you in your individual and group conferring as well.

Once you've chosen your books, read with this question in mind: "What makes this book harder than the one that was one level before it?" You might think in terms of reading skills. That is, how is it that I predict or infer or question differently in this book than I did in the last? Alternatively, you might think about text difficulties. That is, what are the ways in which the text is structured or the vocabulary is chosen that make this book more challenging than the level before it? (See Figure 7.3.)

Often, when I offer this advice, teachers say to me, "Isn't this already written down somewhere?" Although there are guides, like Fountas and Pinnell's *Leveled Books, K–8* (2005) or *Continuum for Literacy Learning* (2007), it is essential to actually do our own reading of children's literature and analysis of what strikes us as difficult. The guides can be used as a reference. In doing so, we develop a *felt* sense for the level, and this helps more than any discrete list of text difficulties you can find in a book. In addition, considering the potential challenges allows you to plan your instruction for a child. Without the firsthand experience to anticipate challenges, it will be difficult to

The Lens of Comprehension Skills*	The Lens of Text Difficulties†
Ask yourself, In what way does this book require the reader to utilize the following comprehension skills in a way that is different? • Retelling/synthesizing • Determining importance • Activating prior knowledge • Questioning • Inferring • Visualizing • Utilizing fix-up strategies Also consider: • Fluency	Ask yourself, How does the book's text appear to be increasingly challenging in the following categories from the level before it? • Sentence complexity/syntax • Vocabulary • Words • Illustrations • Book and print features • Language and literary features • Themes and ideas • Content • Overall text structure

*From *Mosaic of Thought* by Keene and Zimmermann (1997).
†From *Continuum for Literacy Learning* by Fountas and Pinnell (2007).

Figure 7.3 Lenses to Use When Considering What Makes Levels Increasingly More Challenging

articulate and explain them to a child. Also, once you get to know the difficulties at a level, it will help you to begin to create language around the strategies for approaching the difficulty. Often I find myself saying, "What did I do when I encountered that particular challenge in a text?" Or, if it is hard for you as an adult proficient reader to pin down your own strategies, you might think, "What steps would a child reading at this level benefit from learning to handle this challenge?"

A few words of caution with this work. Sometimes you'll find that there aren't such big differences from one level to the next. A to B and P to Q are examples of this. In other levels you'll find there are more drastic differences, such as from J to K or K to L. It's important to not get carried away thinking that there is always this whole huge set of newness at every level. It might even be better to begin by looking at every other level of books that represents the range in your classroom, arranging them in a continuum. This way, you'll see the differences in texts more clearly as you gain a sense for how challenges and difficulty increase.

The second caution is that doing this work puts a lot of faith in the levels that are provided to you for the books in your classroom library. Be sure that when you go to use a book for this inquiry, it's been leveled correctly from a reliable source. Know that there are books out there that are leveled in surprising ways.

For example, *Donovan's Word Jar* by Monalisa DeGross (1998) is a short chapter book with a very simple narrative about a boy who collects words. One day, his jar of words gets full and he doesn't know what to do about it. He asks around, discounting everyone's suggestions until one day he visits his grandmother's nursing home and finds his solution. The residents at the home begin taking words out and appreciating them, and Donovan realizes that words are best used when shared with people. Very simple, nothing too hard. Looking at it, I'd think it's probably an L. When I looked up the level, it turns out it's an N. N?! The only thing I can figure is that it's higher than I would have expected because there are some complex vocabulary words throughout—the words in his word jar. I've also seen books that are leveled very differently than I would have thought because of some more mature content, or a setting that might be unfamiliar. Just one challenging element can throw a book into a much higher level.

Leveling children's literature—which wasn't written with the constraints of a basal reader, controlling words and sentence length and content (and thank goodness it's not)—is not an exact science. You should not extrapolate that all N books are the same, but you can make some generalizations from this inquiry that will help inform your practice. Also, readers bring different experiences and prior knowledge to a book as well as different understandings of syntax based on the language spoken at home. These may make a text more accessible to one reader than another. Again, leveling is not an exact science, but it does offer us ways to more closely match readers and texts, making instruction more precise and productive.

Let's get back to the procedure for the inquiry. After reading, I find it helpful to create a sort of strategy menu or cheat sheet to synthesize all of the information I've gotten from the book together with possible strategies to teach and questions to ask to assess and research. If you begin by thinking about text difficulties, you can follow this procedure to develop your own strategy menu:

Procedure for Determining Text Levels

1. Text features: Identify a text feature that is unique to the level you're studying.

2. Skills: Think about what skill or skills might challenge a reader.

3. Strategies: Think about what strategies would help a reader be successful in this level text.

4. Questions: Think about questions you would ask to assess how a reader is handling the text difficulty.

Alternatively, if you begin by thinking about the skills and how they are different from level to level, you might follow this procedure:

1. Think skill by skill about all of the ways the text might force a reader to use each comprehension skill.

2. Consider strategies to help a reader who would struggle with that skill.

3. Consider questions that you could use to assess the use of the skill.

Regardless of what procedure you follow, I recommend a four-column chart with one column for the text difficulty, one column for the skill, one for a question you might ask while assessing the reader, and one for possible strategies. Such a chart might look something like Figure 7.4, which I created with teachers at PS 277. To make this chart, we read a few level P books to get to know the level; then we used Fountas and Pinnell's *Continuum for Literacy Learning* (2007) to cross-check what we were noticing in the texts with a reliable reference; finally we came up with the questions, skills, and strategies we might use to assist the reader.

Text Feature	Questions	Skills	Strategies
Ideas and themes that require the reader to take an unfamiliar perspective	"What are some big ideas showing up in your book? What do you think about them?"	• Acknowledge perspective • Activating prior knowledge • Inferring	"Ask yourself, 'What idea or theme do I see in the book that is also true in the world?' Think about what your ideas are about that theme in the world, compare that to your ideas from the book."
Ideas and themes that require a reader to understand cultural diversity	• "How is the character similar/different from you?" • "How does that affect your big idea about your character?"	• Activating prior knowledge • Making inferences	"Identify how characters are similar/different from yourself, for example, where they live, daily life, family structures. Use what you know about what makes your character unique to add to your thoughts about him or her."
Extensive use of figurative language that is important to understanding the plot	Find an example of figurative language. • "What do you think that means?" • "What do you think is really happening here?" • "What picture do you have in your mind?"	• Activating prior knowledge • Visualizing • Making inferences • Monitoring for meaning	• "Use what you know already about the story to determine what might be happening." • "Make a movie in your mind of the scene to help you figure out what's really happening."
Settings distant in time and space from students' experiences	"Can you describe the setting?"	• Activating prior knowledge • Visualizing • Making inferences	• "Think about your own experiences that may be similar to the setting in the book."

Figure 7.4 Level P Strategy Menu

Text Feature	Questions	Skills	Strategies
			• "Have you been in places like this one? Use what you know to help you picture this setting." • "Think about other books, movies, TV shows that may be set in a similar setting."
Complex elements of the genre of fantasy	"What do you picture when you read the part about [magical element]?" (e.g., dragon)	• Activating prior knowledge • Visualizing	"Visualize something you have done that's similar to what's being described as being magical in this book (maybe you haven't ridden a dragon, but have you ridden a horse?)."
Longer (fifteen-plus words), complex sentence structures, including dialogue and many embedded clauses and phrases	Identify complex sentence. "Please read this aloud for me." Listen for fluency, phrasing, and intonation.	• Utilizing fix-up strategies: monitoring for meaning • Fluency	• "Read the dialogue in a voice your character would use." • "If a sentence is not making sense, a comma can be a clue of where to break the sentence up, for example—what do I understand about the first part of this sentence?"
Many longer descriptive words—adjectives and adverbs	"What does this word mean?"	Utilizing fix-up strategies: decoding	"Identify root words and make sure you know the meaning of the root word."

Figure 7.4 *(Continued)*

Text Feature	Questions	Skills	Strategies
Many new vocabulary words that readers must derive from context	• "Were there any words you read that you could sound out but didn't know what it meant?" • "What does this word mean?"	• Monitoring for meaning • Making inferences • Utilizing fix-up strategies: figuring out new vocabulary	• "Stop when you get to a word that doesn't make sense." • "Read the sentences before and after the tricky word to look for clues about the meaning of the word, for example, partner sentences."
Many complex multisyllable words that are challenging to take apart	Have the student read aloud, noticing what he does when encountering a difficult word.	• Utilizing fix-up strategies: decoding • Utilizing fix-up strategies: monitoring for meaning	• "Chunk the word into pieces—read the word syllable by syllable." • "Look for root words you know, prefixes you know, and/or suffixes you know."
Many books with only a few or no illustrations	"What picture do you have in your mind?"	• Visualizing • Synthesis/Retelling	• "Use what the author is describing together with what you know about the place/people like that to develop a picture." • "Add details to your mental picture using all of your senses: what do you hear? See? Smell?"

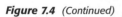

Figure 7.4 (Continued)

Text Feature	Questions	Skills	Strategies
Increased text density: many lines of print on a page	Ask the child to read aloud.	Fluency	"Read it in a smooth voice, like talking. To do this, try to find phrases inside of each sentence. Sweep your eyes under the line, chunk by chunk."
Large variation among print styles and font size (related to genre)	Ask the child to read aloud.	Fluency	"Let your eyes sweep ahead of what you're reading aloud or in your head."
Varied space between lines, with some texts having dense print	Ask the child to read aloud.	Fluency	• "Let your eyes sweep ahead of what you're reading aloud or in your head." • "Use an index card to mark your line. Once that becomes comfortable, use the index card to mark a paragraph at a time and finally get rid of the card altogether."

Figure 7.4 (Continued)

QUESTIONS TO ASK YOURSELF AND TO EXPLORE WITH YOUR COLLEAGUES

✔ How can you set up a study team with colleagues across grade levels to start learning about text difficulties? Perhaps you could each take on one level, and then meet and jigsaw what you've learned? Or each grade level can take on a span of three or four, and then teach each other at a whole-school faculty meeting?

Getting to Know Your Readers Within a Level

Once you gain insight about different reading levels, it is equally important to get to know each reader individually. What a reader is able to do within a level will vary from child to child. Therefore, targeted assessment in terms of how well a child is handling the text difficulties and is demonstrating good command of comprehension skills within a text level will let you know how to best support him in the current level, and how to best support his movement into the next level.

Trends in Student Performance and Cross-Checking with Text Difficulties

One way in which you might use your newfound knowledge of text levels to inform your teaching is to compare what you know about the level of a book with what you already know about a student. It is likely that unless it's the first week of school, you have some information about the student as a reader.

The first assessment tool you have is a running record. It helps you gain insight about a student's miscues, fluency, and comprehension when reading a text that is just right and reading a text that is at an instructional level. I recommend not only using running records to find where students can read with a high degree of accuracy, with fluency and strong comprehension, but also taking a running record using a text one level above that child's just-right level to give you a window into what the child does when she encounters difficulty. This running record will be particularly helpful for readers at lower levels, and less so once readers reach levels M and higher. Still, you can analyze miscues, consider responses to comprehension questions, and evaluate fluency. Advice for doing these analyses is in Chapter 2.

You have also likely learned about the reader through one-on-one or partnership conferences. If you have taken notes on the kinds of skills and strategies that the reader has needed support with so far, you can use those notes to look for a pattern, or use them to get a big picture of the kinds of work the reader is able to do.

You may also have a reading portfolio, which includes information about the reader during read-alouds, about the reader during partnership work, or about the reader's reading notebook. (See Chapter 2 for more ideas for ways to make reading visible, and advice for assessing in reading.)

The goal now is to look across all of the information you have and think about the instructional support the reader may need. Providing instruction within the child's ZPD (Vygotsky 1978) will increase the potential for successful learning. When considering the ZPD, you provide the scaffolding necessary so that the child is able to approximate the new skill with support. Eventually, the child will gain control and no longer need support by a more proficient other. This way, you are not looking for a deficit, but instead you are looking for connecting what the child knows and supporting the beginning of new learning that you will work to strengthen.

For example, I recently worked with a student who had been stuck in a level K for months. It was the winter of her third-grade year, and her teachers told me that any time they tried to assess her in a level L, to see if she was ready to move to the next level, she demonstrated perfect accuracy and strong comprehension but had a hard time with fluency. I looked at her conferring notes and found that her fluency had been strong in her level K books, and she had worked on inferring, a higher-level comprehension skill.

We determined that in order to support her as she moved to the next level, we might work with her on reading fluently in level L texts by relying on her strength of reading fluently in level K books. When I looked at the level K books she was reading, and then at the level L books that I wanted her to read, I saw that there were a number of new text formatting changes at level L that might be affecting her ability to read fluently. Words were now stretched across a whole line, instead of being broken up in phrases. Words were sometimes hyphenated across a line. Sentences were longer and more complex. There was more text on the page, and less white space. To teach her to use her strengths in level K—being able to read phrases fluently when the author had broken it up for you—I needed to teach her how to phrase a sentence herself when the lines and the sentences were longer and more complex. I could also show her how in a level K book, a page is often equal to about a paragraph in a level L book, so she'd have to pause and think within a page instead of at the end of each page in order to maintain her comprehension, thereby affecting her fluency.

Conducting Assessment-Only Conferences

Assessment-only conferences are helpful opportunities to get to know a reader within the context of the level difficulties, characteristics, and skills that I've just studied. It may be the case that looking back at conferring notes or running records or the child's writing about reading won't help me determine the next steps for a reader. This might be because I find that most of my conferences are focused on the unit of study goals, and those goals don't align perfectly with what I've just learned about the text-level difficulties. It may be that when I look at a student's notebook, I discover that the child has a pattern in the way she responds—always responding with retellings, for example—which may not mean that she is unable to respond in other ways, just that she hasn't. In these cases, I may need to do further research or assessment before determining a way to work with the student to support progress to the next level.

An assessment-only conference is a short, approximately ten-minute opportunity to meet with a student and ask questions from the strategy menu. In doing so, I can ascertain how the student handles text difficulties. By determining areas of strength and need in terms of print work, fluency, and comprehension, I can more easily identify next steps for the reader. I decide to do assessment-only conferences whenever I don't have the information I need from other assessment measures about how a student handles the difficulties of a particular text.

I recently worked with Jasmine, a fourth grader, who was reading a level P for months. The teacher was trying to figure out what else it would take to move her to a level Q. We began by looking at the strategy menu we'd made for level P. I went down the "Question" column, asking Jasmine to read aloud to me or to talk about the big ideas she had about the themes and characters in the book. At the end of our time together, I discovered that Jasmine was actually reading her level P books very superficially. I concluded that in order for her to be able to work with a more difficult level of text, we had to first work to strengthen her skill work in the level P text. In fact, in my opinion the P books were books she could read with some support, but O books were really a better fit for her to be reading independently. The classroom teacher had never noticed this because he had been so focused on working on the student's retelling skills. Equipped with information from our assessment-only conference, we set some concrete goals for Jasmine and developed a plan for how we'd work together over the next few weeks. We first deepened her reading in level P texts. Then, when we were ready to move to a level Q, we used the newly established strengths to build on as we introduced the next, more challenging text level.

Text-Level Introduction Groups: An Alternative to Guided Reading

The beauty of using this kind of small group as an alternative to guided reading is that we give students support with the next level while still allowing choice of book, and the support that is given is *strategic* in nature, not based on the specific vocabulary or plot of a specific book. Giving strategic support will likely help the child transfer this learning from book to book, because strategies generalize to other texts. Capitalizing on the element of choice also positively influences engagement.

As with all small groups described in this book, it's imperative that the children who are grouped together need the same instruction. Though groups are flexible and ever-changing based upon students' growth, having children with like needs in the same group offers us better opportunities to meet individual needs. It's best to pull together a group of level L readers who need the same support. Depending on the size of a class, and the diversity of levels within a classroom, it could be more productive to make a few different groups of readers, even though they are reading at the same level. In other classrooms, it may work out that all of the readers at the same level could benefit from the same instruction.

In a text-level introduction group, readers with like needs are pooled together with a book of their choice at the next level in hand. For example, I might pull a group of fifth graders together who are going to be new to level U books and need support handling multiple plotlines. I want to teach them about how there may be switches between the plots from chapter to chapter, and that they'll have to keep up with those changes and consider how one plot affects the other. Unlike in guided reading where I introduce the *book*, in this type of small group, I will introduce the *text characteristics or features, along with strategies to handle those characteristics*. Introducing the book would be impossible, as each child is holding a different book! It is important, however, that children are reading the same genre, as text characteristics and difficulties will vary with different genres.

Structure and Example of the Group

The group came together with a book each member had chosen from the library that was one level higher than their current independent level. This was a big day—they got to read that book they'd been eyeing in the library or the book their friend had been reading that they had coveted. I began the lesson by *telling them why they were gathered*, then *taught* some text characteristics that they would encounter, and offered strategies they might use to make reading successful. Then, I *engaged* by having them start reading, coaching them and offering support as needed. At the end, I sent them off with a *link* and encouraged them to keep working independently.

CONNECT AND COMPLIMENT: TELL THEM WHY THEY WERE GATHERED AND REINFORCE A STRENGTH "So readers, today is a big day! We're going to learn how to tackle a new book—one that may be a bit more challenging. I know you all have been so eager to start reading these books you've chosen. I see you picked a Horrible Harry book, Michael. I think you're going to find Harry quite a funny character! And Josephine, you chose *Pinky and Rex and the New Baby*, huh? Is that because you have a new baby at home? You'll have to see how Pinky and Rex deal with that. And it looks like you've chosen an Amelia Bedelia book, Jonas. She is something else!

"Part of enjoying these new books is going to be reading them with excitement and expression just like you read your last set of books. Whenever I would come over to you in partnership time and you were rereading scenes with dialogue, acting out the characters, it was so convincing! I felt like I had jumped right into your story. I want you to have the same feeling when you read these books.

"I can tell by the way you're all holding your book that you can't wait to dive in. Before you start, I want to talk to you about a few strategies that are going to help you when you come across some tricky parts in your new book. When you tackle a more challenging book, reading smoothly is sometimes challenging. Let's investigate a few strategies that will help you read smoothly in these books."

TEACH: INTRODUCE DIFFICULTIES AND STRATEGIES "There are a number of ways in which these books make it harder to read smoothly than the books you've been reading. The first is that you'll notice that in these new books, the words go all the way across a line, whereas in the other books, the lines are shorter. That's because in many of the books you've been reading, the author is trying to help you to read in chunks, or phrases. Now, when you get to your new book, you're going to have chunk these longer lines for yourself. Watch me read this part in chunks." I briefly demonstrated how I swept under about five words, then another five, and then another four, and reached the period at the end of the sentence. I used my finger so they would not only hear, but also see, what I demonstrated.

"The next thing I want to tell you about is that sometimes in these books you've just chosen, when the word won't fit on a line, the author will break the word up and it will go across two lines. On the first line, you'll see a part of a word and then a hyphen, and on the second line you'll see the rest of the word." I pointed to a few examples so they could see what I was describing. "To keep reading smoothly, you'll need to notice when words are broken apart and then whip your eyes around to the next line quickly.

"A third thing that's going to make reading smoothly a challenge is that there are many more lines of words on a page in these new books." I showed them an example of a page from a level K book and a page from a level L book to demonstrate my point. "Authors who write these books have more to say when they are telling their stories, and you'll need to really think about what's happening because a lot more is going to happen on each page. To read smoothly, focus your eyes on the book and make sure that your eyes go straight across the line. If you feel like it's challenging, you might take a note card like this one, and put it halfway down your page so that you read part of a page, take a little break and think, and then read the rest of the page." Again, I demonstrated what I was talking about.

ENGAGE: COACH THE STUDENTS IN TRYING THE STRATEGIES "OK! The time has come for you to start reading. I'm going to have you stay here for just the next few moments while you're reading your books. Remember to do all the great work you were doing in your other books—think about what's happening and think about your ideas and make sure your reading is making sense. Another goal is going to be for you to be reading smoothly. So if things get tricky, remember those strategies I taught you to help you chunk the words within a line, put words together that are broken up across two lines, and use a card to break up a page that's really full of words."

At this point, the students each began to read and I made my way around, coaching each one as needed. I helped the children reflect on whether or not they'd benefit from using a card to split up a page, I coached them to move their eyes quickly to the next line, and I coached them with breaking up a long line of print into sensible phrases that sounded right and made sense.

LINK: SEND THE CHILDREN OFF TO CONTINUE INDEPENDENT READING After I offered each child about two forty-five seconds' to one minute's worth of coaching, I called their attention back to me.

"Readers, you're doing great work. As you keep reading this book you've chosen, you're going to have to keep working on that smooth reading we've been talking about. Make sure you're chunking within each line, whipping your eyes around when you see a word broken up across two lines, and using a card if it helps you to break the page up into smaller parts. Keep in mind that this reading smoothly shows that you're understanding what you read, and that when you read smoothly, it helps you to better understand as you read. Take a moment before you go back to your seats to jot some of the things you practiced with me today on a bookmark that you'll keep in your book as a reminder." At this point, the children jotted down the strategies in their own language. This helped to hold them accountable and was a support to them as they continued independently back at their seat.

"When you feel like you're starting to get tired, or you're losing track of your reading in any way, you may decide to take a break. The rest of your baggie still has level K books in it, which should feel very comfortable to you. You can take a break whenever you need to and get back to the level L book when it feels like it's time.

"I'm going to meet with you all in a few days to coach you some more with your reading so you'll have some more help very soon. Congratulations, readers! You should each be so proud of yourself for your hard work."

One Teacher's Story

Laurie Faber, a third-grade teacher at PS 158, was gracious enough to share many stories of how she used text-level introduction groups in her classroom. One story

> ### Text-Level Introduction Groups
> - Children get to choose their own books.
> - Children are grouped because they are all working to move to the same new level.
> - The teacher doesn't introduce a book—the teacher introduces text difficulties.
> - The teacher gives strategic support to the readers for text difficulties.
> - The group follows the "connect and compliment, teach, engage, link" structure.
> - A child should keep texts at their "old" level and the one book that was practiced in the group to work on that week. More group work is often necessary before a child is secure in the new level.

describes a group of three readers—Mary, Caroline, and Emily—whom Laurie was trying to move from level O to P in late March. Figure 7.5 shows the notes she took across six days of meetings with this group.

You can see in her notes that each meeting took on a different strategy that was important to the new level and important to the individual readers. Laurie took notes on each individual student within the group, and tailored her coaching, and the application of the strategy, to meet them within each student's ZPD.

The meetings on March 25, 27, and 29 were all focused on helping the girls read a self-chosen book. Each was reading a different title. The meetings on April 1, 3, and 6 were when the children were working in a book club together, all reading *Circle of Gold* (Boyd 1996). Even though they were all reading the same book, the instruction was not about the book, it was about strategies to help them with text difficulties at this level. The April meetings revisited the same teaching points from late March, asking the girls to apply what they'd learned to a new context. This is an important aspect of releasing scaffolding because they were more independent with the strategies and could easily apply them to the next book they read at this level.

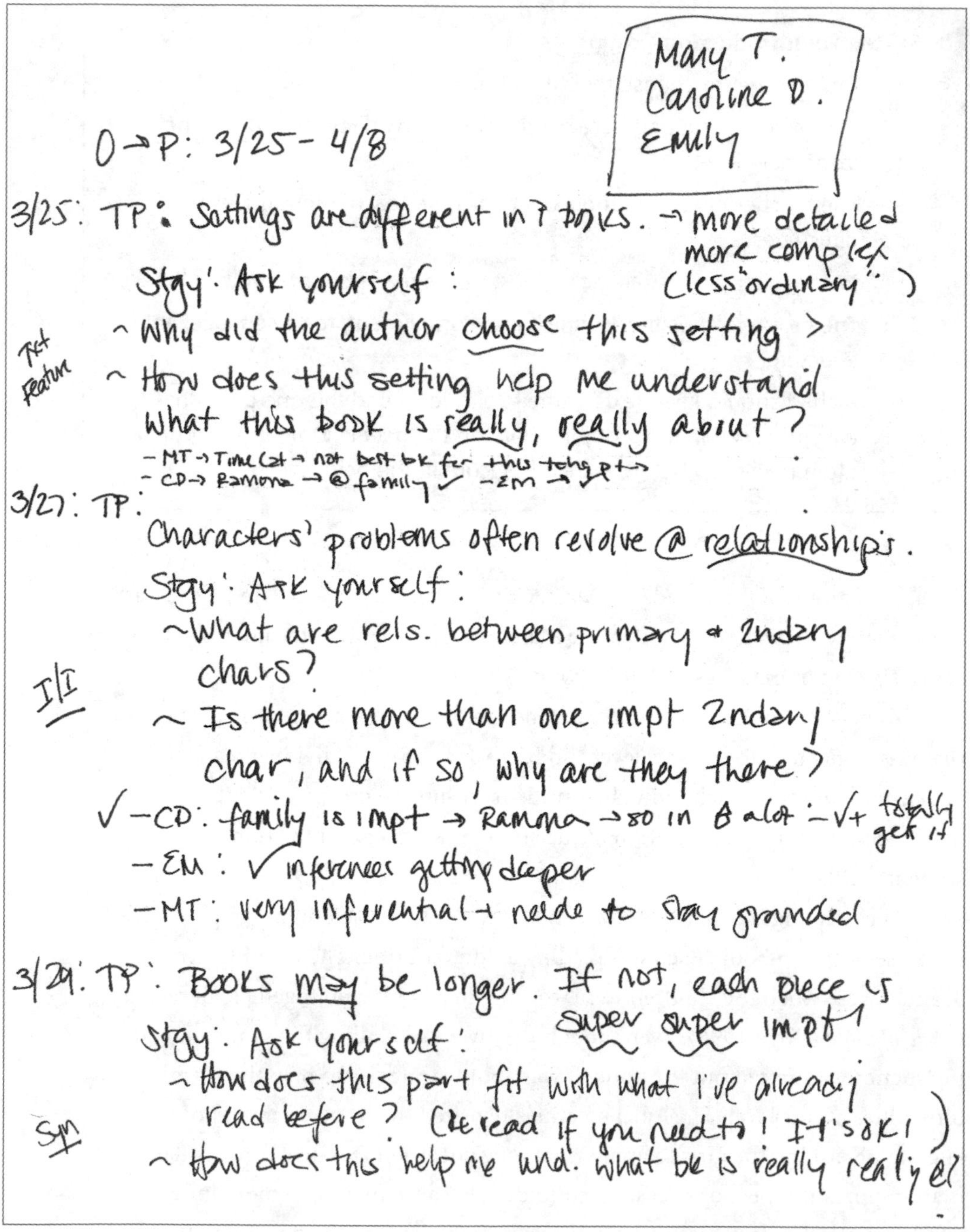

Mary T.
Caroline D.
Emily

$0 \rightarrow P$: 3/25 - 4/8

3/25: TP: Settings are different in 7 books. → more detailed
more complex
("less ordinary")

Stgy: Ask yourself:

Txt
feature

∧ Why did the author choose this setting >

∧ How does this setting help me understand
what this book is really, really about?
— MT → Time Cat → not best bk for this tchg pt
— CD → Ramona → @ family ✓ — EM → ✓ ←

3/27: TP:

Characters' problems often revolve @ relationships.

Stgy: Ask yourself:

∼ What are rels. between primary & 2ndary
chars?

I/I

∧ Is there more than one impt 2ndary
char, and if so, why are they there?

✓ — CD: family is impt → Ramona → so in B alot — ✓+ totally
get it

— EM: ✓ inferences getting deeper

— MT: very inferential → needs to stay grounded

3/29: TP: Books may be longer. If not, each piece is
super super impt!

Stgy: Ask yourself:

∧ How does this part fit with what I've already
read before? (reread if you need to! It's ok!)

SM

∧ How does this help me und. what bk is really really ∂

Figure 7.5 Note Taking from a Third-Grade Text-Level Introduction Group

4/1   Put Circle of Gold in hands of girls - gave 3 goals
        revisited TP → setting (their voices)   (pgs.)
      MT - setting will be impt so I need to   ~ plans.
          think @ it
      EP - it might be different
      CD - it'll help us und. what bk is @.

4/3   revisited TP @ char rels / probs
        EP - why did Mom slap Mattie is impt prob
totally ✱ CD - absent char. is the father. Maybe not b/c of
get it   Mattie but she's just really upset @ so
             many other things.
        MT - (agrees)

4/6   revisited TP of synthesis - what bk is really really @
      MT - can take what life throws at you

      CD - st life is not always fair

      EP - st special can make a diff (even if you dont
                                          know it)

4/7 - EP → assess √+   ⎫
4/8 - CD assess √+   ⎬ all O → P !
      MT assess √+   ⎭

Figure 7.5 (Continued)

You can see from the notes that they all demonstrated proficiency with level P when assessed using a running record the following week. These students went on one month later to a group designed to help them move from P to Q, and by June each of the readers in this group was assessed to be able to read level R independently. That is a lot of growth in a short period of time!

The Last Word

This chapter offered advice for ways to get to know text levels better, in order to get to know how readers work within a text level better and in order to help support students' movement to the next level. Remember that knowing what level a child is reading in is only one piece to the puzzle. It's important to study a child's work within books at that level to determine whether she needs continued support with the level she is in, or if she might be ready to move to the next level with some support.

Small-group work that helps children work in books that they've chosen themselves, while still providing support with the new text level, is both engaging and highly effective. Targeting instruction to small groups of children around text features that pose specific challenges to them means that the instruction is tailored and differentiated to what students need most. Being part of a small group also allows children to support each other's growth into the new level.

Revisiting the Tenets

Let's consider together how some of the ideas from this chapter align with the tenets established in the first chapter. We agreed that reading instruction should . . .

❏ *match the individual reader.* When introducing a new text level to a group of readers, it's important to remember that you're not introducing *all* of the new text difficulties. You are choosing a few text difficulties, and appropriate corresponding strategies, based on what you know about the individuals in the group. Your decisions are based on your assessment of what new strategies you think are within their ZPD.

❏ *teach toward independence.* These groups were conceived of with the hope of helping children transition to a new level so that eventually they could read at that new level independently. It's important not to move too fast into a new level to ensure that when a child *does* move, she can read that new level text with independence and security.

❏ *teach strategies explicitly so that readers become proficient and skilled.* It is not enough to introduce what's hard in a new level, it's also important to offer the readers strategies for how to handle that new difficulty. Learning text levels by reading actual texts and reflecting on how you, as a teacher, would handle those challenges is some of the best preparation you can do to lead these groups.

❏ *value time spent, volume, and variety of reading.* When children are stuck in a level for a while, it is not uncommon to find that their engagement level, volume, and interest in reading might drop. I often hear children say, "But I already read all the books at my level!" in protest. This is one of many indicators that a child is disinterested in the books at her level and wants help transitioning to the next level.

❏ *follow predictable structures and routines.* The text-level introduction group follows a very familiar structure: connect and compliment, teach, engage, link. This predictability helps children know what is expected of them and what their role is throughout the course of the lesson. What's new is how you engage the children from the start and the teaching that fits inside of this lesson. Maintain what you know about good coaching as explained in other chapters in this book.

Organizing and Managing Small-Group Conferring: Common Questions

*A*fter reading this book, you might be thinking, "Wow, I have a lot of planning to do." Truly differentiating instruction—tailoring teaching points and teaching methods and teaching materials to individuals and small groups—does take forethought. However, careful systems for management, organization, and scheduling will make the integration of the ideas presented in this book realistic and attainable.

At one point I realized that as a teacher, I put my planning time and energy almost exclusively into my workshop minilessons—the part of the reading workshop that lasts seven to ten minutes—and then I operated "on the fly" for the remaining forty minutes of small-group and individual conferring. A major shift occurred in the quality of my teaching, and consequently in the results I saw in my students' performance, when I shifted to spend more time planning the independent reading time of my workshop while still continuing to plan minilessons based on careful assessments.

Throughout this book, I've shared ideas on how to create conferring menus—lists of questions, skills, strategies, and prompts that will equip you with a variety of ways to respond to children's reading while conferring. These conferring menus are one way to prepare for group conferences. In addition to this planning and preparation, it's also helpful to have a clear sense of how to manage and organize the reading time. In this section, I answer questions that often arise in regard to managing it all. I will:

❏ *review reading workshop basics* to give you a possible context in which to conduct the small groups described in this book.

❏ help you to *visualize the room* by offering classroom management principles that allow small-group work to take place

❏ give advice on how to *keep track* of the small-group work through effective note-taking systems that allow you to follow up on past teaching

❏ offer tips on how to *schedule yourself* to ensure you meet individual needs in a way that is fair and balanced across the week

Reading Workshop Basics

Throughout this book, I refer to different components of reading workshop under the assumption that many readers of this book have a reading workshop up and running. Having a reading workshop is not essential, however, to be able to lead the type of quality, small-group instruction described in this book. If you are new to reading workshop, I recommend reading *The Art of Teaching Reading* (Calkins 2000).

In this section, I briefly review and define the terms used throughout this book and by the Teachers College Reading and Writing Project (TCRWP) community relating to a reading workshop.

In *Conferring with Readers* (2007), I wrote about my experience in high school art class. I had a wonderful teacher, Ken Vieth, who ran our class like a workshop. Each month, we began a study together—watercolors, clay sculpture, portraiture—and Mr. Vieth planned a sequence of lessons for the whole class with the study in mind. These whole-class lessons lasted only minutes of our entire class period, though, because it was essential that we got to our own work as quickly as possible. As we worked, Mr. Vieth made his way around the classroom, providing compliments and coaching as he saw fit. Sometimes, he sat beside one or a group of us and modeled a new technique that he thought might help our piece. Other times, he just gave a passing tip or reminder or compliment based on what he saw. At the end of the class period, he gathered us back to the corner of the room where we began the period. Before the bell rang, he shared one student's successes and offered us advice on how we might emulate that same technique in our work, if we so chose.

Reading workshop makes independent reading an instructional time.

This art studio class is a perfect example of what happens in a reading workshop. There are certain predictable structures in place: there is a lesson at the start of the period, there is lots of time for independent work, the teacher confers and works with small groups of students, and the period ends with a teaching share. Even when the whole class is engaged together in study of a particular medium or form of art, there is still choice within the framework for students to choose the topic of their emerging work.

Reading workshop makes independent reading an instructional time. It is a highly structured and predictable framework in which we as teachers provide direct, explicit instruction at the beginning called the minilesson, which supports students in conferences and small groups, allows time for students to discuss their books and reading work with others in partnerships and book clubs, and ends with a teaching share. The TCRWP's vision of reading workshops is one that follows units of study, about one per month, where the whole class is engaged in inquiry into a common topic such as a genre, story element, or a reading habit or skill.

For example, a class might spend a month studying nonfiction reading, then move into a unit on inference and interpretation, and then move on to a character study. Across a child's elementary school career, units of study are revisited with increasing complexity so that there is a spiraling effect to the curriculum, each year building on the next. For example, in first grade, children might be in a character unit of study focused on getting to know their characters like friends and learning all they can about the characters. Then, in second grade, a character unit might be focused on inferring about character, determining character traits beyond what's explicitly stated. Then, in upper elementary school, children might track a character throughout a series of books, synthesizing information across texts. In fourth or fifth grade, students might study how secondary characters impact main characters and/or how to track a character's internal and external journey across a text.

Reading workshops have been written about extensively by Lucy Calkins in *The Art of Teaching Reading* (2000), Sharon Taberski and Shelley Harwayne in *On Solid Ground* (2000), and Kathy Collins in *Growing Readers* (2004). Even when there is an ongoing class unit of study, children still have choice of books and work to read those books at their own independent level. Reading workshop is a highly effective way to manage students who each read self-selected books and to engage in rigorous, assessment-based instruction. Below I describe each of the components of the workshop in more detail. It should be noted, though, that even if you don't have a reading workshop up and running, it is still possible to implement the types of small-group work described in this book instead of, or in addition to, the types of small-group work you currently use with your students.

What Are Minilessons?

The minilesson is the whole-class teaching that begins the workshop (Calkins 2000). The lesson may be focused on a habit of reading, print work (decoding), fluency, or comprehension. The lesson will ground the class in the ongoing work of the unit of study, and is based on our assessment of what most of the students in the class need. The minilesson is often not the assignment of the day. Instead, the minilesson helps students to build a repertoire of different strategies they will use at an appropriate time while independently reading. Because not all lessons are expected to be applied immediately, we often create charts that chronicle the strategies we teach, which students refer back to while independently reading.

Although the term *minilesson* is used by many, the TCRWP has developed an architecture that we've found to be helpful to keeping the lessons short—each lesson lasts about ten minutes—and to ensure both elements of teacher demonstration as well as student guided practice. The parts of our minilessons are called *connection*, *teach*, *active involvement*, and *link*.

The minilesson begins with a *connection* in which we give a context for the day's learning. At times, we begin with a brief story or anecdote that can serve as a metaphor for the teaching. Other times, we review the strategies that children have learned so far in the unit, which set the foundation for today's strategy. Other times, we might highlight one or two students whose work can serve as a model for today's lesson.

The second part of the lesson is the *teach*. During this part, we usually demonstrate but sometimes use a different method such as example and explanation or inquiry. The students' job during this part of the lesson is to watch and listen attentively as they will soon have a chance to practice the same strategy. Most teachers find it helpful to refrain from calling on students to be involved with this part, or answering questions, as that sometimes interferes with the clarity of what's being demonstrated and often causes the lesson to run longer.

Next, the students have an opportunity to practice the strategy during the *active involvement*. We find it important that *all* students have a chance to try the strategy, not just a few, so we typically ask children to do one of three things: turn and talk to a partner, stop and jot on a sticky note or in their notebook, or practice out loud or quietly to themselves. Each of these options is instead of calling on one or two children to demonstrate their understanding.

The final part of the lesson is the *link*. In this part, we review what's been taught and reframe that day's teaching point in the context of the larger goal. Often, I will remind children that they are building a repertoire and that today's lesson is not an assignment, but is instead intended to help them when they encounter a challenge that would warrant the use of the strategy.

What Happens During Independent Work Time?

Immediately following the minilesson, students return to their self-chosen or teacher-assigned reading spots with a baggie or bin full of books. Inside of this baggie or bin are the books that the student has self-selected from the classroom library. Often, we allow students to visit the classroom library once a week and ask students to plan a week's worth of reading during that visit. In a primary classroom where students are reading and rereading short books with little text, they may have as many as twelve to fifteen books for a week's worth of reading. In a fifth-grade classroom, students might only take two or three books for the whole week.

Also in the baggie or bin, students may keep a reading notebook, a pencil, some bookmarks, and a pad of sticky notes. Having each of these additional tools in their baggie allows students to stay put during reading time. The sticky notes and notebook are to encourage students to jot thoughts, ideas, and questions about their books as they read. The notebook might also be used for longer responses to reading that could take place at the end of a workshop period or at home.

Once situated, students spend a large chunk of time reading independently, and on some days meet with a reading partner or a reading club for a variety of purposes including discussing their reading, stretching and elaborating on their ideas, helping each other clarify confusion, practice reading fluently, or role-playing favorite scenes. We may choose to structure the weeks in different ways. Many primary teachers make time for partnerships every day, whereas in the upper elementary grades and middle school, students might meet a few times a week. This is because children in primary grades often need help sustaining independent reading for an entire workshop period. Children in older grades can sustain independent reading and conversation for longer periods of time and are better off having conversational time set aside fewer times in the week, for longer each time.

During independent reading time and partnership or book club time, we are actively involved in instruction. We make our way around the classroom working with individuals and small groups of students in conferences. During this time, the small-group instruction described in this book takes place. This independent time is essential as we tailor instruction to individual needs, keep careful notes on what we've taught, and follow up on past teaching.

Can You Define Partnerships, Reading Clubs, and Book Clubs?

Reading partnerships and clubs are an essential part of reading workshop. Vygotsky (1978) believes that reading is socially constructed and that children need to be part of a community of readers. These social groupings allow students to work with apprentices (their peers, and at times, their teacher). This valuable talk time has been shown to help students to make incredible amounts of progress in their thinking and comprehension, even in low-income areas or with students who would otherwise be thought of as "struggling" (Raphael and McMahon 1994; Gavelek and Raphael 1996; Murphy et al. in press).

Reading partnerships in primary (K–2) classrooms achieve this same goal of making reading a social activity. Partnerships help students stay with print longer than they would be able to do independently. In the very beginning of kindergarten, we might switch the children between reading alone and reading with a partner every ten minutes. In a second-grade classroom, children might work with a partner after fifteen to twenty minutes of reading alone, and then return to reading alone for the remainder of the class period. (See sample schedules in Figure 8.1.)

During partnership time, students in primary classrooms often choose between the book that each student is independently reading, place the single copy of one book between them, and do an activity with the book. Sometimes, the students read the book together, taking turns with each page. Other times, students read and then act out their favorite part or discuss the ideas and reactions they had in certain parts. They also might practice reading and rereading the same few pages, trying to make their reading sound more fluent and proficient with each rereading. Ideas for differentiating this partnership work are found in Chapter 5. Because students need to be able to read a text from either baggie, partnerships are ability-based, and, when possible, students are partnered by reading interests.

In the primary grades, students might also move to reading clubs at some point in the year. Described by Kathy Collins in her book *Reading for Real* (2008), these social groupings allow students to work with groups of peers around a common topic, reading with engagement, purpose, and excitement. Perhaps a club forms to find out how to take care of the class' new hamster, or they all love Poppleton by Cynthia Rylant and want to read every book they can find written about him. The children in these clubs won't necessarily be reading the same book at the same time, but they share a collection of books and talk about what they learn and think based on what they read.

In third grade and above, partnerships are often used more heavily in the first half of the school year, providing scaffolding before students move to book clubs. Early in the school year, students find a partner with help from their teacher. This partner must read at or about the same reading level and have comparable book tastes to the student. The partners choose some books that they'll read together (requiring the classroom

Second-Grade Reading Workshop				
Monday	**Tuesday**	**Wednesday**	**Thursday**	**Friday**
Minilesson (7 minutes) Read alone (15 minutes) Partnership (10 minutes) Read alone (15 minutes) Share (5 minutes)	Minilesson (7 minutes) Read alone (15 minutes) Partnership (10 minutes) Read alone (15 minutes) Share (5 minutes)	Minilesson (7 minutes) Read alone (15 minutes) Partnership (10 minutes) Read alone (15 minutes) Share (5 minutes)	Minilesson (7 minutes) Read alone (15 minutes) Partnership (10 minutes) Read alone (15 minutes) Share (5 minutes)	Minilesson (7 minutes) Read alone (15 minutes) Partnership (10 minutes) Read alone (15 minutes) Share (5 minutes)

Fourth-Grade Reading Workshop, September Through December (Partnerships)				
Monday	**Tuesday**	**Wednesday**	**Thursday**	**Friday**
Minilesson (7 minutes) Read alone (30 minutes) Partner (10 minutes) Share (5 minutes)	Minilesson (7 minutes) Read alone (40 minutes) Share (5 minutes)	Minilesson (7 minutes) Read alone (30 minutes) Partner (10 minutes) Share (5 minutes)	Minilesson (7 minutes) Read alone (40 minutes) Share (5 minutes)	Minilesson (7 minutes) Read alone (30 minutes) Partner (10 minutes) Share (5 minutes)

Fourth-Grade Reading Workshop, January Through June (Book Clubs)				
Monday	**Tuesday**	**Wednesday**	**Thursday**	**Friday**
Minilesson (7 minutes) Read alone (25 minutes) Book club (15 minutes) Share (5 minutes)	Minilesson (7 minutes) Read alone (40 minutes) Share (5 minutes)	Minilesson (7 minutes) Read alone (40 minutes) Share (5 minutes)	Minilesson (7 minutes) Read alone (30 minutes) Book club (15 minutes) Share (5 minutes)	Minilesson (7 minutes) Read alone (40 minutes) Share (5 minutes)

Figure 8.1 Workshop-at-a-Glance: Sample Schedules

library to have double copies of those titles for the children to borrow), and also keep up an independent reading life outside of the partnership. These partnerships meet a few times a week for about ten minutes each time for discussions. In the upper grades, where the books are more complex and the instruction is often more likely focused on comprehension skills and strategies, the partnership time is spent sharing their writing about reading and using that writing about reading as a springboard for longer discussions where partners come to new insights and ideas about their books.

When we decide to launch book clubs in our class, we often put two partnerships together to form a group of four. Again, each member of the club reads at the same reading level and has similar tastes in books. When part of a book club, members choose books together and set plans for how many pages they'll read before their next meeting time and the kind of work they'll do as readers. They meet a few times a week to discuss their books, using their own writing about reading and ideas from reading the book independently to ground their discussion.

What Happens During the Teaching Share?

The teaching share is the part of the workshop where we gather the students back together at the end of the time period. During this time, we might reinforce something that we taught that day or week, highlight some success a student had, or set up for the work of tomorrow. The best teaching shares aren't simply opportunities for children to share something, but instead are opportunities to teach something, using a student as an example. For instance, perhaps I have been working with my students on jotting meaningful questions as they read. The teaching share might be a time for me to articulate that meaningful questions often can't be answered right in the text, but are questions that need to be discussed. I might find two students who wrote such questions and ask them to read their questions to the class, providing a model for the rest of the group.

Visualizing the Room

To teach effectively in a small-group conference means being able to devote your energy and attention to that group, and the individuals within the group, for the five to fifteen minutes that the group lasts. When one teacher is responsible for a class of thirty plus students, it's important to be able to see the big picture. While I work with one group in the classroom, I need to know what the rest of the class is doing. Also, I need to have a sense of where I will conduct my groups to allow for quick transitions and good use of instructional time.

What Are the Rest of My Kids Doing?

This is no doubt a question that flickers through your mind an awful lot in the course of a day. Conferring—either individual or small-group conferring—can only take place if the rest of the students are engaged in their reading and can self-manage their own behaviors.

In Chapter 2, I suggested ways to conduct inventories to determine levels of engagement during independent reading, and in Chapter 3, I discussed possibilities for group conferences targeted toward engagement problems. One way to enhance the quality of conferring is to ensure students are actively engaged in reading. There are many ways you've already read about including making sure readers are matched to books that are at their just-right reading level and of interest, teaching strategies for refocusing when students get distracted, and giving students agency over their own learning by helping them set goals for their reading work.

Children also need to be taught how to self-manage themselves so that they are able to troubleshoot their problems when they arise instead of relying on the teacher to solve their problems for them. One way I addressed interruptions in my own classroom was by reflecting on the reasons for the interruptions in the first place. Then, using a format I learned from my colleague Colleen Cruz, I considered all the ways I could ensure students better understood expectations by explicit teaching. Not only did this prevent many interruptions, but it also made workshop time much more productive for students.

By putting systems in place in advance, I am often able to set students up for success. See Figure 8.2 for some ideas of ways to plan for a well-managed reading workshop. Notice the emphasis in the left-hand column on being explicit and clear and having a routine or system. This is because children need to be taught clearly what my expectations are. Notice the emphasis on the far right-hand column on saying as few words as possible or even using nonverbal cues and gestures when possible. By emphasizing what I expect students *to do* rather than harping on what they *shouldn't do*, I am able to create a supportive, positive, and productive context for learning.

To Create a Productive Context for Learning . . .	The Result	If the Result Is Not Achieved, You Might . . .
• Create charts from minilessons to show a teaching point and example. • Teach children who need extra support how to work on their individual goal(s) they are being taught in conferences. Have a place in the child's notebook or in the child's baggie where the goal is clearly stated. You may determine the goal with the support personnel.	Children return from pull-out services and know immediately what to do.	• Say, "Check your baggie/folder for your goal." • Say, "Check the chart." • Point to a chart.
• Establish a place in the room where extra supplies are kept. Allow children to go to that center without permission. • Have children keep sticky notes in their book baggie, have a routine for students to check their own supplies before coming to the minilesson. • Teach children to use alternative materials such as a notebook instead of sticky notes or a pen instead of a pencil.	Children know where to find the supplies needed to do their work.	• Point to the spot in the room where supplies are kept. • Say, "Where might you find what you need?"
Create a "book hospital" basket where damaged books can be placed for care.	Children know where to put classroom materials that need repair.	• Point to the book hospital. • Say, "Keep reading."

Figure 8.2 Creating a Productive, Independent, Reading Workshop: Anticipating and Responding to Potential Management Problems

To Create a Productive Context for Learning . . .	The Result	If the Result Is Not Achieved, You Might . . .
• Decide what your rule will be about bathroom and water: can they go during independent reading or do they have to wait? Make your rule clear and post it. • If you decide to allow children to go to the bathroom or fountain during independent reading, establish a system for keeping track of who is out of the room, without having to ask you for permission. Some teachers use systems that involve moving a clothespin, signing out, or flipping a card from red to green on a chart when they leave the room.	Children know what is acceptable to do and what is not acceptable to do during workshop time.	• Say, "You know what to do." • Point to the chart with the posted rule. • Point to the sign-out sheet or whatever system you've established.
• Create a "book shopping" schedule so children know what day they choose new books. • Advise children on how many books they'll need to sustain a week's worth of reading. Err on the side of having them choose too many. • Post a "If you are choosing from the ____ basket, you should have ____ [number of] books" chart by the classroom library. • Arrange books in attractive ways that also help children identify just-right books. • Teach children different purposes for rereading.	Children learn how to choose a week's worth of reading to sustain them.	• Say, "Do whatever you think you're supposed to do." • Say, "Think of what you'll do as you reread."

Figure 8.2 (Continued)

To Create a Productive Context for Learning . . .	The Result	If the Result Is Not Achieved, You Might . . .
• Teach children to set appropriate goals with partners and clubs based on their knowledge of themselves as readers and their own rate of reading. • Make sure that children have independent books as well as partner/club books in their baggie. • Teach a minilesson about what to do if you meet a goal before your partner: you can reread, you can write about your reading, or you can read something else. Create a chart that goes with this lesson.	Students know they will be reading more than one book at a time and have ways to self-manage goal setting.	• Point to a chart that will help the child solve her own problem. • Say, "I'll bet your independent book is just waiting for you." • Say, "Check the chart we made."
• Teach children how to jot down their thoughts during independent reading time. Remind them they can share later. • Spread children out into their own spots so they aren't near anyone while they are reading. • Have children sit back-to-back with their partner so they won't be tempted to talk.	Students learn to respect others' right to some quiet time for reading. They also learn how to "hold their thinking" for sharing later.	• Indicate the child could move. • Have a gesture that communicates "eyes on your book."

Figure 8.2 *(Continued)*

Where Am I Conducting These Groups?

Many teachers create a space in the classroom where most small-group instruction will take place. For some, it is more comfortable to have a kidney-shaped table in a corner of the room with seats for four or five children on the outside, and a chair for the teacher on the inside cutout. These tables make coaching during the engage portion of the lesson easier. Other teachers prefer to pull groups of children back to the rug and work with them in an intimate setting on the floor. This is a particularly helpful solution in small classrooms.

Sometimes, group conferring is impromptu. At times, I find myself working with an individual student, then realize that the whole table could benefit from listening in. In these instances, my small groups take place at the students' tables or independent reading spots. I find it most comfortable to purchase a small foldable camping stool to carry around with me so that I can settle down next to students at their own seats around the classroom. Other teachers use a rolling stool or small kindergarten-size chair that moves with ease.

Keeping Track

In a reading workshop, instruction is differentiated and individualized. Even in classes with small numbers of students, it is impossible for teachers to remember every individual detail about each conference and small-group lesson. The better the teacher takes notes, the more accurately she can follow up with what's been taught and the better she can plan for future instruction.

What Might My Note-Taking System Look Like?

There are many options for a note-taking system. Most important about the system you choose is to make sure that you can keep track of individual students even when they are within a small-group structure. It is also important to create a system where you can take notes quickly, and you don't have to recopy information. Often, group conferring will happen over time, with a teacher seeing some or all of the members of the group more than once. For this reason, it would be wise to have a system where you can look at one student's progress within a group over time.

The first note-taking system I suggest is a system that has the whole class on a single sheet where you can record the teaching point for the small group in one student's square, and then "see _____ [that student's name]" in the squares of the other children who also were part of that group. In each child's square, you could write notes about the amount of support or type of support the child needed during the lesson. See Figure 8.3 for an example of this type of form. To see progress over time

Conferring Table, Week of: **March 16**

Mamotaz 3/16	David 3/18	Patti SG 3/17	Rabbil SG 3/17	Jamel C 3/18
SG – Visualizing char. faces. Needs follow-up, needed coaching	SG accumulating inferences → theory needs more practice in ea. of to accumulate	see Rabbil text level intro L – follow-up w/ fluency	text level intro L – follow-up w/ multi-syllabic words	① Look across series for patterns
Natalia C 3/16	Michael C 3/17	Kayleen 3/16	Malik 3/16	Jonathan SG 3/17
Visualizing – ignores setting – very char. focused Taught using senses	followed up on 3/16 conference visualizing. Story → move to	see Mamotaz-SG ↑ move meeting – try in different book.	C followed up on inference from 3/9. Needs more practice. Maybe SG next week?	see Rabbil – fluent + expressive check comprehension on next mtg.
Sarah SG 3/18	Nelson SG 3/18	Jill C 3/18	Drew SG 3/17	Cesar SG – see Drew 3/17
see David strong – check back next week in another book	see David strong initial inf → needs to lay out to synthesize	① – considering how char. aren't just one way. Look across series	Inferring char. traits based on actions. One more mtg. in diff book.	ready to be ind – check later in week during conf.
Dora SG 3/17	Christian 3/16	Kristian C 3/16	Rick 3/16	Lateek C 3/18
see Drew strong – move to new group or onto new skill next wk.	see Mamotaz-SG needed heavy coaching.	Overly focused on primary char. Taught interaction btwn char + think about both.	SG – see Mamotaz needed heavy coaching	checked on transition to M. story accumulation, taught infer. about sec. character
Cesar 3/19	Kayleen 3/19			
V – still doing a good job w/ 3/17 new book. Independent.	checked 3/16 SG in new book – needed coaching.			

SG = small group
(1-on-1) C = conference

Figure 8.3 Whole-Class at-a-Glance Note-Taking Form

is a little more challenging with this system, but if you keep the same names in the same boxes, it becomes easy to flip from one sheet to the next.

A second note-taking option is to have one sheet for every time a new group is started. Dates go along the top of the grid, and students' names go along the left-hand column. On this type of form, you will record the teaching point for the group at the top of the page. Notes about the amount of support a student needed and ideas for next steps for that student will go in the center boxes on the grid. See Figure 8.4 for fourth-grade teacher Brooke Baron's version of this note-taking form. Note that not all of the boxes are filled; this is because some children were phased out of the group as they became more independent and less in need of follow-up.

Small Group Sessions – ~~Interpretation~~ Ms. Baron

GROUP GOAL: Envisioning – setting, character Envisioning

Name	Session 1 11/4	Session 2 11/7	Session 3 11/10	Session 4
Bujana	Started to retell ↓ at bedroom— boys picture	Setting – be quiet in the scenable at night— Nice job	—in the woods really picturing the woods	
Jessica	She's crying broke Ked leg + fell down	Not making the Scenery Pictures — needs to fill in the big picture	What does the persons face look like?	
Billy	Retelling having a hard time to use the clues in the book to envision	— Can't describe the Baseball field— What do the people look like? What do you hear?	Need to really break it down for him— keeps on saying whats in the book	— doing much better w/ describing the scene.
Ellie	had differently w/ Visionary talked abt Cafeteria	Shelia's scared at dogs –she looks, peter laughing	Fantastic job, got it!	

Figure 8.4 Ms. Baron's Small-Group Note-Taking Form Shows Notes on the Individual Within a Group

A third option is to take notes on separate sheets of paper for each student (see Figure 8.5). Many teachers with whom I work have a three-ring binder with a divided section for each child in the class. All note taking during one-on-one conferences goes in that student's separate section. When the teacher takes notes on small groups, she writes "GC" for "group conference" next to the notes she takes, but still has the information in the divided sections of the three-ring binder. Teachers who use this form of note taking say they like being able to see one student's progress over time.

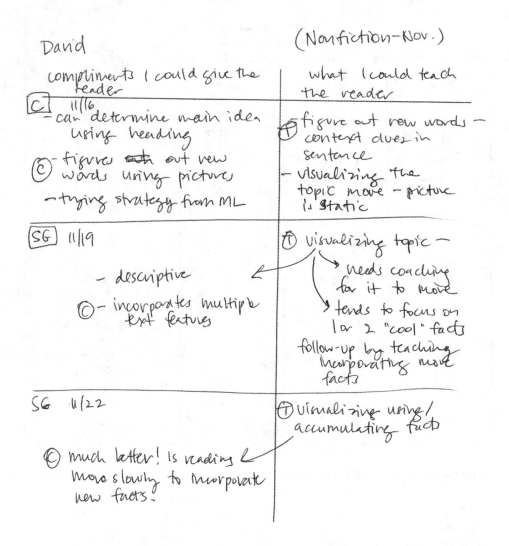

Figure 8.5 A Note-Taking Form for an Individual Student with One-on-One and Group Conferring Notes Together

When children are grouped for a longer period of time, as is the case with partners or clubs, you might find it helpful to preprint sheets that have students' names on them and record notes about what you noticed during the conference, and what the students in the partnership were taught. Figure 8.6 shows Tara Goldsmith's version of this for her first-grade partnerships.

NF Reading (Science Topics)

Partner Notes for Reading Workshop

Lucas and George Date: 6/10 Research: Sharing their "what I learned" post-its - would stop there Teach: "I learned... This makes me think..."	**Amelia and Miles** Date: 6/12 Research: No post-its, reading favorite parts to each other Teach: Having post-its ready for partner talk "This page is mostly about"
Allie and Sydney Date: 6/5 Research: Syd. shared all her post-its about what she learned - Allie didn't get a chance to share. Teach: Take turns sharing one post-it talking off of it	**Philippe and Lilian** Date: 6/5 Research: Sharing post-its, engaged Teach: Asking "what do you think?" to keep convo. going
Lucy and Nikki Date: 6/12 Research: Noticed they were learning some of the same info about earthworms Teach: Saying "I learned that too" → "I think that's important b/c..."	**Kyle and Maria** Date: 6/8 Research: Talking about what they noticed in the pictures Teach: "That reminds me of..."
Raf and Jonathan Date: 6/8 Research: Showing pictures to each other Teach: "This page is mostly about..." - point to pics.	**Nichole and Chrishelle** Date: 6/8 Research: lining up the books, no engagement, flipping through books Teach: Choral reading to support one-to-one correspondence f engagement
Makenzie and Lois Date: 6/10 Research: Sharing "what I learned post-its" - no further convo. Teach: "I think that's important b/c... What about you?"	James and Ryan Date: 6/5 Research: Couldn't decide who would share/talk first Teach: Gave them a partner A/B- A shares first today, B shares first tomorrow

Figure 8.6 Ms. Goldsmith's Partnership Notes for a Nonfiction Study

When Do I Take Notes?

I find it helpful to take notes as I confer because my memory isn't always good enough to write down detailed notes after the fact. Sometimes, I pause for a few minutes in between conferences to record notes before calling another group or going over to an individual for a one-on-one conference. Or you could take notes home at the end of the day or find time during a preparation period in the school day, to record what you remember from conferences. However, I find it more effective to capture the information as quickly as possible to help in future planning and instruction.

Some small-group conferences will be easier to record as you teach, and others might be more challenging. I almost never record notes during a shared reading lesson, as I find that my attention is too focused on each of the students and finding ways to respond in the moment to them. I usually take notes after the lesson has ended. Strategy lessons are much easier for me to write as I teach. My advice is to experiment and see what works best for you. Remember that charts made during instruction often serve both students and teachers well.

What Do I Write Down?

Write down whatever information you find to be helpful. At the very least, I want to have information about what was taught and what would be important next steps for each student in the group. I want to make sure that each student is represented as an individual, even though they are in a group. I also like writing down the amount of support I had to give each student and sometimes even the prompts I used during the engage portion of the lesson so that when I see the group for a follow-up, I can reference my specific individualized teaching for each student.

Scheduling Yourself

In this book I offer many options for types of small-group work to address different needs. In *Conferring with Readers*, Gravity Goldberg and I (2007) offer multiple types of individual conferences as well. This section gives advice for how to keep all of these options in mind to create a balanced schedule that is equitable to all of the students in your class.

How Do I Balance Individual and Group Conferring?

The way you balance individual and group conferring will likely depend on the size and makeup of your class. On years when I had thirty-two or more children in a class, I found that I did much more small-group conferring than individual conferring. I didn't drop individual conferring altogether, however, because I found those conferences were important opportunities to assess students and to maintain a more personal relationship with each child in my class. I work with some special education teachers who teach twelve children in a multiaged classroom and find that they do mostly one-on-one conferring because of the incredibly drastic range of each of the readers in their class. Often, when they do pull small groups, they are groups of two or three, but almost never four or five. These are each extreme examples to prove the point that the real answer is: it depends.

If I were to take the average of these two situations, I would say that it's likely that you'll attempt one individual reading conference for each child in your class each week. However, you may see some children who need specialized or more support a second or even third time across the week.

Keep in mind that what seems equitable isn't always what's fair to students. Some children will need more support than others at certain times of year or with certain types of new learning. It's important to keep in mind, however, that ample time to practice independently is an important component of making this work. Although students who find reading challenging may need more instructional time and greater support, Allington (2000) reminds us that for students to grow as readers, they need lots of time for reading accessible texts. So, if you find that you are working more intensively with some children one week, make sure to balance it with less teacher time in subsequent weeks.

I also keep in mind the extra support services that students in my classroom receive. Students that receive pull-out or push-in services during my reading period still need time to practice reading. In fact, these children probably need it more than others. Often, the children who receive English as a Second Language (ESL) and Resource Room instruction are also the children who get over-seen by their classroom teacher in small groups or one-on-one. Too many teachers telling these children too many different teaching points will do nothing but confuse them. I find it most helpful to focus and simplify. The support teachers and I all communicate through a shared folder that houses all conference notes. We work together to help the student with one common goal at a time, and we make sure that across the week the child has a good balance of instructional time and practice time.

Figure 8.7 is one sample of how you might organize your time (not taking into account pull-out or push-in schedules). To make such a schedule, I sat with all of my individual and group conference notes and class-at-a-glance grids created from past notes and/or from assessments of the students in my class. I thought about how children fit together. I kept track on a separate class list of names when I put a child into a group to ensure that I was not overwhelming any

	Monday	Tuesday	Wednesday	Thursday	Friday
Total time:	40	40	40	40	40
One-to-One Conferences	Mamotaz ⑮ Sarah Nelson	Patti ⑳ Jonathan Cesar Kristian	Rick ⑤	Mamotaz ⑮ Patti Kayleen	
Guided Reading	Dora Christian } I→J Lateek ⑮		Dora Christian } I-J Lateek ⑮		Dora Christian } I→J Lateek ⑮
Group Conferences	David ⑩ Natalia Malik Jill Move away from literal post-it	Rabbil, Jamel, Michael — ⑦ Visualizing setting	text intro — level M ⑩ Kayleen Drew	David, etc — revisit ⑩ Monday	Rabbil, etc — revisit Tues ⑦
Conferring During Talk (partners)	n/a (partner share)	Dora + Christian ⑩ Rick + Lateek	n/a (partner share)	Kristian + Cesar ⑩ Drew + Nelson	Jonathan + Sarah ⑩ Mamotaz + David
Observation/Check-in time	n/a	observe ③ engagement	revisit ⑩ to check in w/ M, Tu conf + groups	observe ⑤ engagement	check-in, ⑧ conf. as needed.
# of children seen:	10	11	6	11	10

Figure 8.7 Sample Schedule for Organizing a Week of Group and Individual Conferring

Mamotaz	C	C	P	
David	SG	SG	P	
Patti	C	C		
Rabbil	SG	SG		
Jamel	SG	SG		
Natalia	SG	SG		
Michael	SG	SG		
Kayleen	SG	C		
Malik	SG	SG		
Jonathan	C	P		
Sarah	C	P		
Nelson	C	P		
Jill	SG	SG		
Drew	SG	P		
Cesar	C	P		
Dora	GR	GR	GR	P
Christian	GR	GR	GR	P
Kristian	C	P		
Rick	C	P		
Lateek	GR	GR	GR	P

Figure 8.7 (*Continued*)

one student with many too many conferences, or that I wasn't forgetting to put someone into a group at all. Notice that I also have time set aside each day that is not scheduled or planned to allow myself to be responsive and pull impromptu groups, do some kid-watching, conduct a few more individual conferences, or revisit a group as needed.

How Can I Keep My Groups Flexible?

Remember that just because you begin with four students in a group, and plan to see that group for a few meetings, doesn't mean that all four students will be in all of the meetings. As children demonstrate proficiency with the new learning, they can be phased out of a group. Also, if you notice a student could benefit from a group, you can add a student by keeping your groups flexible. Figure 4.6 from Chapter 4 illustrates this point nicely.

The Last Word

Making the most of your instructional time during reading workshop requires a bit of choreography and forethought. Having a sense for how you'll take notes, where you'll conduct your groups, and how you will manage the whole class will help make this time feel productive. Think about your own classroom and any challenges to management or organization that you anticipate, and use the advice in this chapter to help you get off to a strong start.

References

Afflerbach, Peter, David Pearson, and Scott Paris. 2008. "Clarifying the Difference Between Reading Skills and Reading Strategies." *The Reading Teacher* 61 (5): 364–73.

Allington, Richard. 2000. *What Really Matters for Struggling Readers: Designing Research Based Programs.* Columbus, OH: Allyn & Bacon.

Anderson, Carl. 2000. *How's It Going? A Practical Guide to Conferring with Student Writers.* Portsmouth, NH: Heinemann.

Angelillo, Janet. 2003. *Writing About Reading: From Book Talk to Essays, Grades 3–8.* Portsmouth, NH: Heinemann.

Ash, G. E. 2002, March. "Teaching Readers Who Struggle: A Pragmatic Middle School Framework." *Reading Online* 5 (7).

Beers, Kylene. 1996. *Into Focus: Understanding and Creating Middle School Readers.* Norwood, MA: Christopher-Gordon Publishers.

———. 2002. *When Kids Can't Read—What Teachers Can Do: A Guide for Teachers 6–12.* Portsmouth, NH: Heinemann.

Biggs, Marie, and Susan Homan. 2005. "Using an Interactive Singing Software Program: A Comparative Study of Struggling Middle School Readers." In *Reading Psychology.*

Bomer, Randy, and Katherine Bomer. 2001. *For a Better World: Reading and Writing for Social Action.* Portsmouth, NH: Heinemann.

Burroughs, Augusten. 2006. *Running with Scissors.* New York: St. Martin's Paperbacks.

Calkins, Lucy. 2000. *The Art of Teaching Reading.* Needham Heights, MA: Allyn & Bacon.

Clark, K. F., and M. F. Graves. 2005. "Scaffolding Students' Comprehension of Text." *The Reading Teacher* 58 (6): 570–80.

Clay, Marie M. 1985. "Beginning Literacy in Two Languages." *Asia Pacific Journal of Education* (2): 3–14.

———. 1991. *Becoming Literate: The Construction of Inner Control.* Portsmouth, NH: Heinemann.

———. 1993. *An Observation Survey: Of Early Literacy Achievement.* Portsmouth, NH: Heinemann.

———. 2001. *Changes over Time: In Children's Literacy Development.* Portsmouth, NH: Heinemann.

Collins, Kathy. 2004. *Growing Readers: Units of Study in the Primary Classroom.* Portland, ME: Stenhouse.

———. 2008. *Reading for Real: Teach Students to Read with Power, Intention, and Joy in K–3 Classrooms.* Portland, ME: Stenhouse.

Cooper, H. 2003. "Summer Learning Loss: The Problem and Some Solutions." Champaign, IL: ERIC Clearinghouse on Elementary and Early Childhood Education.

Cruz, M. Colleen. 2004. *Independent Writing: One Teacher—Thirty-Two Needs, Topics, and Plans.* Portsmouth, NH: Heinemann.

Cunningham, P. M., and D. Hall. 1998. "The Four Blocks: A Balanced Framework for Literacy in Primary Classrooms." In: K. Harris, S. Graham, and M. Pressley, eds. *Teaching Every Child Every Day* (32–76). Cambridge, MA: Brookline Books.

Cunningham, Patricia, and Richard Allington. 1994. *Classrooms That Work: They Can All Read and Write.* Needham Heights, MA: Allyn & Bacon.

Daunis, Sarah, and Maria Cassiani Iams. 2007. *Text Savvy: Using a Shared Reading Framework to Build Comprehension, Grades 3–6.* Portsmouth, NH: Heinemann.

Dickinson, D. K., and S. B. Neuman, eds. 2001. *Handbook of Early Literacy Research.* Volume 1. New York: Guilford Publications.

Dubner, S., and S. Levitt. 2009. *Freakonomics: A Rogue Economist Explores the Hidden Side of Everything.* New York: Harper Perennial.

Duke, N. K., and P. D. Pearson. 2002. "Effective Practices for Developing Reading Comprehension." In: A. E. Firetrap and S. J. Samuels, eds. *What Research Has to Say About Reading Instruction, 3d. ed.* (205–42). Newark, DE: International Reading Association.

Durkin, D. 1981. "Reading Comprehension Instruction in Five Basal Reader Series." *Reading Research Quarterly* 16 (4): 515–45.

Eggers, D. 2000. *A Heartbreaking Work of Staggering Genius.* New York: Vintage Books.

Fader, D. N. 1968. *Hooked on Books: Programs and Proof.* California: Berkley Books.

Fitzgerald, J. 1999. "What Is This Thing Called 'Balance?'" *The Reading Teacher* (53) 2: 100–108.

Flippo, R. F. 2001. *Reading Researchers in Search of Common Ground.* Newark, DE: International Reading Association.

Ford, M. 1992. *Motivating Humans: Goals, Emotions, and Personal Agency Beliefs.* Newbury Park, CA: Sage.

Fountas, Irene, and Gay Su Pinnell. 1996. *Guided Reading: Good First Teaching for All Children.* Portsmouth, NH: Heinemann.

———. 2000. *Guiding Readers and Writers, Grades K–8.* Portsmouth, NH: Heinemann.

———. 2005. *Leveled Books, K–8: Matching Texts to Readers for Effective Teaching.* Portsmouth, NH: Heinemann.

———. 2006. *Teaching for Comprehending and Fluency: Thinking, Talking and Writing About Reading K–8.* Portsmouth, NH: Heinemann.

———. 2007. *Continuum for Literacy Learning, Grades K–8.* Portsmouth, NH: Heinemann.

Gavelek, James, and Taffy E. Raphael. 1996. "Changing Talk About Text: New Roles for Teachers and Students." *Language Arts* 73 (3): 182–92.

Gladwell, M. 2002. *The Tipping Point: How Little Things Can Make a Big Difference.* New York: Back Bay Books.

———. 2008. *Outliers: The Story of Success.* New York: Little Brown and Company.

Guthrie, J. T., and A. Wigfield. 1997. "Reading Engagement: A Rationale for Theory and Teaching." In: J. T. Guthrie and A. Wigfield, eds. *Reading Engagement: Motivating Readers Through Integrated Instruction* (1–12). Newark, DE: International Reading Association.

Harris, A. J., and E. R. Sipay. 1990. *How to Increase Reading Ability* (9th Ed.). New York: Longman.

Holdaway, Don. 1984. *The Foundations of Literacy (Grades K–6).* New York: Ashton Scholastic.

Johnston, P. H. 2004. *Choice Words: How Our Language Affects Children's Learning.* Portland, ME: Stenhouse.

Keene, E. O., and S. Zimmermann. 1997. *Mosaic of Thought.* Portsmouth, NH: Heinemann.

Kelley, M. J., and N. Clausen-Grace. 2007. *Comprehension Shouldn't Be Silent: From Strategy Instruction to Student Independence.* Washington, DC: International Reading Association.

Kim, Jimmy. 2004. "Summer Reading and the Ethnic Achievement Gap." *Journal of Education for Students Placed at Risk (JESPAR)* 9 (2): 169–88.

Kuhn, Melanie. 2008. *The Hows and Whys of Fluency Instruction.* Boston: Addison-Wesley.

Laminack, Lester, and Reba Wadsworth. 2006. *Learning Under the Influence of Language and Literature: Making the Most of Read-Alouds Across the Day.* Portsmouth, NH: Heinemann.

Martel, Y. 2003. *Life of Pi.* Orlando, FL: Harvest Books.

Mraz, M., and T. V. Rasinski. 2007, May. "Summer Reading Loss." *The Reading Teacher* 60 (8): 784–89.

Murphy, P. K., I. A. G. Wilkinson, A. O. Soter, M. N. Hennessey, and J. F. Alexander. "Examining the Effects of Classroom Discussion on Students' High-Level Comprehension of Text: A Meta-Analysis." *Journal of Educational Psychology* (in press).

National Endowment for the Arts. 2007. *To Read or Not to Read: A Question of National Consequence.* Available at: www.nea.gov/research/ToRead.PDF.

———. 2008. *Reading on the Rise: A New Chapter on American Literacy.* Available at: www.nea.gov/research/ReadingonRise.pdf.

National Institute of Child Health and Human Development (NICHD). 2001. *Teaching Children to Read: An Evidence-Based Assessment of the Scientific Research Literature on Reading and Its Implications for Reading Instruction.* Reports of the Sub Groups:

Comprehension. Report of the National Reading Panel. Washington, DC: National Institutes of Health.

Nell, Victor. 1988. *Lost in a Book: The Psychology of Reading for Pleasure.* New Haven, CT: Yale University Press.

Nichols, Maria. 2006. *Comprehension Through Conversation: The Power of Purposeful Talk in the Reading Workshop.* Portsmouth, NH: Heinemann.

Parkes, Barbara. 2000. *Read It Again! Revisiting Shared Reading.* Portland, ME: Stenhouse.

Pearson, P. D., and M. Gallagher. 1983. "The Instruction of Reading Comprehension." *Contemporary Educational Psychology* 8: 317–44.

Pearson, P. D., T. E. Raphael, V. L. Benson, and C. L. Madda. 2007. "Balance in Comprehensive Literacy Instruction: Then and Now." In: L. Gambrell, L. Morrow, and M. Pressley, eds. *Best Practices in Literacy Instruction* (30–54). New York: Guilford Press.

Raphael, T. E., and S. I. McMahon. 1994. "Book Club: An Alternative Framework for Reading Instruction." *The Reading Teacher* 48: 102–106.

Rasinski, Timothy. 2003. *The Fluent Reader: Oral Reading Strategies for Building Word Recognition, Fluency, and Comprehension.* New York: Scholastic.

Santman, Donna. 2005. *Shades of Meaning: Comprehension and Interpretation in Middle School.* Portsmouth, NH: Heinemann.

Serravallo, Jennifer, and Gravity Goldberg. 2007. *Conferring with Readers: Supporting Each Student's Growth and Independence.* Portsmouth, NH: Heinemann.

Shin, F., and S. Krashen. 2007. *Summer Reading: Program and Evidence.* Needham Heights, MA: Allyn & Bacon.

Shirai, S. 1992. "Phylogenetic Relationships of the Angel Sharks, with Comments on Elasmobranch Phylogeny (Chondrichthyes, Squatinidae)." *Copeia* 1992 (2): 505–18.

Sittenfeld, C. 2009. *American Wife: A Novel.* New York: Random House Trade Paperbacks.

Taberski, S., and S. Harwayne. 2000. *On Solid Ground: Strategies for Teaching Reading K–3.* Portsmouth, NH: Heinemann.

Tomlinson, C. A. 2001. *How to Differentiate Instruction in Mixed-Ability Classrooms.* Association for Supervision and Curriculum Development: Alexandria, VA.

Tovani, C. 2000. *I Read It but I Don't Get It: Comprehension Strategies for Adolescent Readers.* Portland, ME: Stenhouse.

Trelease, J. 2001. *The Read Aloud Handbook.* New York: Penguin.

Von Spreken, D., J. Kim, and S. Krashen. 2000. "The Home Run Book: Can One Positive Reading Experience Create a Reader?" *California School Library Journal* 23 (2): 8–9.

Vygotsky, L. S. 1978 (1934). *Mind in Society: The Development of Higher Psychological Processes.* In: M. Cole, V. John-Steiner, S. Scribner, and E. Souberman, eds. and trans. Cambridge, MA: Harvard University Press.

Wood, D., J. S. Bruner, and G. Ross. 1976. "The Role of Tutoring in Problem-Solving." *Journal of Child Psychology and Psychiatry* 17: 89–100.

Children's Literature

Abbot, T. 2003. *Secrets of Droon*. New York: Scholastic.

Appleby, E. 2001. *Three Billy Goats Gruff: A Norwegian Folktale*. St. Louis, MO: San Val, Incorporated.

Benton, J. 2005. *The Invisible Fran (Franny K. Stein, Mad Scientist)*. New York: Simon and Schuster.

Berger, M. 1995. *Discovering Jupiter*. New York: Scholastic.

Bos, B. 1995. *Meet the Molesons*. Perfection Paperbacks. New York: North-South Books.

Boyd, C. D. 1996. *Circle of Gold*. New York: Scholastic.

Bunting, E. 2001. *Riding the Tiger*. New York: Clarion Books.

Cameron, A. 1981. *The Stories Julian Tells*. New York: A. Knopf Paperbacks.

Caple, Kathy. 2000. *Worm Paints*. Cambridge, MA: Candlewick Press.

Cleary, B. 1985. *Ramona*. New York: William Morrow & Co.

Curtis, Christopher Paul. 1999. *Bud, Not Buddy*. New York: Random House Children's Books.

Curtis, Gavin. 2001. *The Bat Boy and His Violin*. New York: Aladdin.

Dahl, Roald. 1970. *Fantastic Mr. Fox*. New York: Puffin Books.

———. 1988. *James and the Giant Peach*. New York: Puffin/Scholastic.

Davidson, M. 1987. *The Story of Jackie Robinson: The Bravest Man in Baseball*. New York: Dell Yearling.

DeGross, M. 1998. *Donovan's Word Jar*. New York: Harper Trophy.

Dussling, J. 1998. *Bugs! Bugs! Bugs!* New York: DK Publishing.

Editors of *Time for Kids*. 2005. *Time for Kids: Sharks!* New York: Harper Collins.

Falconer, I. 2000. *Olivia*. New York: Atheneum/Anne Schwartz Books.

Fox, P. 1993. *Monkey Island*. New York: Yearling.

Frank, A. 1953. *Anne Frank: The Diary of a Young Girl*. New York: Pocket Books.

Greenburg, Dan. 1996. *Zack Files: My Great-Grandpa's in the Litterbox*. New York: Penguin.

Gutelle, A. 2009. *Baseball's Best: Five True Stories*. New York: Random House.

Howe, James. 1999. *Pinky and Rex and the School Play*. New York: Scholastic.

———. 1999. *Pinky and Rex and the New Baby*. New York: Aladdin.

Janeczko, P. 2009. *A Foot in the Mouth: Poems to Speak, Sing, and Shout*. Cambridge, MA: Candlewick.

Kinney, Jeff. 2007. *Diary of a Wimpy Kid*. New York: Amulet Books.

Kline, Suzy. 1986. *Herbie Jones*. New York: Penguin Books.

———. 1998. *Horrible Harry in Room 2B*. New York: Scholastic.

Llewellyn, C. 1999. *The Best Book of Sharks*. Boston: Kingfisher.

Lobel, A. 1984. *Days with Frog and Toad*. New York: Harper Collins.

McGovern, A. 1978. *Shark Lady: True Adventures of Eugenie Clark*. New York: Scholastic.

Mead, A. 1995. *Junebug*. New York: Bantam Doubleday Dell Books for Young Readers.

Munoz Ryan, Pam. 2005. *Becoming Naomi Leon.* New York: Scholastic.

Neri, Greg. 2007. *Chess Rumble.* New York: Lee and Low.

Osborne, M. P. 1992. *Dinosaurs Before Dark: Magic Tree House, No.1.* New York: Scholastic.

Parish, P. 1985. *Amelia Bedelia.* New York: Harper Collins Publishers.

Patterson, K. 1977. *Bridge to Terabithia.* New York: Harper Trophy.

Paulsen, Gary. 1987. *Hatchet.* New York: Aladdin.

Pilky, D. 1997. *The Adventures of Captain Underpants.* New York: Scholastic.

Riordan, Rick. 2008. *The Maze of Bones (The 39 Clues).* New York: Scholastic.

Rodda, E. 2002. *Deltora Quest: Enter the World of Deltora.* New York: Scholastic.

Roy, R. 1997. *A to Z Mysteries: The Absent Author.* New York: Scholastic.

Rylant, Cynthia. 1996. *Henry and Mudge Under the Yellow Moon.* New York: Aladdin.

———. 1997. *Poppleton.* New York: Scholastic.

———. 2004. *Mr. Putter & Tabby Write the Book.* Orlando, FL: Harcourt.

Sachar, L. 1978. *Sideways Stories from Wayside School.* New York: Avon Books.

———. 1992. *Dogs Don't Tell Jokes.* New York: Yearling Books.

Scieszka, J. 2008. *Knucklehead: Tall Tales & Mostly True Stories About Growing Up Scieszka.* New York: Viking.

Scieszka, J., and L. Smith. 2004. *Time Warp Trio.* New York: Puffin.

Silverstein, Shel. 1974. *Where the Sidewalk Ends.* New York: Harper & Row.

Thomson, S. L. 2006. *Amazing Sharks!* New York: Harper Collins.

Van Allsburg, Chris. 1992. *The Widow's Broom.* New York: Houghton Mifflin Books for Children.

Index